T0292022

PSYCHOPHYSICS AND EXPERIMENTAL PHENOMENOLOGY OF PATTERN COGNITION

PSYCHOPHYSICS AND EXPERIMENTAL PHENOMENOLOGY OF PATTERN COGNITION

JIRO HAMADA
Tokushima University, Tokushima, Japan

ELSEVIER

ACADEMIC PRESS
An imprint of Elsevier

Academic Press is an imprint of Elsevier
125 London Wall, London EC2Y 5AS, United Kingdom
525 B Street, Suite 1650, San Diego, CA 92101, United States
50 Hampshire Street, 5th Floor, Cambridge, MA 02139, United States
The Boulevard, Langford Lane, Kidlington, Oxford OX5 1GB, United Kingdom

ISBN 978-0-323-95286-6

For information on all Academic Press publications
visit our website at https://www.elsevier.com/books-and-journals

Publisher: Nikki Levy
Acquisitions Editor: Megan McManus
Editorial Project Manager: Maria Elaine D. Desamero
Production Project Manager: Punithavathy Govindaradjane
Cover Designer: Mark Rogers

Typeset by STRAIVE, India

Working together
to grow libraries in
developing countries

www.elsevier.com • www.bookaid.org

Dedication

Dedicated to psychologists Munehira Akita (Ph.D. at Columbia University, 1930–2006), T. Satoru Aiba (Ph.D. at University of London, 1930–2021), and Shiro Imai (Ph.D. at Johns Hopkins University, 1929–2021), and respectfully presented to mathematician Toru Ishihara (D.Sc. at Kyoto University).

Contents

PART THREE Symmetry cognition

Preface

This book traces a long history of symmetric cognition and organizations of perception and memory from the standpoint of psychophysics and experimental phenomenology. The emphasis is on psychological experiments and theoretical models. The book starts with experiments based on a theoretical background, and follows a path of theoretical convergence through repeated experiments that modify the theoretical framework. In the course of this process, I have selected experiments that seem to contradict theoretical expectations. I believe that theoretical progress is possible only when experimental support is obtained, and that only in this way can new discoveries be made. I also believe that psychological experimental data is valuable when it is put together into a mathematical system. However, this research is not complete, and many problems remain to be solved. I would like to leave the resolution of these issues to the next generation.

In Part 1, Mach (1865) was a pioneer in the field of contour perception, represented by the Mach bands discussed. Obonai (1955, 1957) and Békésy (1959, 1960) proposed a one-dimensional antagonistic process of excitation and inhibition. Fujii, Matsuoka, and Morita (1967), based on Obonai's qualitative psycho-physiological induction, extended a difference of two Gaussians (DOG) to two-dimensional space to simulate geometric illusions, following Obonai's psycho-physiological induction. Based on this model, Hamada (1976a, 1976b, 1984b) developed a one-dimensional serial processing model by adding luminance dependence to DOG in which inflection points are detected as edges and are subjected to information reduction. I then simulated a border contrast in brightness perception with this model. Using the results as a reference, I conducted psychophysical experiments on a contour perception and brightness illusions. In these experiments, I distinguished between dark and light Craik-O'Brien illusions and clarified the relationship between them and the Cornsweet illusion. I also examined simultaneous contrasts of brightness and the Ehrenstein illusion. These experiments revealed an asymmetry between dark and light, and an anisotropy in the Ehrenstein illusion. Furthermore, I showed that the addition of a local luminance step (i.e., edge) to a uniform field caused a decrease in brightness levels without exception, including my unpublished experiments. This decrease in brightness levels is thought to indicate the processing in the upper level of the antagonistic process of excitation/inhibition and information reduction of Hamada (1976a, 1976b, 1984b). Then, the brightness levels decrease due to luminance steps (edges), and the difference in brightness and darkness between adjacent surfaces becomes more noticeable. The theoretical basis for Part 1 is the antagonistic process of excitation and inhibition (i.e., DOG) and a decrease in brightness levels.

In Part 2, Hamada (1990a) measured the negative time-order effect in two weighted stimuli, which were raised in succession, not only by relative but also by absolute judgments, and found that the preceding stimulus was judged lighter, and the following stimulus was judged heavier than a single stimulus in the control condition. The mechanism of this negative time-order effect was explained by a disinhibition based on the antagonistic process of excitation and inhibition.

In Part 3, we examined symmetry cognition using the free-viewing tasks by printing two- and one-dimensional dot patterns on cards in order to elucidate cognitive psychological facts. Mach's (1918) pioneering work on this topic is also worth mentioning. He showed the effects of translation, rotation, reflection, and dilation transformations on symmetry cognition. Early perceptual claims about the role of symmetry in vision were made by Gestalt psychologists. Koffka (1935) discussed a principle of Gestalt psychology introduced by Wertheimer (1880–1943), who called it the Law of Prägnanz. It can be formulated as follows: psychological organization will always be only as "good" as the prevailing conditions allow. In this definition, the term "good" is undefined. It embraced regularity, symmetry, and simplicity. We extended works of Garner and Clement (1963), Imai, Ito, and Ito (1976a, 1976b), and Imai (1977b) to examine the goodness, complexity, disjointness (the inverse of unifiedness), and similarity of dot patterns. For example, based on group theory, Hamada and Ishihara (1988) drew dot patterns in a two-dimensional hexagonal grid and I drew them in square grids and studied symmetry cognition experimentally and theoretically. As a result, the effects of group order (i.e., the number of transformations), grids, contrast polarity, numerosity (i.e., 8, 13, and 21 dots), configuration of the dot patterns, and linearity or collinearity on cognitive judgments were clarified. In addition, the complexity and disjointness of the D_2 linear pattern with parallel edges were found to be affected by an anisotropic spatial filter based on DOG. The anisotropy of symmetry cognition also appeared in the goodness and complexity of the 72-dot repetitive patterns. Moreover, not only the similarity of black–white filled pattern pairs in one and two dimensions

(1D and 2D) but also the goodness and complexity of 1D black-white filled patterns were also determined by group theory.

The theoretical basis of Part 3 is group theory, and the cognitive system seems to judge goodness, complexity, disjointness (the inverse of unifiedness), and similarity based mainly on group order and configuration of dot patterns. In addition, it is thought that the cognitive system is affected by the antagonistic process (DOG) in the early levels before group order is involved. The group theoretical approach to the study of symmetry cognition is expected to be developed in the future.

In Part 4, Mach (1918) was a pioneer in the size illusion. He showed that when a square is tilted by 45° to form a diamond, there is a large psychological difference in spite of geometric congruence, that is, an anisotropy of a geometrical illusion appears. We experimentally investigated the distance and tilt angle of the periphery of the Ebbinghaus patterns to reveal the effects of four or eight surrounding circles on the central circle and the anisotropic effect of the geometric illusion. In contrast, the Delboeuf illusion measured by the comparison method and an illusion by the absolute judgment method differed greatly in appearance. Therefore, we distinguished these two illusions and named the former the Delboeuf illusion and the latter the concentric circle illusion. In the concentric circle illusion, when the order of judgments of the inner and outer circles of the concentric circle was changed, the amount of the illusion was different and a judgment-order effect appeared.

In Part 5, Hamada (1986, 1988b, 1990b) examined modality effects on random digit sequences by successive recall instead of immediate one and found that visual and auditory memories exist independently in the cognitive system, and that auditory digits have an inhibitory effect on visual memory but not vice versa. Furthermore, when visual and auditory digits were presented one after the other in interchanging conditions, I found that each other's memory interferes during memorization.

As described above, I believe that the theoretical origins of contour perception and brightness illusion (Part 1), the negative time-order effect on weight sensation (Part 2), symmetry cognition (Part 3), the size of the circle in geometric illusions (Part 4), and visual and auditory memory in successive recall (Part 5) in this book lie in the antagonistic process of excitation and inhibition.

Acknowledgments

First, I would like to review my history as a researcher, with acknowledgments. A native of Tokushima City, Japan, I was born in Fukui Prefecture, in August 1947, and grew up in Chiba and Kochi Prefectures. I don't remember Fukui, but I grew up on the coast of Chiba, where when the sky is clear the majestic Mt. Fuji can be seen clearly across Tokyo Bay. There, in the summer, I enjoyed swimming in the sea, and I have fond memories of shell gathering at low tide. In Kochi, I grew up in the mountains of the Monobe River system in the Shikoku Mountains. This place was full of nature. In the severe winters, the water splashed down on the waterwheel shed of the stream where the spring water flowed, forming many icicles, and the surrounding green grass and trees were also covered with ice and shone beautifully.

However, in August 1962, when I was in the third year of junior high school, my father, who was working for a construction company, collapsed due to a cerebral thrombosis and became paralyzed on the left side of his body. Therefore, I entered Yamada High School in Kochi Prefecture in the countryside. However, our family could not make a living, and we had to return to Tokushima, where my father was born. I then applied to transfer to a regular high school in Tokushima City. However, the barriers between the different prefectures prevented me from doing this, so I had no choice but to re-enroll in the mechanical department of Tokushima Technical High School. I enjoyed studying here and was good at industrial mathematics and drafting, but I had a strong desire to go to university and applied to the Faculty of Education of Tokushima University to become a junior high school math teacher. However, I was not accepted for my first choice, a junior high school mathematics course, but was admitted to my second choice, an elementary school course. In Japan, entering a national university from a technical high school was possible, but extremely difficult. The fact that I was able to do so gave me significant confidence. In addition, the drafting skills I learned in high school became indispensable for my research on pattern cognition in an age without computers. It was also extremely fortunate for me that I was able to enroll in an elementary school course at the institution that had a psychology department.

My earliest encounter with experimental psychology was when I was a first-year student at Tokushima University; Associate Professor Mitsuyo Ito of the College of Liberal Arts was looking for participants for an experiment in his psychology class. I immediately accepted the invitation. There, in the darkroom of his laboratory, the light threshold was being measured. As a second-year student, I joined the psychology department in the Faculty of Education, majoring in psychology and minoring in mathematics. There, I was able to learn a wide range of psychology in general from Associate Professor Takao Matsuda, who specialized in perceptual psychology, and his assistant Hiroyuki Kaiho. I also continued to be a participant in the light threshold measurement experiment, and when I became a fourth-year student, I stated to my advisor, Prof. Matsuda, that I would like to write my bachelor's thesis under the guidance of Prof. Ito, and he allowed me to do so. This illustrates the free atmosphere that existed in the psychology department. Based on the results of experiments conducted over a period of 4 years, I hypothesized that the standard deviations of the difference of two Gaussians (DOG) of excitation and inhibition became smaller as luminance increase. That is, the DOG became more acute as luminance increased. I then proposed a mathematical luminance-dependence model based on convolutional integration of luminance and DOG in my bachelor's thesis (Hamada, 1971). For the calculation of convolution integrals, I received guidance from Toru Ishihara, an assistant in the mathematics department. The fact that I minored in mathematics helped me a lot.

As a senior in college, I was wondering whether I should become an elementary school teacher or further study psychology. That fall, I thought both options were possible, so I took the entrance exam for the master's program of Osaka Kyoiku University and was accepted at the top of my class. However, since I had conceived of the luminance-dependent model in my bachelor's thesis, I had an unshakable desire to continue that research. I therefore consulted with Associate Professor Motohiko Kitao, who specialized in learning psychology, about writing my master's thesis on perceptual psychology. He told me that there were no instructors at Osaka Kyoiku University who could teach me, but that I could ask someone at another university to teach me. Encouraged by these words, I built an experimental apparatus on my own. However, I did not have an ultra-fine illuminance meter, which was necessary for the measurement of the light threshold. I therefore asked the manufacturer, Toshiba Corporation, if I could borrow it. The Toshiba employee in charge of this replied that he could not lend me the illuminance meter but told me that there was it in the laboratory of Professor Munehira Akita at the Kyoto Institute of Technology. Therefore, I consulted with my advisor, Professor Toshitaka Tanaka, and he asked Prof. Akita to lend me the illuminance meter and to give me some guidance. Fortunately, Osaka Kyoiku University also had a free atmosphere.

When I met Prof. Akita in the early summer of 1971 with my graduation thesis, he appreciated it and lent me his ultrafine illuminance meter. He also gave me the opportunity to present my experimental results and mathematical model at a research meeting held regularly in Osaka City, and I was able to successfully complete the presentation. Moreover, he took a look at my experimental apparatus at Osaka Kyoiku University and confirmed that it was fully functional. I then carried out an experiment to measure the light threshold. However, inspired by Prof. Akita's research on color vision using the latest Maxwell's optical apparatus, I switched my theme from light threshold measurement to color vision research and wrote my master's thesis, entitled "Duplicity found in dark-adapted curves and the effects of surrounding-adapted color light." The research here was exciting and novel (Akita, 1969; Akita & Hamada, 1973). Prof. Akita also introduced me to Claude Bernard's *Introduction to Experimental Medicine*, translated into Japanese, which impressed me greatly, and the spirit of this book became a pillar of my psychological experiments (Bernard, 1865). In the meantime, the luminance-dependence model continued to linger in my mind, and under the guidance of Prof. Akita, I came up with a mathematical model in 1972 that assumed that the cognitive system detects inflection points of DOG as edges. In other words, I learned from him that the cognitive system perceives change. And if this were so, I believed that inflection points must have an important meaning. In addition, I questioned Ratliff's (1972) explanation for the Craik-O'Brien-Cornsweet illusion using an extrapolation model based on DOG vertices, and thought that the inflection points, not vertices, were detected as edges. Then, when I returned to my city, Tokushima, I found a book by Robinson (1972) on the bookshelf in Prof. Matsuda's laboratory. In the book, I found that Bergström (1966) described the inflection point of the luminance distribution as an edge, which convinced me of the importance of the inflection point. After that, when I was about to complete my master's course, I took the entrance examinations for Kyoto University Graduate School of both Letters and Education, Doctoral Program, but failed to pass either of them. Nevertheless, Prof. Akita strongly recommended me to enter the doctoral program at the Graduate School of Letters, Hokkaido University, where Associate Professor T. Satoru Aiba was enrolled. He wrote a letter of recommendation for me, and I was successfully admitted.

In Sapporo, I completed my doctoral thesis on brightness contrast induction under the guidance of Prof. Aiba (Hamada, 1980a). In the process, I experimentally investigated the brightness illusion and found a decrease in brightness levels (Hamada, 1980b, 1980c). Earlier than this, I visited

Associate Professor Tomozo Furukawa of the Research Institute of Applied Electricity, Hokkaido University, through Prof. Akita's introduction. When I explained to him the mathematical model I had developed from my bachelor's thesis, he gave me a high evaluation. He also recommended that I should perform computer simulations on the contour perception and gave me detailed instructions for it. As a result, after about a year of trial and error, I was able to simulate the border contrast. The final point of contention was to treat the inflection points of a difference of two Gaussians (DOG) as edges, and to make DOG have luminance dependence using Stevens' power law. Then, under the guidance of Prof. Aiba, I wrote an English draft about the simulation and presented it at the 21st International Congress of Psychology in Paris (Hamada, 1976a). Here, Professor Yoshihisa Tanaka of Tokyo University reviewed the draft at the Steering Committee of the Commemorative Fund for the International Congress of Psychology, and the Steering Committee adopted me as a *Young Psychologist* of the Congress. I was then able to publish it as Hamada (1976b). I would like to thank Prof. Akita, Professor Mathew Alpern of the University of Michigan, and Professor Miguelina Guirao of University of Buenos Aires for their valuable advice on this paper. I submitted it to a certain international journal twice, but it was not understood, and was rejected. However, the research was highly valued, and I was hired as an assistant to Associate Professor Shiro Imai of Hokkaido University, where I continued my research on the brightness illusion. With his careful guidance, I was able to publish three papers (Hamada, 1980b, 1982, 1983).

I continued to experiment with the brightness illusion after I was transferred to Tokushima University, my alma mater, in 1982. Shortly after, Professor Michael J. Morgan of University College London, who was visiting Prof. Aiba's laboratory, carefully read Hamada (1976b), which describes a mathematical model of edge detection for a border contrast. He highly valued the paper, saying that it was surprising that a paper that surpassed Marr and Hildreth (1980) had been published in Japan in 1976. He then recommended that I resubmit this paper to *Biological Cybernetics*. As a result, I was able to publish my work as Hamada (1984b); however, it was 17 years, counting from my first year at Tokushima University, before I could publish it in an international journal.

Professor Lothar Spillmann of University of Freiburg and Dr. Walter H. Ehrenstein of Dortmund University improved the drafts of my research on contour perception and brightness illusion, which have been published in *Perception & Psychophysics*, *Biological Cybernetics*, and other journals. I also received valuable advice from Professor Stephen Grossberg of Boston

University, among others. I would like to thank Walter in particular for his support. My encounter with him began with a letter dated May 2, 1977 from him. There was one question on my mathematical model that simulated the border contrast by treating inflection points as edges, which I presented at the 21st International Congress of Psychology held in Paris (Hamada, 1976a). He asked me if this mathematical model could explain the Ehrenstein illusion that his father had discovered. I tried to simulate the illusion using a digital computer with Mr. Kaname Amano, who was a program consultant at Hokkaido University Computing Center. However, the mechanism of the illusion was too complicated to simulate using only the idea of inflection points. Meanwhile, this letter was the beginning of our friendship and joint research with Walter. And he improved my English drafts, and I was able to publish many papers on the brightness illusion in international journals. Without him, this would not have been possible. In addition, when I was sent to Dortmund University as an overseas researcher with my family for 10 months from March 1991, with the support of the Japanese Ministry of Education and the German Academic Exchange Service (DAAD), I conducted an experiment of brightness contrast induction with Walter, Mr. Manfred Müller, and Professor Carl Richard Cavonius. The result is Hamada and Ehrenstein (2008), but it took 18 years after the experiment to achieve publication. Professor Kaname Amano of Ehime University, who had moved there from Hokkaido University, carefully improved sections of Part 1.

After I returned to Tokushima University, I came up with the idea of what would happen if I compared the time-order effect in weight judgments between relative and absolute judgments, and worked with students in my psychology laboratory class to collect data.

My research on symmetry cognition began when I was working as a research assistant under Prof. Imai of Hokkaido University, who taught me about it. This was at the time when he published the work on transformational structure theory (Imai, 1977a, 1977b) and when it was born. I was also greatly influenced by Prof. Matsuda of Tokushima University, who was conducting joint research with Prof. Imai at the same time. In February 1984, soon after I returned to Tokushima University, Professor Toru Ishihara, a mathematician, read Imai (1977a) and proposed patterns with three reflection axes instead of four, and we started some joint research. His idea represented a world-leading breakthrough. He also introduced me to several mathematical books on group theory. In the early days of my research on symmetry cognition, he gave me precise guidance on group theory, which allowed me to proceed linearly many subsequent experiments without losing my way, as group theory illuminated my path. Without my encounter with Prof. Ishihara, I would never have completed Part 3 of this book. I still find the group theoretical approach to be a treasure trove of symmetry cognition. I was also surprised to find that the mathematical model of Hamada (1976a, 1976b, 1984b), which simulates the border contrast of brightness, is closely related to Hamada, Fukuda, Uchiumi, Fukushi, and Amano (2019), which deals with complexity judgments in symmetry cognition, through an anisotropic spatial filter. It was truly moving to see the connection between these two themes, which had previously been thought to be unrelated, after 43 years of separation.

Many of my friends have contributed to the discussion and improvement of sections of Part 3. For example, when I sent a draft of Hamada and Ishihara's (1988) paper on symmetry cognition to Walter, he and Dr. Cees C. van Leeuwen of Katholieke University carefully improved it. The starting point of my research on symmetry cognition is in this paper. Furthermore, when I sent a draft of Hamada et al. (2016) to Professor Galina V. Paramei of Liverpool Hope University, she encouraged me to submit it to *Acta Psychologica*. Kaname and Associate Professor Steve T. Fukuda, who had moved from Tokushima University to Bunkyo University, carefully improved it. Then, Professor Peter A. van der Helm of the University of Leuven (KU Leuven) gave us precise instructions on how to redo the data analysis, which also benefited the paper. Associate Professor Marco Bertamini of University of Liverpool gave me valuable advice on another section of Part 3. In particular, Kamame has made careful improvements to all the recent papers on symmetry cognition, as well as to Part 3, Chapter 8, Experiment 2 on similarity, Chapter 9 on goodness and complexity in cluster condition, and Chapter 11 on transformational group structure theory. Therefore, his corrections and advice at key points helped to maintain the theoretical consistency of Parts 1 and 3. Professor Kohji Fukushi of Kawamura Gakuen Women's University, who served as a program consultant at Hokkaido University Computing Center around 1975 also gave me good advice on an anisotropic space filter and other topics. In addition, I received valuable advice from Associate Professor Chikusa Uchiumi and Professor Yutaka Sato of Tokushima University. Dr. Menno M. Hogeboom of University of Amsterdam, who worked in my laboratory for 1 year from April 1994 under Tokushima University International Education and Research Exchange Fund, developed D_n and C_n curve patterns

($n = 1$, 2, 4) with four corners by modifying the dot patterns of Hamada (1988a).

I have also studied circle size illusions as a geometrical illusion. This research started when I was sent to Dortmund University as an overseas researcher in 1991. Walter invented the mixed pattern on the Ebbinghaus illusion. Then, he worked in my laboratory from March 2 to April 11, 1992, under the Fujii-Otsuka International Education and Research Fellowship of Tokushima University. We exchanged views on the light-dark contrast induction and the size illusion. After his return to Germany, I came up with the idea of measuring the size of the inner or outer circle in the concentric circles by absolute judgments and found that the amount of illusion changes when the order of judgments of the inner and outer circles is changed, that is, the concentric circle illusion and the judgment-order effect. In addition to working with Walter, I was able to collaborate with Galina on this theme. That is, she stayed in Tokushima and Kyoto by Tokushima University International Education and Research Exchange Fund. In other words, she stayed in my laboratory from May 20 to 25, 1997, and after fruitfully discussing it with me, she stayed for five days at the 8th Congress of International Colour Association held in Kyoto.

I presented visual and auditory random digit sequences in succession, and then had them recalled in succession to examine the modality effects (Hamada, 1986, 1988b, 1990b). This research dates back to the work of Prof. Imai of Hokkaido University, who conducted experiments on successive recalls using visual random digit sequences (Imai, 1979). The experiments on visual memory were conducted in his laboratory where digits were written one by one on a response sheet to a sound signal. Thus, when I was assigned to Tokushima University, I wanted to examine the differences in memory when random digits were presented in visual and auditory form, and I conducted experiments with my students as the theme of their graduation research. Ms. Lonneke S. Frie, an undergraduate student of University of Amsterdam, was a scholar of the Japanese-German Centre Berlin and worked in my laboratory for 8 months from April 1993 to advance this theme.

I would like to thank the approximately 3000 students who participated in the pattern cognition experiments in my psychology class at Tokushima University. In the experiments, I not only collected data, but also assigned each student to carry out a brief analysis and discussion of the data to experience the significance and fun of cognitive psychology. This helped to motivate them and to ensure clean data was obtained. These experiments required me to be sensitive and careful with the participants, since I was collecting experimental data from real students without compensation. The well-controlled experimental data never lied. The lecture room was like a laboratory for me. I would also like to thank the students of Hokkaido University and Tokushima University for their personal cooperation as experimenters and participants. In addition, I would like to express my sincere gratitude to my wife Kayoko, a good collaborator and companion, who devotedly took care of me when I was seriously ill in October 2014, gave me time to rest after my recovery, and fully supported the writing of this book.

The above sets out the trajectory of my research on pattern cognition, which I have conducted for about 50 years with the guidance and cooperation of many people. My life has not been smooth, and I have encountered some difficulties, but I think I have grown each time. My research life has been blessed with many miraculous fortunes.

Finally, I would like to thank Natalie Farra, PhD, who was promoted from Senior Acquisitions Editor of Neuroscience at Elsevier/Academic Press to her current position as Regional Marketing Manager of North America, for her efforts throughout the development of this book.

Jiro Hamada
Tokushima University, Tokushima, Japan

PART ONE

Contour perception and brightness illusion

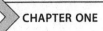

CHAPTER ONE

Mathematical models for an antagonistic process of excitation and inhibition

1.1 Mach bands and a border contrast

Mach (1865) rotated the black–and–white windmill pattern in Fig. 1.1A at high speed and generated a luminance distribution with three different gradients from the center toward periphery as shown in (C). As the result, the apparent brightness of the pattern appeared as shown in (B and D) (see Ratliff, 1965; Mori, 1977). Here, two light bands were observed at β' and γ', which correspond to the refractive areas β and γ where the gradient of the luminance distribution changes. According to him, the area between α' and β', which should be white, was grayish, while the area between β' and γ' was slightly darker toward the outside but appeared almost uniformly gray. Similarly, when Fig. 1.1a, in which the black–and–white pattern is inverted, is rotated at a high speed to generate the luminance distribution shown in (c). The apparent brightness is shown in (b and d), and dark bands are seen in β' and γ'. These light and dark Mach bands indicate that the cognitive system perceives contours with emphasis. He attributed the generation of Mach bands to neural interactions in the retina, which occur in areas where the luminance distribution of the retinal image is convexly or concavely refracted with respect to the spatial axis. In other words, he hypothesized that the neural circuitry in the retina has an inhibition that subtracts the second-order differential coefficient from the retinal image, as described in detail later.

Fig. 1.2a shows five types of stepes ranging from dark gray to light gray, and their intensity (reflectance) distribution has five steps as in (b). However, when (a) is observed, it is not a uniform and simple five-step brightness sensation but rather dark and light Mach bands that do not objectively exist appear especially at the boundaries of each step as shown in (c). This is called a border contrast (Cornsweet, 1970; Rigss, 1971). The mechanism of this

Psychophysics and Experimental Phenomenology of Pattern Cognition
https://doi.org/10.1016/B978-0-323-95286-6.00001-6

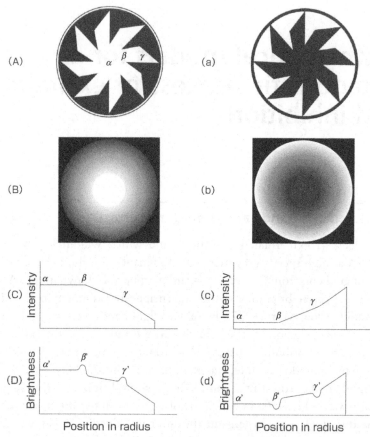

Fig. 1.1 Mach bands of light *(A–D)* and dark *(a–d)*. *(Adapted from Mach, E. (1865). Über die Wirkung der räumlichen Vertheihung des Lichtreizes auf die Netzhaut.* Sitzungsberichte der mathematisch-naturwissenschaftlichen Classe der kaiserlichen Akademic der Wissenschaften, 52, 303–322. *(Ratliff, 1965); Mori, T. (1977). Mach bands. In: O. Fujita, T. Mori, Y. Isogai (Eds.),* Psychological laboratory *(pp. 93–123). Vol. 2. Tokyo: Fukumura Press (Japanese text).)*

phenomenon can be explained as follows, based on Mach's theory shown in Fig. 1.3. Here, like Helmholtz (1867), he hypothesized that light stimuli pass through media such as the cornea and the lens and are therefore subject to aberration, resulting in a blurred image on the retina. That is, the retinal image for Fig. 1.2a was not a staircase with right-angled corners as in Fig. 1.2b but a blurred image with rounded cliffs at each step, as shown by the solid curve in Fig. 1.3a. In the supposedly blurred image, the dark and light contours shown by the dotted curve in Fig. 1.3a can be observed. Why do we see sharp contours in the blurred areas? Mach's answer to this

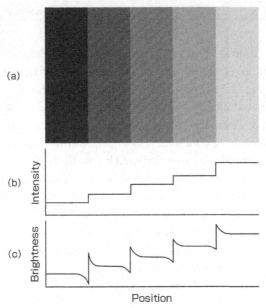

Fig. 1.2 A border contrast (a and c) and intensity distribution (b). *(From Cornsweet, T.N. (1970). Visual perception.* New York: Academic Press.)

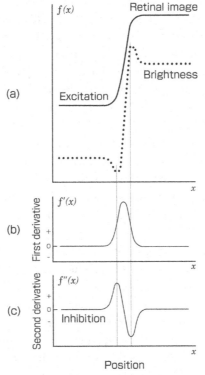

Fig. 1.3 Mach's second-order differential model (a–c) for the Mach bands. *(From Hamada, J. (1984c). How humans perceive things.* Publicity from Tokushima University, 49, 12–16. (Japanese text).)

question was as follows. First of all, he postulated that the strength of stimuli on the retina induces the excitation and inhibition of neural activity. The solid curve in Fig. 1.3a represents the excitation by the retinal image, and when differentiated against the spatial axis, the first derivative coefficient in Fig. 1.3b is led. Then, the locations of the maximum and minimum values of the second derivative coefficients in Fig. 1.3c correspond to the locations of the dark and light Mach bands depicted by the dotted curve in Fig. 1.3a. If we subtract the solid curve in Fig. 1.3c from the solid curve in Fig. 1.3a and treat them as an inhibition and an excitation, respectively, the Mach bands appear at the cliff as shown in the dotted curve in Fig. 1.3a. Therefor, he proposed a second-order differential model, in which the second-order differential coefficients are calculated in the neural network of the retina. Hering (1920) also explained the border contrast as the inhibition of an unclear retinal image (see Metzger, 1953).

1.2 Békésy's neural unit

Békésy (1959, 1960) conducted an experiment on the tactile two-point threshold of cutaneous sensation as shown in left side of Fig. 1.4. He applied a single or two equal-weight pressure stimuli to the palm of the hand and observed the pressure sensation in response. A single point stimulus produced one sensation (A). However, when the distance between the two stimuli was close (B, 2.0 cm), they became one sensation. The sensation was much stronger than that of the single point stimulus. But when the distance was further away (C, 3.0 cm), the two stimuli were perceived as two separate sensations, and the sensation for each stimulus was much weaker than when the single stimulus was presented. When the distance was further increased to 3.5 cm, the sensation of the two stimuli was the same as that of the single one. Although the same pressure was applied to both stimuli, different pressure sensations were obtained depending on the distance between the stimuli.

Békésy explained this phenomenon in the right side of Fig. 1.4, in which a single point stimulation on the skin produces neural activity as a Mexican hat consisting of sensation and inhibition (Fig. 1.4a). In this figure, the gray area above the horizontal line in (a) represents the intensity of sensation, and the area below represents that of inhibition. When the two stimuli are presented 2.0 cm apart in Fig. 1.4b, the neural activity to them is such that the sensory parts overlap with the sensory one and the inhibitory parts overlap with the inhibitory one. If we treat excitation as positive (+) and inhibition

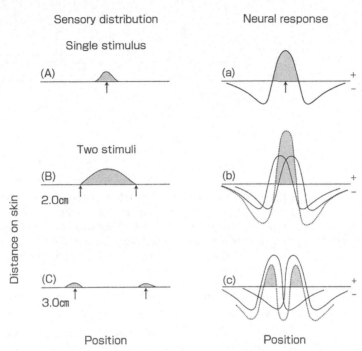

Fig. 1.4 Békésy's experimental results on the tactile two-point threshold in cutaneous sensation *(A–C)* and his neural unit-based explanation *(a–c)*. The *up arrow* indicates the location of the stimulus. *(Adapted from Békésy, G.v. (1960). Neural inhibitory units of the eye and skin. Quantitative description of contrast phenomena. Journal of the Optical Society of America, 50, 1060–1070; Hamada, J. (2020). Psychophysics of pattern cognition. Tokyo: Kazama Press (Japanese text).)*

as negative (−) and add the neural activity of the two Mexican hats, we get a higher and deeper Mexican hat, as shown by the dotted curve (b). When the two stimuli are presented 3.0 cm apart in Fig. 1.4c, the sensory and inhibitory portions of the two Mexican hats overlap, and they form two vertices as indicated by the two gray areas in Fig. 1.4c. The height of these vertices is lower than that of the solid curves. Finally, if the distance between the two stimuli is set to 3.5 cm, which is not shown in Fig. 1.4, the two Mexican hats do not overlap each other. Békésy explained the results of the tactile two-point threshold experiment consistently by assuming that the cognitive system perceives the amount of sensation for the two stimuli. Next, we would like to introduce his study that simply explains the Mach bands in vision based on the antagonistic process of excitation and inhibition.

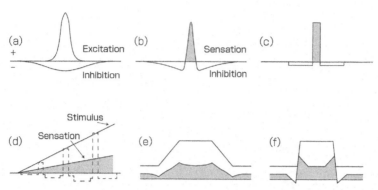

Fig. 1.5 Obonai's psycho-physiological induction (a and b) and Békésy's simplified neural unit (c), and an application of the neural unit to gradient-like light intensity starting from zero (d) and trapezoidal intensity stimuli (e and d). *(Adapted from Obonai, T. (1957). The concept of psycho-physiological induction. Psychologia, 1, 3–9; Békésy G.v., Neural inhibitory units of the eye and skin. Quantitative description of contrast phenomena. Journal of the Optical Society of America, 50, (1960) 1060–1070.)*

Obonai (1955, 1957), earlier and independently for Békésy (1959, 1960), proposed the qualitative psycho-physiological induction theory shown in Fig. 1.5a and b. Békésy (1960, 1967a) postulated that a single stimulus induces a wide range of inhibition for a narrow range of excitation as in Fig. 1.5a, but that neurophysiologically, self-inhibition is applied to the excitation to produce a Mexican hat-like neural activity, resulting in sensation and inhibition as in Fig. 1.5b. He named the combination of sensation and inhibition in the shape of a Mexican hat a neural unit. For simplicity, he represented the neural unit as squares in Fig. 1.5c. There is no essential difference in the Mexican hat and the simplified neural unit, since inhibition surrounds sensation. He also set the observation distance at 25 cm and fixed the width of the sensory area at 0.1 mm and the inhibitory one at 9 times that width. He also set the ratio of sensory to inhibitory strength to 1.6.

The following two assumptions were made when converting the stimulus distribution into the sensation by neural units. (1) Each division point generates a simplified neural unit, and its strength is proportional to the stimulus intensity at each division point. (2) The strength of a neural unit at any point on the spatial axis is the algebraic sum of the height of the neural unit at the point and the heights of all the neural units around it. Under these two assumptions, the neural units were applied to the stimulus distribution in Fig. 1.5d, which starts from zero and has a constant gradient. As a result, the gradient of sensation becomes constant and weaker due to the effect of inhibition. In this way, he made the height of the sensory area and the depth of the inhibitory area depend on the stimulus intensity. However, the range of sensation and inhibition is fixed.

Next, he applied the same graphical manipulation to the trapezoidal light intensity distribution where the stimulus gradient is changing as shown in Fig. 1.5e and f. Here, the intensity at left and right is not zero. The dark and light Mach bands appear in the area where the gradient of the stimulus distribution is changing. The width of this band is equal to that of the neural unit. The operation of transformation from stimulus distribution to sensation is mathematically equivalent to convolutional integration. His theory is essentially equivalent to Mach's theory described previously. That is, dark Mach bands are produced by strong inhibition from surrounding areas of strong light stimuli, while light Mach bands are induced by only slight inhibition from the areas of weak light ones. The existence of inhibition, first hypothesized by Mach in 1865 and about 100 years later reasserted by Békésy, has been confirmed by neurophysiology. That is, the existence of inhibition was dramatically demonstrated by developments in neurophysiology as the fact of lateral inhibition (Hartline & Ratliff, 1957; Ratliff & Hartline, 1959; Ratliff, 1965). The inhibition, which corrects blurred retinal image into sharp contours is the purposeful function that allows the cognitive system to perceive the external world efficiently.

1.3 Luminance dependence of DOG

As mentioned above, Obonai (1955, 1957) proposed a Mexican hat-like antagonistic process of excitation and inhibition (see Fig. 1.5b), similar to Békésy's neural unit, based on his studies of the geometric illusions and the light threshold (Kaneko & Obonai, 1952, 1959; Obonai, 1977). The following is an overview of the results of Fujii, Matsuoka, and Morita's (1967) simulation of the geometric illusion and their psychological experiment.

1.3.1 Fujii et al.'s two-dimensional lateral inhibition model

Fujii et al. (1967) extended the antagonistic process of excitation and inhibition, which had been proposed qualitatively in one dimension by Obonai, to a two-dimensional lateral inhibition model. They expressed the relationship between the stimulus pattern $i\,(\xi, \eta)$ and the output response $o(x, y)$ as a convolution integral of the following equation.

$$O(x, y) = \int_{-\infty}^{+\infty} \int_{-\infty}^{+\infty} W(x - \xi, y - \eta)i(\xi, \eta)d\xi d\eta \qquad (1.1)$$

Then, referring to Kuffler's (1953) on-center-off surround type receptive field, the coupling function $w(x, y)$ was approximated by DOG (a difference of two Gaussians) and expressed by the following equation.

$$W(x, y) = \frac{K_1}{2\pi\sigma_1^2} \exp\left(-\frac{x^2 + y^2}{2\sigma_1^2}\right) - \frac{K_2}{2\pi\sigma_2^2} \exp\left(-\frac{x^2 + y^2}{2\sigma_2^2}\right) \quad (1.2)$$

Here, α_1 and α_2 represent the standard deviations of excitation and inhibition, respectively. In addition, the strengths of the excitation and inhibition were equal and $K_1 = K_2 = 1$, indicating no luminance dependence. The result of applying Eqs. (1.1) and (1.2) to a square is shown in Fig. 1.6. The output response is excitation (+) inside the square and inhibition (−) outside. The output response is stronger in the inner corners and edges of the square, indicating that the model has a feature extraction function. They hypothesized that the cognitive system performs a pattern recognition based on this

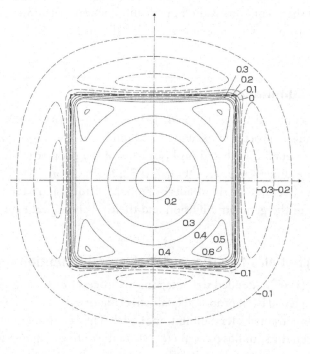

Fig. 1.6 Feature extraction for a square by the lateral inhibition model. *(From Fujii, K., Matsuoka, A., & Morita, T. (1967). Analysis of the optical illusion by lateral inhibition. Japanese Journal of Medical Electronics and Biological Engineering, 5, 117–126. (Japanese text with English abstract and captions).)*

feature extraction. Next, we will explain their psychological experiment on geometric illusion and theoretical considerations based on their model.

1.3.2 Method

1.3.2.1 Stimulus patterns

Stimulus patterns were drawn in black ink on white cards 10×15 cm in width and length. The rectangular patterns in a control condition was 5 mm wide and 50 mm long (about $5°$ in visual angle). The experimental condition consisted of eight illusory patterns as shown in Fig. 1.7. The comparison patterns were rectangles of 5 mm in width and 46 to 60 mm in length, and 15 patterns were prepared at 1 mm intervals. Fig. 1.7a and b is rectangles with a trapezoid added. And (h) is a horizontal rectangle with a vertical one added to its center, that is, it is an inverted T-shape. The length of each of them is 50 mm. On the other hand, (c) and (d) add a semicircle to the rectangle, (e) and (f) add a half-key bracket, and (g) rotates the figure (h) by $90°$. The length between these tips is 55 mm.

1.3.2.2 Procedure

The patterns in the experimental and control conditions were placed on the left and the comparison pattern on the right, and they were arranged on a desk so that their long axes were aligned. The participants were students at Miyakojima Technical High School in Osaka City, and the observation distance was 60 cm. First, they selected one of the 15 comparison patterns that they felt was equal in length to the rectangle in the control condition. Only the participants who correctly judged the length of the control pattern within an error of ± 1 mm performed the experimental condition. Therefore the number of participants for each illusion pattern ranged from 100

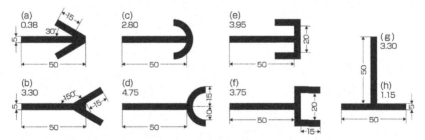

Fig. 1.7 Modified Müller-Lyer patterns (a–h) and the amounts of illusion (mm). *(From Fujii, K., Matsuoka, A., & Morita, T. (1967). Analysis of the optical illusion by lateral inhibition. Japanese Journal of Medical Electronics and Biological Engineering, 5, 117–126. (Japanese text with English abstract and captions).)*

to 103. In the experimental condition, participants compared the length of the 50 mm portion of the eight illusory patterns in Fig. 1.7 with that of the comparison pattern.

1.3.3 Results and discussion

The average measured illusion is shown in Fig. 1.7. All the illusion patterns showed overestimation compared to the 50 mm control. In Fig. 1.7a and b, the outward arrowhead shows a larger illusion than the inward one. Similarly, in (c) and (d), the outward semicircle ring cause more illusion than the inward one. In (e) and (f), the amount of the illusion is almost the same and the effect of the square bracket direction is weak. The base of the inverted T-shape (h) causes less illusion than the horizontal rectangle (g) rotated by 90°. The illusion of (d) is the largest, while that of (a) is the smallest.

1.3.3.1 Computer simulation

They analyzed the amount of illusion by convolutional integration of the patterns and DOG using the lateral inhibition model described previously. They assumed that the cognitive system detects the vertexes of excitation in DOG and that the geometric illusion is produced by the movement of these vertexes. That is, as shown in Fig. 1.8, the output response of the model to the control pattern (A) is (a), and the cognitive system judges the distance L between the vertices at both ends as the length of the pattern. Similarly, the

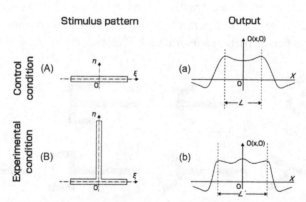

Fig. 1.8 Stimulus patterns (A and B) and output responses (a and b) of the lateral inhibition model. (From Fujii, K., Matsuoka, A., & Morita, T. (1967). Analysis of the optical illusion by lateral inhibition. Japanese Journal of Medical Electronics and Biological Engineering, 5, 117–126. (Japanese text with English abstract and captions).)

output response to the base of inverted T-shape shown in (B) is (b), and the cognitive system judges the distance L' between the vertices appearing near both tips as the length of the pattern. Here, L' is longer than L, and this is the amount of illusion. They calculated the theoretical amount of illusion ε by the following formulas. For illusory patterns (a), (d), and (h), $\varepsilon = (L_i - L)/L \times 100\%$, and for the others, $\varepsilon = (L_i - L - 5)/L \times 100\%$ after correcting for the rectangle end being 5 mm longer. Then, they calculated α_1 and α_2, which corresponded to the experimental relative amounts of illusion and the theoretical illusions based on their model, by an extreme value search method. After computer simulation, they set $K_1 = K_2 = 1$ and determined the standard deviations of excitation and inhibition to be $\sigma_1 = 0.23°$ and $\sigma_2 = 1.8°$ in visual angle. As a result, the correlation coefficient between the amount of illusions obtained by the eight patterns and that of the theoretical value is 0.993, indicating a high correlation.

1.3.4 Hamada's luminance-dependent model

Before Obonai (1955) and Békésy (1959) postulated the antagonistic process of excitation and inhibition, Beitel (1934, 1936), Tevlov (1936), and Kaneko and Obonai (1952) reported that the light threshold in the periphery falls when the luminance in the inducing field is low and rises when it is high (see also Takahashi & Uemura, 1967). Hamada (1971) and Ito and Hamada (1972) proposed a luminance-dependent model based on the light threshold of a small light spot projected at the center of an annulus. In the following, Hamada (1971) will be reviewed.

1.3.5 Method

1.3.5.1 Experimental apparatus and procedure

The experimental apparatus was a box 1.8 m long, 0.9 m wide, and 0.9 m high, having a wall with a test window, corresponding to the observation distance of 1 m, behind which eight 60-W incandescent bulbs were installed. A voltage regulator to adjust the luminance of the annulus and a projector with a voltage regulator to project a small light spot at the center of the annulus were used. The annulus was made by pasting black paper on a white paper (reflectance: 84%). The light from bulbs uniformly illuminated the entire white paper and transmitted through the annulus part. The inner radius of the annulus was 4 mm (14' in visual angle) and the outer radii were 6, 8, 12, and 20 mm.

The experiment was conducted in a dark room and started after 60 min of dark adaptation. Participants wore a 3 mm diameter artificial pupil in the right eye. The participant's head was fixed on a chin rest. Light and shape thresholds were first measured for the annuli. The former was the minimum luminance at which light of the annulus could be perceived in the darkness, and the latter was the luminance at which the shape of it could be perceived. These thresholds are the average of the upper and lower thresholds of the ascending and descending series in the method of limits. These thresholds were measured over a period of two different days by dividing four types of annuli with different outer radii into two groups. The luminance of each annulus was set at six intensities that crossed the thresholds of light and shape. Similarly, the light threshold of a small light spot projected to the center of the annulus was measured. The order of measurement was from the lowest to the highest luminance of the annulus. The measurement of the light threshold of the small light spot was repeated four times on different days, and the order of the four annuli was counterbalanced. The thresholds were measured in descending series of the method of limits starting from the intensity at which they were clearly visible, and the small spot also served as the fixation point. Two participants were a staff member and an undergraduate student at Tokushima University.

1.3.6 Results and discussion

Since the results of the two participants were qualitatively identical, the results of one participant's experiment are shown in Fig. 1.9. A solid circle was the light threshold in the control condition in which the luminance of the annulus was zero. Compared to it, the light threshold of the small light spot decreased when the luminance was slightly higher than that of the annulus and increased when it was much higher. Under the condition in which the luminance of the four annuli was .015 radlux, the light threshold increased as the outer radius increased. The results for the (4:6 mm) condition are located on the right side and deviate, while those for the other conditions are almost parallel to each other. The lowering of the light threshold reflects excitation, and the rising reflects inhibition.

Fujii et al. (1967) set that $K_1 = K_2 = 1$ and $\sigma_2/\sigma_1 = 7.8$ in Eq. (1.2). Hamada (1971) then applied this formula to the annulus with $K_1 = K_2 = 1$ and $\sigma_2/\sigma_1 = 8$ and applied the transformations $\xi = r\cos\theta$ and $\eta = r\sin\theta$ to Eqs. (1.1) and (1.2). He solved for the output response at the center in the (4: 6 mm) condition by the following equation.

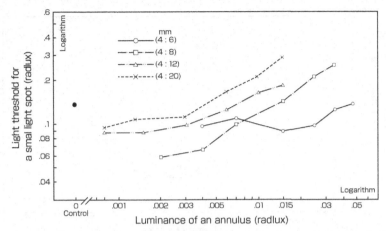

Fig. 1.9 Light thresholds of small light spots with increasing luminance in annuli. *(From Hamada, J. (1971). Inhibitory and facilitational effects in visual field. (Bachelor thesis). Japan: Tokushima University Tokushima, pp. 1–109. (Japanese text).); Ito, M., Hamada, J. (1972). Experimental study on facilitation effects in visual field (continued from the last report). Bulletin of Journal of Cultural and Social Sciences, University of Tokushima, Department of Liberal Arts, 7, 163–172. (Japanese text with English abstract and captions).)*

$$f\sigma_1(0,0) = \int_0^{2\pi}\int_{r_1}^{r_2}\left(\frac{1}{2\pi\sigma_1^2}\exp\left[-\frac{r^2}{2\sigma_1^2}\right] - \frac{1}{2\pi(8\sigma_1)^2}\exp\left[-\frac{r^2}{2(8\sigma_1)^2}\right]\right)rdr.d\theta$$

$$= \left(e^{-\frac{r_1^2}{2\sigma_1^2}} - e^{-\frac{r_2^2}{2\sigma_1^2}}\right) - \left(e^{-\frac{r_1^2}{2(8\sigma_1)^2}} - e^{-\frac{r_2^2}{2(8\sigma_1)^2}}\right) \quad (1.3)$$

Here, r_1 and r_2 are the inner and outer radii of the annulus, respectively. Assuming that σ_1 and σ_2 are the reciprocals of luminance, the output response for an annulus with an inner radius of 4 mm and an outer one of 6 mm was calculated and is shown in Fig. 1.10. This figure shows that when the output response is compared to it (solid circle) for the zero-luminance where σ_1 is infinite, as luminance increases it shifts from downward to upward. This means that the GOD becomes sharper as luminance increases. In this model, as luminance increases further, the σ_2 becomes too small and inhibition becomes weaker at the center of annulus, although not shown in Fig. 1.10. However, the output response in the region of moderate excitation and inhibition is consistent with open circles in Fig. 1.9. In the same way that Békésy explained Mach bands in terms of the light intensity dependence of neural unit, Hamada proposed a luminance-dependent model. In this model, the ratio of σ_2 to σ_1 was changed from 7.8 in the Fujii et al. (1967) model to 8.0, and the two standard deviations were set to decrease

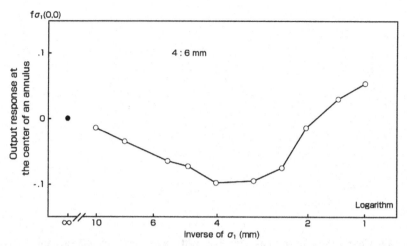

Fig. 1.10 Output response at the center of the annulus. As σ_1 and σ_2 narrow, the output response shifts from excitation to inhibition. *(From Hamada, J. (1971). Inhibitory and facilitational effects in visual field. (Bachelor thesis). Japan: Tokushima University Tokushima, pp. 1–109. (Japanese text); Ito, M., Hamada, J. (1972). Experimental study on facilitation effects in visual field (continued from the last report).* Bulletin of Journal of Cultural and Social Sciences, University of Tokushima, Department of Liberal Arts, 7, 163–172. *(Japanese text with English abstract and captions).)*

inversely proportional to luminance as luminance increases. In addition, Gergeson (1980) pointed out that the size of the receptive field increases at low luminance and low contrast. This is in support of Hamada's (1971) model. However, in his model, the strength of excitation (K_1) and inhibition (K_2) is fixed at 1. Therefor, Hamada (1976a, 1976b, 1980a, 1984b) added luminance dependence not only to σ_1 and σ_2 but also to K_1 and K_2 in the following model. Namely, he developed a four-level serial processing model in which the cognitive system detects the inflection points of GOD as edges and averages the gradient of neural responses between the edges, unlike Fujii et al. (1967) and Ratliff (1972) who focused on the vertices of excitatory and inhibitory neural responses.

1.4 Simulation of a border contrast by a four-level serial processing model

First, we would like to give a short description of Bergström's (1966) experiment on the brightness illusion (see Robinson, 1972). He presented the observer with a smooth-gradient luminance distribution following two overlapping cumulative normal distribution functions as shown in Fig. 1.11. The apparent brightness of 12 positions of that was measured by the

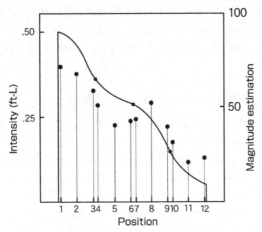

Fig. 1.11 A sloped luminance distribution consisting of two cumulative normal distributions and results of magnitude estimation for 12 points by Bergström (1966). *(Adapted from Hamada, J. (1994). Brightness perception. In: T. Oyama, S. Imai, T. Wake (Eds.), Handbook of sensory and perceptual psychology (pp. 344–348). Tokyo: Seishin Press (Japanese text).)*

magnitude estimation method, and the results are shown as large solid circles. Although the luminance at position 5 is higher than that at position 8, the former appears to be darker than the latter, that is, the relationship between luminance and brightness is reversed. In addition, there were discontinuity lines of brightness at the three inflection points (small solid circles) of the smooth luminance distribution. This discontinuity line is a corroboration of the edge detection in the following Hamada's four-level serial processing model.

Hamada (1976a, 1976b, 1980a, 1984b) added the functions of inflection point detection and information reduction to his luminance-dependent model described previously to construct the one-dimensional four-level serial processing model shown in Fig. 1.12. Since Bergström used the magnitude estimation method to measure the apparent brightness (i.e., a border

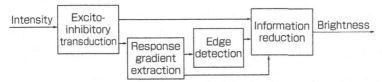

Fig. 1.12 A four-level serial processing model for a border contrast. *(Adapted from Hamada, J. (1976b). A mathematical model for brightness and contour perception. Hokkaido Report of Psychology, HRP-11-76-17, 1–19.)*

contrast) for the five-step luminance distribution shown in Fig. 1.13a, Hamada used its luminance (0.47, 0.33, 0.24, and 0.13 ft-L) and the background (0.10 ft-L) as input stimuli for his four-level serial processing model.

1.4.1 Excito-inhibitory transduction level

The function of this level is expressed by the convolution integral of the luminance distribution and the line spread function (DOG), as in Fujii et al. (1967), Furukawa and Hagiwara (1978), and Wilson and Bergen (1979). In other words, the output $O_1(x)$ for the luminance distribution i (ζ) is given by the convolution integral of Eq. (1.4). The line spread function $W(x)$ is the difference of excitation (narrow normal distribution) and inhibition (wide normal one) and is described as in Eq. (1.5).

$$O_1(x) = \int_{-\infty}^{+\infty} W(x - \xi)i(\xi)d\xi \qquad (1.4)$$

$$W(x) = \frac{K_1}{\sqrt{2\pi}\sigma_1} \exp\left(-\frac{x^2}{2\sigma_1^2}\right) - \frac{K_2}{\sqrt{2\pi}\sigma_2} \exp\left(-\frac{x^2}{2\sigma_2^2}\right) \qquad (1.5)$$

K_1 and K_2 are the intensities of excitation and inhibition, and σ_1 and σ_2 are their standard deviations, respectively. Hamada showed that the luminance dependence of the excito-inhibitory transduction level in the four-level serial processing model is determined by power law of Stevens (1961).[a] According to Stevens, the exponent of brightness function for 5° target amount to 0.33 and that for point source to 0.5.

A 5° target with the exponent of 0.33 is equivalent to an infinite uniform luminance field of view because it is considered to be sufficiently larger than the distribution of inhibition. Assuming that the spatial extent on the retina is homogeneous, K_1 and K_2 can be expressed by the following two equations. Here, I is the luminance of the visual field, and A and B are constants.

$$K_1 = AI^{-0.67} \qquad (1.6)$$

$$K_2 = BK_1 \qquad (1.7)$$

A point source with power law of 0.5 is assumed to be a necessary and sufficient area for the induction of excitation and inhibition. Then, the output response of the excito-inhibitory transduction level to the point light source

[a]The application of Stevens' power law to the luminance dependence of the excito-inhibitory transduction level was proposed by the author, and Associate Professor Tomozo Furukawa formulated (1.6)–(1.9). For details of the equations, see Hamada (1984b).

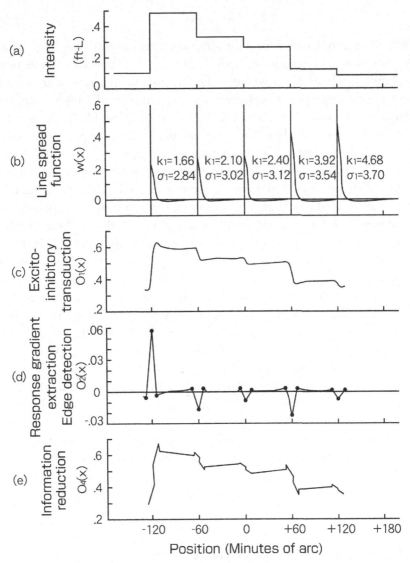

Fig. 1.13 Results of simulation (a–e) for a border contrast by a four-level serial processing model. *(From Hamada, J. (1984b). A multi-stage model for border contrast. Biological Cybernetics, 51, 65–70. (Springer Nature).)*

is the peak value corresponding to the origin of the line spread function. Therefore, σ_1 and σ_2 can be expressed by the following two equations, where C and D are constants.

$$\sigma_1 = CI^{-0.17} \tag{1.8}$$

$$\sigma_2 = D\sigma_1 \qquad\qquad (1.9)$$

In these equations, the stronger the luminance, the narrower the distribution of excitation and inhibition, and the sharper the line spread function becomes. Patel (1966) showed that the linear spread function of the visual system becomes sharper with increasing luminance. His results support Hamada's first level. If we determine the four constants (A, B, C, and D), we can determine the luminance dependence of the four parameters (K_1, K_2, σ_1, and σ_2). Hamada used computer simulations to determine A, B, C, and D so that the final output of his model would match the experimental results of Bergström's (1966) border contrast shown later. As far as the relative values of the outputs are concerned, we can assume that $A = 1$. According to his experiment on the border contrast, the brightness in the center of the second step of the staircase luminance distribution (-30 mins in visual angle in Fig. 1.13) was almost equal to that of the light Mach band in the corner of the third step. Therefore, the values of the three constants (B, C, and D) were determined so that the output at -30 min in the final level of Hamada's model coincided with the peak of the light Mach band around $+60$ min. As a result, the values of B, C, and D were 0.19, 2.5, and 9.0, respectively. The value of B indicates that the ratio of the strength of inhibition to excitation K_2/K_1 is 0.19. The value of C indicates the luminance-dependent spread of the excitation. The value of D indicates that the ratio of the standard deviation of the inhibition to that of the excitation σ_2/σ_1 is 9.0. For example, for 0.33 ft-L in Fig. 1.13b, σ_1 and σ_2 are 3.02 and 27.18 min in visual angle, respectively. Also, (b) shows the results of K_1 and σ_1 for each luminance, and (c) shows the output response of the excito-inhibitory transduction level. The output response shows the prototypes of Mach band and border contrast.

1.4.2 Response gradient extraction level

The gradient of the output response in the first level is extracted in this second level. In other words, it is to calculate the first derivative of the output of the first level. The output of this second level is given by the following equation, and the result is shown as the curve in Fig. 1.13d. This output is used for the third and fourth levels.

$$O_2(x) = O_1'(x) \qquad\qquad (1.10)$$

1.4.3 Edges detection level

This third level detects the inflection points in the output of the first level, that is, the vertices of the output response of the second level shown in Fig. 1.13d (small solid circles). Mathematically speaking, the edge is the point that satisfies the following two equations, where x_i is the inflection point in the output of the first level. The position of the edge detected in this third level is sent to the fourth level.

$$O_2'(x_i) = 0, \tag{1.11}$$

$$|O_2(x_i)| > |O_2(x)| \text{for } 0 < |x - x_i| < \delta$$
$$(i = 1, 2, \ldots\ldots n), \tag{1.12}$$

This inflection point depends on the output of the first level (Watt & Morgan, 1983), unlike the zero-crossing model later proposed by Marr and Hildreth (1980) and Marr (1983). In the zero-crossing model, the ratio of σ_2/σ_1 is about 1.6, while in Hamada's model, the ratio is 9.0. Similarly, Fujii et al. (1967) estimated the ratio to be 7.8 based on actual measurements of the geometric illusion. Furthermore, Hamada (1971) estimated the ratio to be 8.0 based on the measurement of the light threshold. Thus the ratio of σ_2/σ_1 in the zero-crossing model is too small (see Robson, 1983). In addition, Marr and Hildreth's model has no luminance-dependent parameters and assumes that the intensity of excitation and inhibition are equal and $K_1 = K_2 = 1$. This assumption is also made by Fujii et al. (1967) and Hamada (1971). On the other hand, Békésy's neural unit sets the ratio of sensation to inhibition at 1.6, and Hamada's (1976a, 1976b, 1984b) four-level model sets the ratio of inhibition to excitation at $K_2/K_1 = 0.19$.

Bergström reported in Fig. 1.11 that discontinuous lines can be observed at three inflection points in a smooth continuous luminance distribution consisting of two cumulative normal distribution functions (see three small circles in Fig. 1.11). This phenomenon supports the edge detection in Hamada's third level. In other words, when the luminance distribution is convoluted and integrated by GOD, three inflection points are generated.

1.4.4 Information reduction level

The fourth level averages the response gradients processed in the second level between the edges detected in the third one and keeps the total output processed in the first one constant. This means that the total output from the first level is preserved, but the response gradient from the second one is lost except for its average value. The excitatory and inhibitory neural activity processed at the first level is sent to the second one, where the gradient of the response output is extracted. At the third level, the inflection points are detected, and at the fourth one, the inflection points become intervals and the output response of the first one undergoes linearization between them. The output of the fourth and final level is obtained by the following three equations; the calculation results of which are shown in Fig. 1.13e.

$$O_4(x) = \left(x - \left(x_{j+1} + x_j\right)/2\right)S + T/\left(x_{j+1} - x_j\right)$$
$$\text{for } x_j \leq x < x_{j+1},$$
(1.13)

$$S = \left(O_1\left(x_{j+1}\right) - O_1(xj)\right)/\left(x_{j+1} - x_j\right),$$
(1.14)

$$T = \int_{x_i}^{x_{j+1}} O_1(x)dx \quad (j = 1, 2, ...n),$$
(1.15)

Here x_i is the position of the edge. By the functions of edge detection and information reduction, Mach bands appear at the corners of the luminance distribution, and a slope appears in the flat part of it, completing the border contrast. The slope corresponds to the Hering-type inhibition postulated by Békésy (1968). In this model, the total output of the final level between adjacent edges keeps the output of the first one, so the final output satisfies Stevens' power law. Then, after an edge is detected in the third level, the output between adjacent edges is linearized and the output response becomes discontinuous at the edge location. This model assumes that brightness information is processed serially from the first to the fourth level.

Gerrits and Vendrik (1970) emphasized the filling-in process in the visual system from experiments with Mach bands and stabilized retinal images (Ratliff and Riggs, 1950; Pritchard, 1961), and postulated antagonistic and symmetric bright and dark processes. The bright process corresponds to the on-center and off-surround receptive fields, while the dark process corresponds to the off-center and on-surround receptive fields. Here, the on response of the bright process and the off response of the dark process correspond to excitation, and conversely, the off response of the bright process and the on response of the dark process correspond to inhibition. The excitation of the bright process (on response) causes brightness, and the excitation of the dark process (off response) causes darkness. In addition, their model has spatial spread activity, which is assumed to be blocked by antagonistic light and dark processes. This model is similar to Hamada's (1976a, 1976b, 1984b) four-level serial processing model, in which the inflection points are detected as edges and serve as intervals of information reduction.

1.4.5 A border contrast for a circular light intensity

Observing the four-step circular luminous distribution in Fig. 1.14B, the brightness sensation is as shown in (A). Here, the luminance of the central circle increases at equal intervals to the outer concentric ones, and the background is pure white. The dark and light Mach bands appear at the edges of the concentric circle, and the brightness of the concentric one, which should be flat, is sloped. This brightness gradient corresponds to the Hering-type inhibition. Although not simulated here, we qualitatively apply Hamada's (1976a, 1976b, 1984b) four-level serial processing model to these phenomena. Since this model has the function to average the gradient between edges, the output response is linearized as shown in Fig. 1.14C. In particular, the region surrounded by the circular dark Mach band that appears at the inner edge of the center circle has a homogeneous brightness.

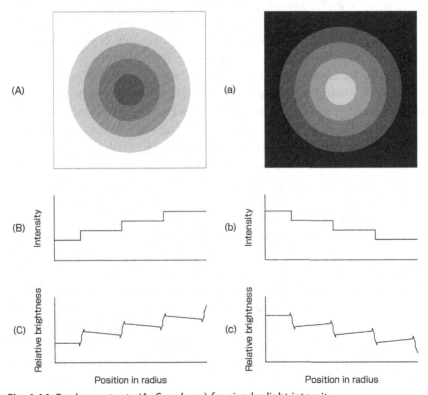

Fig. 1.14 Border contrasts (A–C and a–c) for circular light intensity.

This phenomenon is consistent with Koffka (1923) as shown by Metzger (1953, 2006). On the other hand, when we observe the light four-step circular luminance distribution with the pure black background in Fig. 1.14b, the brightness sensation appears as in (a). Here, light and dark Mach bands are seen on the circular edges, and the Hering-type inhibition with a slope appears in other areas. Then, as in (A and C), the central circle becomes uniformly bright and a light Mach band is visible at the inner edge in (a and c).

Incidentally, the luminance of the center circle in (A) is the same as that of the outermost concentric circle in (a), and that of the center circle of (a) is the same as that of the outermost concentric circle of (A). However, the apparent brightness of those areas is not the same. Moreover, the central circles in (A) and (a) appear to stand out. Experimental and theoretical investigations of these light and dark asymmetries remain to be done.

1.4.6 Koffka's ring

An example of a psychological phenomenon related to edge detection and information reduction in Hamada's (1976a, 1976b, 1984b) four-level model is Koffka's (1915) ring shown in Fig. 1.15 (Metzger, 1953, 2006; Berman & Liebowitz, 1965; Adelson, 2000). In the figure (a), thin black vertical lines are drawn in the center of a uniform gray ring. Here, the left half of the ring is surrounded by a black background and the right half by a white one. As a result, the left half of the ring appears to be lighter while the right one appears to be darker because of the brightness contrast, though they are physically the same luminance. On the other hand, when the lower vertical line is deleted as shown in (b), the right side of the upper vertical line appears to be dark and the left one appears to be light. Here, the brightness strengthens gradually from dark to light when the ring is traced from the right side of the vertical line above in clockwise and reaches the left one. This corresponds to averaging and linearizing the response gradient processed in the second and fourth levels of Hamada's four-level model. When all the vertical lines in the ring are removed, as shown in (c), the whole ring appears to be uniformly gray. This indicates that the loss of vertical lines (i.e., edges) homogenizes the lightness of the entire ring. This phenomenon supports the mechanism that assumes that the neural response between edges is averaged in the final level of Hamada's model. In this way, the cognitive system has the function of highlighting the difference between light and dark by contrasting the brightness around the vertical contour lines and smoothing out the brightness when they are removed.

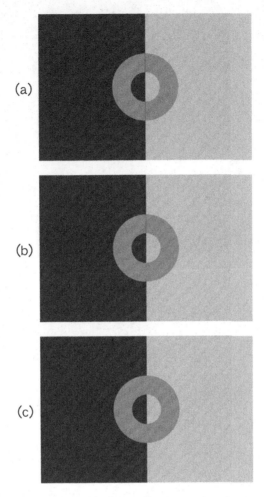

Fig. 1.15 Koffka's ring (a–c). *(Adapted from Metzger, W. (2006). Laws of seeing. (English translated by Spillmann, L., Lehar, S., Stromeyer, M. and Wertheimer, M.) Cambridge: MIT Press.)*

CHAPTER TWO

A five-level qualitative model based on brightness illusions and decrease in brightness levels

2.1 Contour perception and the Craik-O'Brien illusion

O'Brian (1958) generated the luminance distributions shown in the left side of Fig. 2.1. He changed the stepwise luminance distribution shown by the dotted line to a wedge-shape (a) or gentle S-shape (b) shown by the solid curve. Thereupon, the apparent brightness for them was as shown on the right side. That is, when the step intensity was changed to wedge-shaped, the right side was higher than the left one, but the former was darker than the latter, as indicated by single-pointed line. This phenomenon in (a) was reported by Dr. Kenneth Craik in his dissertation in 1940 and is called the Craik-O'Brien illusion (Craik, 1966; Ratliff, 1965, 1972; Jung, 1973). On the other hand, as shown in (b), when the stepwise intensity was made gentle S-shaped, the brightness was uniform despite the different intensities on the left and right sides. These phenomena indicate that the apparent brightness for a pattern is highly dependent on the luminance distribution at the edge. In this section, Hamada (1982) will be reviewed.

Classification of the Craik-O'Brien patterns. Hamada (1982) classified the luminance patterns that produce the Craik-O'Brien illusion into black and white teeth. The characteristic of a black tooth is that the luminance falls suddenly from a certain level and then rises slowly to the original level (negative contrast) as shown in Fig. 2.1. In contrast, the white tooth has a positive contrast. In this chapter the dark and light Craik-O'Brien illusions are defined as the phenomena that when a pattern with black or white tooth is presented, the luminance in the right and left regions is equal except for the tooth, but there is a difference in apparent brightness. In order to understand the induction

Psychophysics and Experimental Phenomenology of Pattern Cognition
https://doi.org/10.1016/B978-0-323-95286-6.00002-8
27

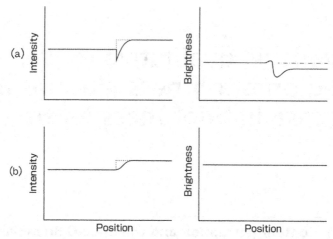

Fig. 2.1 Changing the corner of the light intensity step shown by the *dotted line* on the *left* to a wedge-shaped (a) or a gentle S-shape (b) of the solid curve results in the brightness sensation on the *right*. *(Adapted from O'Brian, V. (1958). Contour perception, illusion and reality.* Journal of the Optical Society of America, 48, 112–119; Hamada, J. (1983). Lightness decrease of the total area accompanying simultaneous lightness contrast. Japanese Journal of Psychology, 54, 115–122. (Japanese text with English abstract and captions).)

mechanism of this illusion, as well as that of the whole light-dark perception, the brightness of the right and left regions in each luminance pattern is compared with that of a uniform field as a control condition. Based on the brightness of this uniform field, the Craik-O'Brien illusion and the contour enhancement effect will be examined by measuring the brightness of the right and left regions as well as that of the contour corresponding to the tooth.

2.1.1 Method

Experimental apparatus and procedure. The front and side views of the apparatus are shown in Fig. 2.2. The front of the presentation box, which was covered with black paper (6% reflectance), was uniformly illuminated at 392 lx by four light sources. In the center of the front of it, there were a test window (50 × 52 mm, 9.2 × 9.5° in visual angle) and a comparison window (18 × 6 mm, 3.3 × 1.1°) below. These windows were opened and closed simultaneously with a black paper shutter that opened for 3 s. A participant observed the pattern at a distance of 30 cm with binocular free vision. To generate the stimulus pattern, a strip of black and white frosted photographic paper was wrapped around a drum (BRAUN Desk Fan HL-70) and fused at high speed at a rotational speed of $2740 \, min^{-1}$. Munsell achromatic paper was presented in the comparison window to

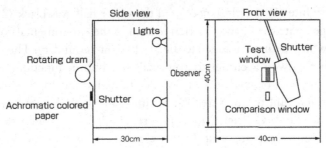

Fig. 2.2 Front and side views of the experimental apparatus. *(From Hamada, J. (1983). Lightness decrease of the total area accompanying simultaneous lightness contrast. Japanese Journal of Psychology, 54, 115–122. (Japanese text with English abstract and captions).)*

measure the apparent brightness of the stimulus pattern. The brightness value of achromatic paper was varied from 1.5 to 9.5 in 18 pieces at 0.5 intervals. The participant's head was fixed using a chin rest.

As shown in Fig. 2.3, a paper used to generate the stimulus pattern had a length of 191 mm and a width of 60 mm. Half of the paper for the uniform

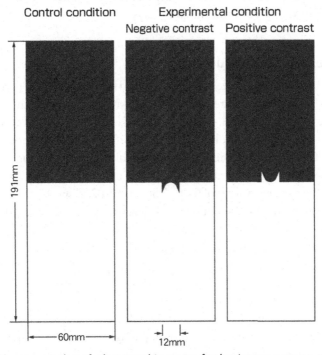

Fig. 2.3 Three examples of photographic paper for luminance pattern generation. *(From Hamada, J. (2020).* Psychophysics of pattern cognition. *Kazama Press Tokyo (Japanese text).)*

field was white (78% reflectance), and the other half was black (2.3%). In order to generate the Craik-O'Brien pattern in the experimental condition, black or white teeth were added to the black–white boundary. The shapes of the tooth followed a cumulative normal distribution function, with the width at the foot of the tooth at 3σ and the height at 0σ. The widths at the sharp and dull tooth were 3 and 6 mm, and their heights were both 8 mm. The Craik-O'Brien patterns were divided into four types: black and white, and sharp and dull. In this experiment, we used a symmetrical pattern of these teeth. The region between the vertices is called the inside area, and the outer region the outside area.

The participants were five students at Hokkaido University and the author. Their task was to judge the apparent brightness of the uniform field and the Craik-O'Brien pattern using the three cases (bright, same, and dark) with that of Munsell achromatic paper. The sites of judgment were the center of the uniform field, as well as the centers of the inside and outside areas in the Craik-O'Brien pattern, and the contour occurring at the edge of the inside one. The point of subjective equality was the average of the upper and lower thresholds measured by the method of limits. Each participant repeated for four sessions on different days.

2.1.2 Results and discussion

The uniform field. Regardless of the sharp and dull patterns, the participants' measured values in each area were also almost the same, so their average values are shown in Fig. 2.4. When Talbot's law was applied to calculate the reflectance of the stimulus pattern, the reflectance of the uniform field was 40.2%, and those of the bottom of the black tooth and the top of the white one were 37.0% and 43.4%. Those reflectance values correspond to Munsell brightness values of 6.80, 6.56, and 7.02, respectively. However, the brightness value for the uniform field shown by the left end and thin line in Fig. 2.4 is 6.06, which does not correspond to 6.80. This difference in brightness value of 0.74 may be due to the difference in areas between the test and comparison stimuli. However, this discrepancy is not a problem in this experiment because the analysis is based on the measurements of the uniform field as the control condition.

As shown in Fig. 2.4, the measured brightness values for both the inside and outside areas around the black tooth are significantly lower than that for the uniform field. Furthermore, the values for the inside and outside areas around the white tooth are significantly lower than that for the uniform field. Similarly, the measured brightness values for the bottom of the black

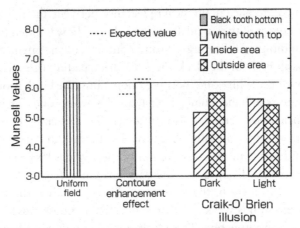

Fig. 2.4 Munsell brightness value matched to the uniform field *(left end* and *thin line)* and to the Craik-O'Brien patterns. The *dotted lines* of *left* and *right* are the expected brightness values for the bottom and top of the tooth, respectively. *(Adapted from Hamada, J. (1982). The contour enhancement effects produced by darkening effects. In H.-G. Geissler & P. Petzold (Eds.), Psychophysical judgment and the process of perception. North-Holland Amsterdam 132–139.)*

tooth are significantly lower than that for the expected values shown by the dotted line of left. On the other hand, the measured brightness value for the top of the white tooth is almost equal to the expected value shown by the dotted line of right.

The brightness value of each area of the Craik–O'Brien pattern does not exceed that of the comparable uniform field, and with one exception (the white tooth top), it is rather significantly darker than that of the uniform field. This result indicates that the Craik–O'Brien illusion is caused by the darkening effect (Cohen & Grossberg, 1984; Horst, 2005). Next, we will discuss the contour enhancement effect.

Contour enhancement effect. If we measured the apparent brightnesses of two uniform fields with the same reflectance as the bottom of the black tooth and the top of the white one, we would expect their measured brightness values to be 0.74 lower than those corresponding to their respective reflectance, as described previously. Assuming the decrease in brightness value of 0.74, the expected values for those uniform fields are 5.82 and 6.28, as shown by the dotted lines of left and right in Fig. 2.4, respectively. In this experiment, we define the contour enhancement effect as $Ec = M/P$, where M is the difference in reflectance corresponding to the brightness value matched for the outside area and that for the bottom or top of the tooth. *P* is the difference in physical reflectance between them, with a value of 3.2%. As a result of the calculation, the value of Ec was much higher than 1.0 in all conditions, indicating a strong contour enhancement effect. The value of Ec is about 5 for the black Craik–O'Brien pattern (negative contrast) and about 3 for the white one (positive one). Thus, the black tooth causes a stronger contour enhancement effect than the white one. Therefore the contour enhancement effect is also caused by the darkening effect.

The Craik–O'Brien illusion. As shown by the dark in Fig. 2.4, there is a significant difference in the measured brightness values between the inside and outside areas, indicating that the dark illusion is caused. On the other hand, on the white teeth, the outside area is darker than the inside one, but the light illusion is weak. Here, the negative contrast caused a stronger illusion than the positive one. This result is similar to that of Magnussen and Glad (1975), who reported that the dark enhancement effect is larger than the light in a flicker situation. Fig. 2.4 shows that the outside areas of both the black and white patterns were significantly darker than the uniform field. That is, the brightness value of the outside area of the pattern with negative contrast is 5.7, and that with positive one is 5.4, while that of the uniform field is 6.1, indicating the decrease in brightness levels (Grossberg, 1987). Thus, the Craik–O'Brien illusion as well as the contour enhancement effect are caused by the darkening effect from the teeth.

2.2 The Craik-O'Brien illusion by a compensation method

According to the matching method described in the previous section, the contour enhancement effect and the Craik–O'Brien illusion were stronger in negative than in positive contrast. In order to investigate the Craik–O'Brien illusion in more detail, the dark and light illusions as a function of the width and height of the tooth are measured by the compensation method (Békésy, 1972a, 1972b). In this section, Hamada (1985) will be reviewed.

2.2.1 Method

Stimulus patterns and procedures. The experimental apparatus was the same as in the previous section, but no comparison stimuli were used. There are eight different black and white teeth. Those teeth were classified into the width-variable condition and the height-variable one. As shown in Table 2.1, a tooth with a width of 3 mm (33′ in visual angle) and a height of 8 mm (3.2% reflectance) is called a prototype (*P*), a tooth with a slower

Table 2.1 Shapes of tooth in the width- and height-variable conditions. P, S, and D indicate prototype, sharp, and dull tooth, respectively.

Width-variable condition	Height-variable condition
(Width: Height)	
S_1 (1.5 mm: 8 mm)	D_1 (3 mm: 4 mm)
P (3 mm: 8 mm)	
D_2 (4.5 mm: 8 mm)	S_2 (3 mm: 12 mm)
D_3 (6.0 mm: 8 mm)	S_3 (3 mm: 16 mm)
	S_4 (3 mm: 20 mm)

From Hamada, J. (1985). Asymmetric lightness cancellation in Craik-O'Brien patterns of negative and positive contrast. *Biological Cybernetics, 52,* 117–122. (Springer Nature).

slope is called a dull (D_n, $n = 1$, 2, 3), and that with a steeper slope is called a sharp (S_n, $n = 1$, 2, 3, 4).

According to the experiment in the previous section, the inside area is darker than the outside one in the dark illusion, while the former is relatively lighter than the latter in the light one. To compensate this difference in brightness between the inside and outside areas, the entire inside area was moved up or down at 1 mm (0.4% reflectance) intervals without changing the shape of the tooth. The stimulus pattern was presented at 392 lx illumination, and the reflectance of the outside area was always fixed at 40.2%. A total of 160 sheets of a pattern-generating photographic paper were prepared.

Five participants were students at Hokkaido University and the author. Sixteen different Craik-O'Brien patterns with black or white teeth were presented in random order. The amount of compensation (mm) required to cancel out the difference in brightness between the inside and outside areas was measured by the method of limits, and the average of the upper and lower thresholds was used as the amount of compensation for the illusion. Their task was to judge the apparent brightness of the inside area based on that of the outside one using the three cases (bright, same, and dark). Each participant repeated four sessions on different days.

2.2.2 Results and discussion

Amount of compensation for the illusion. Fig. 2.5a shows the amount of compensation (mm) for the illusion as a function of the width with the height fixed at 8 mm. The solid and open circles indicate the amount of movement of the inside area required to compensate the dark and light Craik-O'Brien illusions, respectively. The amount of compensation increased linearly as a

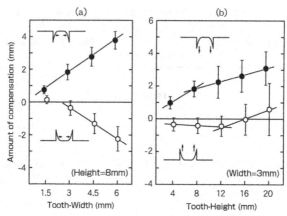

Fig. 2.5 The amount of compensation required to cancel the Craik-O'Brien illusion. The amount of compensation is shown as a function of the width (a) and height (b). *(From Hamada, J. (1985). Asymmetric lightness cancellation in Craik-O'Brien patterns of negative and positive contrast. Biological Cybernetics, 52, 117–122. (Springer Nature).)*

function of the width. In all the widths, it is significantly stronger in the dark illusion than in the light one.

In Fig. 2.5b, the width of the tooth is fixed at 3 mm, and the amount of compensation (mm) as a function of the height is shown. In the case of the dark Craik-O'Brien illusion (solid circles), the amount of compensation increases with increasing the height, divided into two components. On the other hand, in the light illusion (open circles), it is about −0.5 mm even if the height is increased to 12 mm, indicating that the light illusion is weak. However, with further increase in height, the value approaches +0.5 mm, although this is not significant. Thus, the initial compensation amount is negative, and the inside area appears slightly brighter than the outside, and then it turns positive, and the inside one becomes darker. The same phenomenon has been confirmed by Moulden and Kingdom (1990). The tendency of the inside area to darken in the light illusion indicates the reversal of the Craik-O'Brien illusion and is not seen in the dark illusion. In addition, the dull illusion is stronger than the sharp illusion in both dark and light. For example, although the areas of the D_2 (4.5 mm: 8 mm) and the S_2 (3 mm: 12 mm) tooth are equal, the D_2 pattern induces a stronger illusion than the S_2 one, as shown in Fig. 2.5a and b.

Comparison of matching and comparison methods. The results of the previous section and this experiment can be summarized as follows and are in good agreement. (1) The dark and light illusions were asymmetric

in contrast polarity, with the dark illusion being stronger than the light illusion. (2) The dull tooth produced a stronger illusion than the sharp one.
(3) These illusions showed two components as the height of the tooth changed, depending on the shape of it. (4) The reverse illusion appeared in the
light illusion but not in the dark one.

2.2.3 The Craik-O'Brien illusion and Mach bands

In the center of Fig. 2.6A, there is a black gradation. The luminance distribution is illustrated in (B). There is a white semicircle α on the left, and at its
boundary β, the luminance drops sharply, the black shade fades to the right γ,
and then returns to the flat area δ with the same luminance. However,
(A) shows that the right flat area δ' is darker than the white semicircle α'
as shown in (C), and the dark Craik-O'Brien illusion is observed. The effect
of the black shading spills over to the right, and the whole right part is darkened. This dark illusion is caused by the effect of the luminance step (i.e.,
edge) between the white semicircle and the black shadow, which emphasizes
the contour β' (see Fig. 2.4). This means that the difference between light α'
and dark β' areas becomes more pronounced with the contour enhancement
effect. Furthermore, according to Hamada (2010), a bright ring, or a light

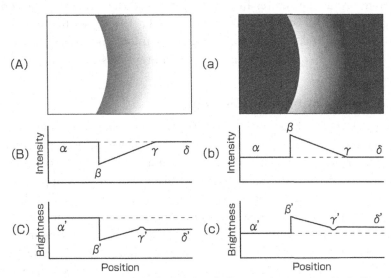

Fig. 2.6 Craik-O'Brien illusions and Mach bands for negative contrast (A, B, C) and for
positive contrast (a, b, c). This illustration shows the dark and light Craik-O'Brien
illusion and the associated light and dark Mach bands. *(Adapted from Hamada,
J. (2010). The same thing looks different in brightness.* Tokushima Newspaper, *October
30 (Japanese text).)*

Mach band, appears in (A), focusing on the boundary γ', which is slightly farther from the white semicircle (C). However, O'Brian (1958) and Jung (1973) did not report the existence of this Mach band. Also, as reported by Hamada (1982), the difference in brightness between the white semicircle α and the bottom of β is accentuated and the black contour β' becomes clearer (see Fig. 2.4). As Jung (1973) pointed out, the trapezoidal angle γ' is moving in the direction of β'.

On the other hand, when Fig. 2.6a is drawn by reversing the black-and-white of Fig. 2.6A, the light Craik-O'Brien illusion appears relatively to be brighter at the right end δ' than at the left side α', though they are the same luminance. However, as shown in Fig. 2.6a and c, the leftmost α' is darker than the rightmost δ' (see Fig. 2.4). In addition, the dark illusion from black shadow in Fig. 2.6A is stronger than the light illusion from white one in Fig. 2.6a (see Fig. 2.4). Furthermore, a dark ring, or dark Mach band, appears in Fig. 2.6a, focusing on the boundary γ' away from the black semicircle (c). The Craik-O'Brien illusion and the contour enhancement effect are caused by the darkening effect due to the edge (Fig. 2.4). Here, the light Mach band tends to be stronger than the dark one.

The relationship between the Craik-O'Brien illusion and Mach bands in negative and positive patterns needs to be investigated experimentally and theoretically in the future. In addition, it is necessary to apply the serial processing model of Hamada (1976a, 1976b, 1984b) to the results of Fig. 2.4 to simulate the Craik-O'Brien illusion and Mach bands in Fig. 2.6 while incorporating the decrease in brightness levels.

2.2.4 Effects of blurring the edge

In Fig. 2.7, the black density of circles (A, B, and C) on a white background is equal to that of circles (a, b, and c) on a black one. However, the latter is brighter than the former because of the simultaneous brightness contrast. The edge with stepwise luminance is gradually blurred from upper left to lower left in a clockwise direction. Here, the radii of the outer circles are 4.4, 5.7, 6.6, and 7.5 clockwise from the upper left circle, respectively.

In Fig. 2.7B with 50% black density, dark Mach bands appear to be relatively thick at the gradations of the lower two disks, while the upper right is weak. Here, light Mach bands appear at the border between the white background and the black gradation. In Fig. 2.7b, the light Mach bands are clearly and relatively thinly observed in three disks: the lower two

Black density in circle

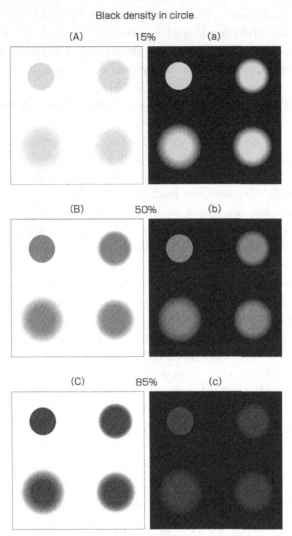

Fig. 2.7 The effect of blurring the edge on the apparent brightness. There are simultaneous brightness contrasts between the disks in (A, B, C) and (a, b, c), and Mach bands are observed when the edges are blurred. *(Adapted from Hamada, J. (2020). Psychophysics of pattern cognition. Kazama Press Tokyo (Japanese text).)*

and the upper-right. In addition, a dark Mach band is visible at the border between the black background and the light gradation. The light Mach band in (b) is sharper and stronger than the dark in (B). This is in agreement with the report of Fiorentini and Radici (1957) (see Ratliff, 1965).

At 15% black density, there are no Mach bands in (A), but strong light and weak dark Mach bands appear at inside and outside of circles in (a), respectively. Similarly, at 85% black density, Mach bands of strong dark and weak light appear at inside and outside of circles in (C), respectively, while these are not observed in (c) (see Mach bands in Fig. 2.6). Thus, the Mach bands clearly appear when the difference in black density between the background and the circles is large.

Evans (1959) made the background of Fig. 2.7B grayish, while the background of (b) was black, and drew eight disks similar to 50% black density condition (Beck, 1972). The luminance at the center of the eight disks was equal, and only the luminance gradient at the edges was different. In this Evans' pattern, the disk with a smooth luminance gradient changes toward to the background region, resulting in brightness assimilation. However, Kingdom (2003) shows that in the background conditions similar to the Evans pattern, the brightness contrast is enhanced when the stimulus pattern is lowpass filtered but diminished when high pass filtered. In the Evans pattern, when the luminance step is blurred and the luminance of the background region is changed as described above, brightness assimilation is observed. However, Mach bands appear, as in Fig. 2.7 (see Arai, 2007). In addition, the brightness contrast is enhanced as in Kingdom's low-frequency pass filter. These phenomena will also need to be examined in the future. Whether blurred contours cause the decrease in brightness levels in these phenomena will also be a future experimental and theoretical issue. For example, in Fig. 2.1b, it is expected to increase or decrease the slope of the S-shape to study the decrease in brightness levels.

2.3 The Craik-O'Brien-Cornsweet illusion

As shown in Fig. 2.8, the dark Craik-O'Brien patterns are (B and b), which added black-teeth to uniform fields (A and a). On the other hand, the light Craik-O'Brien patterns (C and c) have white teeth. In contrast, the Cornsweet patterns (D and d) involve the addition of white teeth to black ones or black teeth to white ones (Cornsweet, 1970; Dooley & Greenfield, 1977). The Cornsweet illusion is a composite of the dark and light Craik-O'Brien illusions, and they are collectively called the Craik-O'Brien-Cornsweet illusion (Fiorentini, Baumgartner, Magnussen, Schiller, & Thomas, 1990; Adelson, 2000; Horst, 2005). In this section, Hamada (1980b) will be reviewed.

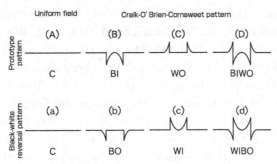

Fig. 2.8 Luminance distribution of stimulus patterns. (A) and (a) are uniform fields, (B) and (b) are black Craik-O'Brien patterns, (C) and (c) are white Craik-O'Brien patterns, and (D) and (d) are Cornsweet patterns. *(Adapted from Hamada, J. (1980b). An inducing mechanism of the Craik-O'Brien and the Cornsweet effects. Japanese Journal of Psychology, 51, 55–62. (Japanese text with English abstract and captions).)*

On the Craik-O'Brien-Cornsweet illusion. We measure the apparent brightness of the uniform field (Fig. 2.8A and a), and that of the inside and outside areas not only of the Craik-O'Brien pattern with black (B and b) or white teeth (C and c), but also that of the Cornsweet patterns (D and d). In this way, we examine how the apparent brightness of each area increases or decreases compared to that of the uniform fields due to the addition of the teeth. We will check whether there is a difference in brightness between the inside and outside areas, that is, whether the Craik-O'Brien-Cornsweet illusion exists. In addition, we will confirm the existence of the decrease in brightness levels compared with the brightness of the uniform fields.

2.3.1 Method

Stimulus patterns and procedures. The experimental apparatus was the same as described previously (Fig. 2.2). Stimulus patterns were illuminated at 250 lx, and the luminance of the uniform field was 30 cd/m^2. The black-and-white boundary area of the frosted photographic paper used to generate the stimulus pattern (e.g., Fig. 2.3) was divided into 14 types. The shapes of the tooth in the patterns are drawn according to the cumulative normal distribution function as described previously, with a sharp pattern of 3 mm in width and 16 mm in height, and a dull pattern of 6 mm in width and 8 mm in height. The areas of these teeth are equal. The experimental conditions were black and white Craik-O'Brien patterns consisting of sharp or dull teeth, and Cornsweet pattern, totaling 12 types. The symmetrical teeth pairs that characterize these stimulus patterns are represented by the symbols shown in Fig. 2.8, combining the black and white teeth (B for black, W for white) and the direction of the foot of the tooth (I for inner, O for outer). Two uniform fields are used as control conditions and are abbreviated as C.

The four participants were students at Hokkaido University and the author. Their task was to compare the apparent brightness of the center of inside and outside areas and that of the uniform field with that of Munsell achromatic paper. Eighteen achromatic papers ranging in brightness value from 1.5 to 9.5 at 0.5 intervals were used as comparison stimuli. The apparent brightness at the site of 14 stimulus patterns was measured by the method of limits of ascending and descending series using the three cases (bright, same, and dark). The order in which the stimulus patterns were measured was randomized for each participant and session and counterbalanced appropriately for the other order. Each participant repeated six experimental sessions on different days.

2.3.2 Results and discussion

The point of subjective equality of the participants tended to be consistent, so they are included in the analysis. Fig. 2.9 shows the average brightness values chosen as subjective equivalents for the prototype and the black–white reversal patterns in the sharp and dull conditions, and for the uniform field.

Decrease in brightness levels. The reflectance of the uniform field was 40.2%, which corresponds to a Munsell value of 6.80. On the other hand, that value of the comparison stimulus, which was chosen as the subjective equivalent to the uniform field, was 5.58, as shown by the dotted line in Fig. 2.9. This discrepancy is not a problem because the analysis is based on the apparent brightness against the uniform field, as described previously. The Munsell value of the inside area (white bars) and the outside one (gray bars) in all experimental conditions is significantly lower than that of the uniform field (dotted line). Since there is no qualitative difference between the sharp and dull patterns and they show similar trends, we include them. Therefor, a total of six patterns will be analyzed: the prototype and the black–white reversal patterns for each of black and white Craik-O'Brien patterns and the Cornsweet patterns. To elaborate on this result, Table 2.2 shows the values obtained by subtracting the value in the control condition (5.58) from the Munsell value for the inside and outside areas for the six patterns. According to the results, the inside and outside areas are all significantly darker than the uniform field. This result means that all areas with

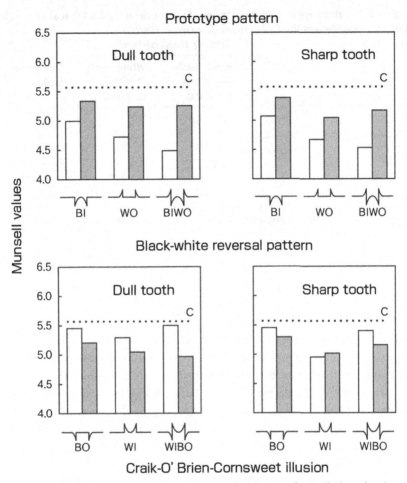

Fig. 2.9 Munsell brightness value for the inside *(white bars)* and outside *(gray bars)* areas in the Craik-O'Brien-Cornsweet patterns. The *dotted line* indicates the measured Munsell value for the uniform field (C). *(From Hamada, J. (1980b). An inducing mechanism of the Craik-O'Brien and the Cornsweet effects. Japanese Journal of Psychology, 51, 55–62. (Japanese text with English abstract and captions).)*

teeth, whether black or white, appear darker than the uniform field, confirming the decrease in brightness levels (see also Fig. 2.4).

The Craik-O'Brien-Cornsweet illusion. To confirm the existence of the Craik-O'Brien illusion, we examined how much darker the inside area was perceived compared to the other one, and vice versa. As a result, the illusion appeared with no significant difference only in the sharp (WI in Fig. 2.9)

Table 2.2 The decrease in brightness levels of the inside and outside areas caused by black or white teeth in the Craik-O'Brien-Cornsweet pattern.

		Craik-O' Brien pattern		
		Black teeth (Negative contrast)	White teeth (Positive contrast)	Cornsweet pattern
		BI	WO	BIWO
Prototype pattern	Inside area	-0.56^{**}	-0.92^{**}	-1.09^{**}
	Outside area	-0.22^{**}	-0.43^{**}	-0.39^{**}
		BO	WI	WIBO
Black-white	Inside area	-0.13^{*}	-0.44^{**}	-0.14^{*}
reversal pattern	Outside area	-0.35^{**}	-0.54^{**}	-0.53^{**}

Negative signs indicate that the brightness value of each area is darker than the uniform field.
$^{*}P < .05.$
$^{**}P < .01.$
From Hamada, J. (1980b). An inducing mechanism of the Craik-O'Brien and the Cornsweet effects. *Japanese Journal of Psychology*, 51, 55–62. (Japanese text with English abstract and captions).

and significant difference in the others. On the other hand, in order to see the existence of the Cornsweet illusion, we examined how much darker the black tooth side was perceived than the white and found that the former was significantly darker than the latter. It can be concluded that the addition of teeth to the uniform field produces the illusion that the brightness level of the entire pattern decreases while the amount of brightness decrease in each area is relatively different. Next, we will analyze the relationship between the illusions observed in this way.

Interaction of the Craik-O'Brien and Cornsweet illusions. As shown in Fig. 2.9, the Cornsweet illusion is stronger than the Craik-O'Brien illusion. This indicates that the Cornsweet illusion is produced by the addition of white or black teeth to the black or white teeth of the Craik-O'Brien pattern. We will further analyze how the brightness value of each area changes when a different kind of teeth is added to the Craik-O'Brien pattern to produce the Cornsweet illusion. That is, we will examen when the Cornsweet patterns were created by adding different kinds of teeth to each Craik-O'Brien pattern, the brightness of the inside and outside areas of each pattern changed in either direction (brighter in the positive case) and by how much. The value in the left column of Table 2.3 is the difference between column 3 and column 1 of Table 2.2, and the value in the right column is the difference between column 3 and column 2 as well.

Table 2.3 Changes in the apparent brightness of the Cornsweet pattern due to the addition of different teeth to the Craik-O'Brien pattern.

		White teeth	Black teeth
		WO	BI
Prototype pattern	Inside area	−0.53*	−0.17*
	Outside area	−0.17*	+0.04
		WI	BO
Black-white reversal pattern	Inside area	−0.01	+0.30*
	Outside area	−0.18*	+0.01

$^{*}P < .01.$
From Hamada, J. (1980b). An inducing mechanism of the Craik-O'Brien and the Cornsweet effects. *Japanese Journal of Psychology*, 51, 55–62. (Japanese text with English abstract and captions).

In Table 2.3, when white teeth were added to the black teeth (left column), the brightness level of each area decreased significantly, except for one case (the inside area of the WI) where the brightness value hardly changed. On the other hand, when black teeth were added to white teeth (right column), the brightness value of the outside area was almost unchanged regardless of whether the direction of the foot of the tooth was inward or outward (outside areas of BI and BO). However, the brightness value of the inside area was significantly darker when the black teeth were added to the inside area (BI), and the opposite was true when it was added to the outside one (BO), where it was significantly lighter. Thus, when we add different types of teeth to the Craik-O'Brien pattern to create the Cornsweet one, the effect is small, unlike when we add the Craik-O'Brien teeth to the uniform field. Moreover, it does not necessarily mean that the brightness level of each region is simply reduced. Therefore, the black and white teeth must act additively to increase the difference in brightness between the inside and outside areas in the Cornsweet illusion, and at the same time there must be a complex interaction between the light and dark Craik-O'Brien illusions.

2.4 Explanation of the contour enhancement effect and the brightness illusion

The Craik-O'Brien-Cornsweet illusion is produced by the darkening effect, in which the brightness of the pattern becomes darker than that of the uniform field. The illusion is caused by the presence of luminance steps (i.e., edges) that decrease the apparent brightness levels to different degrees.

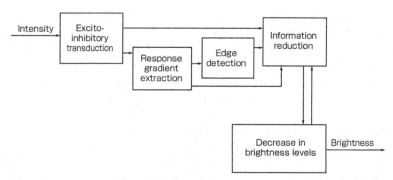

Fig. 2.10 A five-level qualitative model illustrating the contour enhancement effect and the brightness illusion. *(Adapted from Hamada, J. (2020). Psychophysics of pattern cognition. Kazama Press Tokyo (Japanese text).)*

Hamada (1976a, 1976b, 1984b) proposed a four-level serial processing model and simulated a border contrast (Fig. 1.13). In the model, a Mexican hat-like neural response (DOG) is induced by excitation and inhibition in the first level, then the gradient of the neural response is extracted, then the inflection points of the neural response in the first level are detected as edges, and finally in the information reduction level, the gradient of the neural response between edges in the first level is averaged and linearized (Fig. 1.13e). Fig. 2.10 shows a five-level qualitative model in which the decrease in brightness levels occurs in the level upstairs the four-level mathematical model. The decrease in brightness levels processed in the fifth level enhances the difference between light and dark on the adjacent areas, producing the Craik-O'Brien-Cornsweet illusion. Mach (1865) pointed out that the center of a white windmill pattern becomes gray when it is rotated at a high speed (see Fig. 1.1A). His point also indicates a decrease in brightness levels. However, at present, the nature of the decrease in brightness levels in the fifth level cannot be expressed mathematically, and it is only qualitatively described here. The decrease in brightness levels by the addition of the edge is thought to cause the simultaneous brightness contrast in the next chapter. Hamada's model in Fig. 2.10 assumes that brightness information flows serially from the first to the fifth level, but the feedback at fourth and fifth level may be examined in the future (Grossberg & Kelly, 1999; Sokolov, 2005).

CHAPTER THREE

A five-level qualitative model on various aspects of brightness contrast

3.1 Simultaneous contrast of brightness

According to Woodworth and Schlosberg (1954), a simultaneous contrast as a sensory response is defined as a phenomenon that emphasizes the difference between two stimuli. For example, four rectangular gray paper placed in the center of the different backgrounds shown in Fig. 3.1 has an equal reflectance, but it does not appear to be the same brightness. Gray (a) in the black background appears to be brighter, while gray (e) in the white appears to be darker, emphasizing the difference in brightness between the central regions and the backgrounds (Hering, 1920; Cornsweet, 1970). This relationship is still observed between (b) and (d). The gray in (c) is the same reflectance as the four central rectangles.

In order to investigate the change in brightness due to the simultaneous contrast, conventional studies have used a test, an induction, and a comparison field and measured the brightness of the test field by changing the luminance and shape of the induction or test fields, and matched it with the comparison field (Diamond, 1953; Fry & Alpern, 1953; Heinemann, 1955; Horeman, 1963, 1965; Torii & Uemura, 1965). As a result, when the luminance of the induction field was lower than that of the test field, the brightness of the test field hardly changed. However, when that of the induction field was higher than that of the test field, the brightness of the latter decreased in accordance with the luminance of the former. Thus, the effect of the simultaneous brightness contrast was thought to be reflected in the effect of the induction field to reduce the brightness of the test field, and only that of the latter was measured. However, even if it is reduced, it is not clear whether there is an enhancement of the difference in brightness between the two fields without measuring the brightness of the induction field. Therefore, in order to

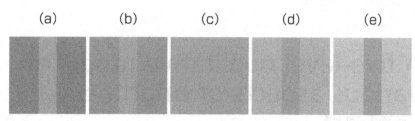

Fig. 3.1 Simultaneous brightness contrast (a and e or b and d) and the uniform field (c). *(Adapted from Hamada, J. (2008).* The excitation and the compound inhibition in brightness illusion. *Tokyo: Kazama Press (Japanese text).)*

investigate the simultaneous brightness contrast, it is necessary to measure the apparent brightness of the test and induction fields, respectively, and directly study the relationship between the brightness of the two fields (a and e or b and d in Fig. 3.1). In other words, the test and induction fields are considered to be interacting with each other. So, we measure the brightness in both the test and induction fields of the contrast induction pattern as the experimental condition and measure the brightness of the uniform field as the control condition (see Fig. 3.1c), to examine the simultaneous brightness contrast and the decrease in brightness levels (Hamada, 1980c). In this section, Hamada (1983) will be reviewed.

3.1.1 Apparent brightness of contrast induction patterns
3.1.1.1 The uniform field and contrast induction patterns
A schematic diagram of reflectance distribution is shown in Fig. 3.2. Parts (a) to (c) are uniform fields, and (d) to (g) are contrast induction patterns with reflectance differences (Hamada, 1991). The sizes of areas of them are equal. Contrast induction patterns are divided into two types, depending on whether the area in which the reflectance is changed and the area in which the reflectance is fixed are inside or outside. That is, in Fig. 3.2 we set not only the inside change conditions (d and e), in which the reflectance of the outside area is fixed and that of the inside one changes, but also the outside change conditions (f and g), in which the reflectance of the inside area is fixed and that of the outside one change.

Simultaneous brightness contrast and decrease of brightness levels. First, we examine the relationship between the brightness of the high- and low-reflection areas of the contrast induction pattern by comparing them to that of uniform fields with the same reflectance as those areas. For example, we measure and compare the brightness of the uniform field (b) with the

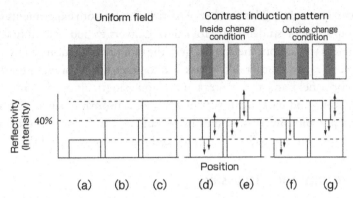

Fig. 3.2 Reflectance distribution (a–g) and assumed changes in neural responses. The *solid up* and *down arrows* indicate increases in excitation and inhibition, respectively, and the *dotted down arrow* indicates a decrease in brightness levels (see also Fig. 3.5). *(From Hamada, J., (2008).* The excitaion and the compound inhibition in brightness illusion. *Tokyo: Kazama Press (Japanese text).)*

high-reflectance area of the contrast induction pattern (d), as shown in Fig. 3.2. The brightness of the low-reflectance area of (d) and that of the uniform field (a) are also compared. In this way, the brightness of each area of the contrast induction patterns and the uniform fields are directly compared. Thus, in order to examine the decrease in brightness levels, we then confirm that the apparent brightness of the low- and high-reflectance areas are darker than those of uniform fields with the same reflectance.

Second, we define the occurrence of simultaneous brightness contrast using contrast induction patterns and uniform fields as follows. Let D_e be the difference in brightness values between the high- and low-reflectance areas of the contrast induction pattern (d) in Fig. 3.2. Furthermore, let Dc be the difference in brightness values between two uniform fields (a) and (b) that have reflectance equal to that of those areas in (d). Then, when $D_e/D_c > 1$, the simultaneous brightness contrast is generated. Thus, the brightness of the high- and low-reflectance areas and that of the two uniform fields corresponding to these areas are compared and examine the enhancement of the difference between light and dark, that is, the occurrence of simultaneous brightness contrast.

Experimental apparatus and procedures. The apparatus was the same as described previously (Fig. 2.2), and stimulus patterns were generated under an illuminance of 370 lx. Thirty-three achromatic papers ranging from 1.5 to 9.5 in Munsell brightness intervals of 0.25 were used as comparison stimuli. The inside and outside change conditions were conducted separately as different experiments. The number of participants for both experiments was 3, each consisting of students at Hokkaido University and the author. The brightness of the uniform field and that of the contrast induction patterns were measured in random order. Their task was to judge the apparent brightness of the uniform field and the contrast induction pattern using the three cases (bright, same, and dark) with that of Munsell achromatic paper. The mean of the upper and lower thresholds by the method of limits was used as the points of subjective equality. They repeated the six sessions on different days.

3.1.2 Results and discussion

The uniform fields. Fig. 3.3 shows the average values of the brightness for the uniform fields and the contrast induction patterns. The measured brightness values for uniform fields with reflectance from 31% to 49% increased linearly with increasing reflectance, as shown by the solid lines connected by × symbols. For later comparison, the value for the uniform field with a reflectance of 40% is shown as a horizontal dashed line.

3.1.2.1 Brightness of reflectance fixed areas

Fig. 3.3 shows that the measured brightness values for the fixed areas with 40% reflectance (outside area of the inside change condition, and inside area of the outside change one) are significantly lower than those for the uniform

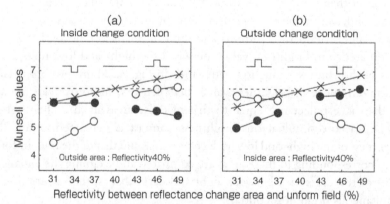

Fig. 3.3 Mean value of Munsell brightness values matched to uniform fields and contrast induction patterns (a and b). *(From Hamada, J., (2008). The excitaion and the compound inhibition in brightness illusion. Tokyo: Kazama Press (Japanese text); adapted from Hamada, J., (1983). Lightness decrease of the total area accompanying simultaneous lightness contrast. Japanese Journal of Psychology, 54, 115–122. (Japanese text with English abstract and captions).)*

field with the same reflectance (dashed line). This result shows the decrease in brightness levels that we confirmed in the previous chapter. When the reflectance of the fixed area is higher than that of the changing area, this brightness value hardly changes even if the reflectance of the changing area increases. In other words, the three solid circles on the left of the inside change condition (a) and the three open circles on the left of the outside change condition (b) correspond to this case. On the other hand, the value of the fixed area decreases as the reflectance of the changing area increases. That is, the three solid circles on the right of the inside change condition (a) and the three open circles on the right of the outside change condition (b) correspond to this case.

3.1.2.2 Brightness of the reflectance change areas
Fig. 3.3a shows the brightness matched to the inside area (open circles), where the reflectance varies from 31% to 49%. Similarly, Fig. 3.3b shows the measured values for the outside areas (solid circles). The measured brightness values for both the inside area in the inside change condition and the outside one in the outside change condition are all significantly lower than the values for the uniform field with the same reflectance (×'s connected by solid lines). This indicates that the brightness level of the changing area is lower than that of the uniform fields with the same reflectance.

3.1.2.3 Paradoxical decrease in brightness levels
There is a noteworthy phenomenon regarding the decrease in brightness levels in the changing area. For example, in the inside change condition of Fig. 3.3a, the measured brightness value (open circle: 6.19) for the inside area with 43% reflectance is significantly lower than that (dashed line: 6.35) for the uniform field with 40% reflectance. This phenomenon indicates that if the reflectance of the area corresponding to the inside area is locally increased by 3% on the uniform field, that is, when edges are added, the brightness level of the entire contrast induction pattern will decrease. This means that the brightness of the reflectance-increasing area is significantly and paradoxically lower than that of the uniform field. Similarly, in the outside change condition shown in Fig. 3.3b, the outside area of 43% was significantly darker than the uniform field of 40%, resulting in the paradoxical decrease in brightness levels.

3.1.2.4 Simultaneous brightness contrast

As mentioned previously, the brightness contrast is indicated by whether the difference between the measured values for the two adjacent areas in the contrast induction pattern (De) is greater than that for the two corresponding uniform fields (Dc). If we denote the strength of the brightness contrast by C, we say that the brightness contrast appears when $C = D_e/D_c > 1$. For example, in Fig. 3.3a, the measured brightness values for the inside and outside areas with 31% and 40% reflectance are 4.44 (open circle) and 5.87 (solid circle), respectively, for the inside change condition shown on the far left. Therefore, $D_e = 1.43$. On the other hand, the values for uniform fields with 31% and 40% reflectance are 5.83 ($\times$) and 6.35 (dashed line), respectively, and $D_c = 0.52$. That is, in these conditions, there is a relationship $C = D_e/ D_c = 2.8$, and the simultaneous brightness contrast occurs. That is, the value of C at 31% ($= 40 - 9\%$) is 2.8, but the value at 49% ($= 40 + 9\%$) is 1.8. Thus, in contrast induction patterns with negative and positive contrasts with the same 9% reflectance difference centered at 40%, the former negative contrast induces the simultaneous brightness contrast that is stronger than the latter positive one. This phenomenon appears in all pairs where the reflectance difference is symmetrically related. In the outside change condition, the negative contrast is stronger than the positive contrast in all pairs as well. Therefore, in contrast induction patterns with negative and positive contrasts, the former significantly induces the simultaneous brightness contrast stronger than the latter. This result is consistent with that of the contour enhancement effect and the Craik-O'Brien illusion in the previous chapter, where the negative contrast was stronger than the positive one. As described previously, when a luminance step (i.e., edge) is added to a uniform field, the decrease in brightness levels in the low-reflectance area becomes stronger than that in the high-reflectance area, and the brightness contrast occurs. Therefore, the five-step qualitative model can explain the decrease in brightness levels and the brightness contrast (see Fig. 2.10).

3.2 Brightness contrast and assimilation in half-wave patterns

In Fig. 3.4a, the gray of the left semicircle appears darker than that of the right, even though the reflectance of the gray is the same in all cases. This phenomenon is called brightness assimilation because it reduces the difference of brightness between the gray parts and the eleven semicircles. The same assimilation is also observed when only the outermost semicircle is

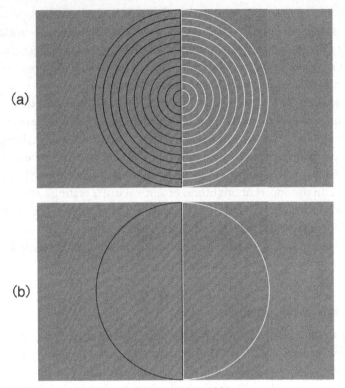

Fig. 3.4 Brightness assimilation and contrast (a and b).

used, as in Fig. 3.4b. On the other hand, when we observe the gray color outside the circumscribed circle, the left side appears darker than the right side, indicating a contrast in brightness. Thus, in this figure, brightness assimilation and contrast occur simultaneously.

Helson and Roles (1959) drew thin black vertical lines at the left side and thin white ones at the right side on a gray paper. The left side appeared to be darker and the right one appeared to be lighter, even though the gray paper was the same reflectance (Helson, 1964; Sokolov, 2013). This brightness assimilation remained even when the gray spacing between the lines was increased by a factor of about 12. Helson (1963) used gray papers with white and black vertical lines as stimulus patterns and compared the brightness of the gray paper between the white and black lines using a nine-category rating method. As a result, assimilation appeared when the width of the black and white lines was narrow, and weakened as it became thicker. Finally, when he made the width of the black and white lines even thicker, it reversed into a brightness contrast. In other words, the apparent brightness of the left gray paper appeared darker when thick white lines were adjacent to it, while it appeared lighter when thick black lines were adjacent to it, creating a brightness contrast. Therefore he concluded that the phenomena of assimilation and contrast are located on a continuum.

Cornsweet (1970) used vertical striped gratings to measure the modulation transfer function of the human visual system. Campbel and Robson (1965) and Patel (1966) measured the contrast threshold at which sinusoidal gratings could be detected. Furthermore, Davidson (1968) developed a contrast matching method. Although these data are informative, they do not shed light on the apparent brightness of vertical stripe gratings. In this experiment, we examine whether a decrease in the brightness levels is observed when the contrast and assimilation of brightness occurs in the square wave patterns shown in Fig. 3.5. In this section, Hamada (1984a, Experiment 2) will be reviewed.

3.2.1 Half-wave patterns

In the paired square wave patterns G_1 and G_2 in Fig. 3.5, D_1 and D_2 are called low-reflectivity areas because their reflectivity is lower than that of L_1 and L_2, and conversely, L_1 and L_2 are called high-reflectivity ones. The reflectance of L_1 and D_2 are both equal to that of the corresponding uniform field U_2 (40%), and they are in a symmetrical relationship to that of U_2. In this way, the square wave patterns of G_1 and G_2 have a reflectance

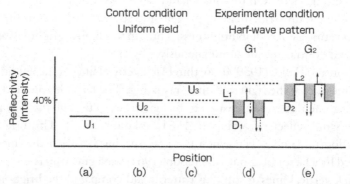

Fig. 3.5 Reflectance distribution and assumed changes in neural responses (a–e). The *solid up* and *down arrows* indicate increased excitation and inhibition, respectively, and the *dotted down arrow* indicates a decrease in brightness levels (see also Fig. 3.2). *(From Hamada, J., (1984a). Lightness decrease and increase in square-wave gratings. Perception & Psychophysics, 35, 16–21. (Springer Nature).)*

distribution that is symmetrical with respect to the uniform field U_2, and these are called half-wave patterns.

3.2.1.1 Stimulus patterns and procedures

The same apparatus was used as the previous section (see Fig. 2.2). The stimulus patterns were observed under an illuminance of 600 lx. The half-wave patterns were longitudinal striped gratings and four different wavelengths were used. The wavelengths were 8', 24', 72', and 110' in visual angle (i.e., 7.5, 2.5, 0.83, and 0.55 cycles/deg). The reflectance values of the measurement sites, that is, the half-wave pattern (L_1 and D_2) and the uniform field (U_2), were all fixed at 40%. In other words, in the experimental conditions, the apparent brightness of areas with high- or low-reflectance of 40% was measured in 40 ± 12, 40 ± 24, and $40 \pm 36\%$ reflectance conditions. As a control condition, the brightness of the uniform field with 40% reflectance (U_2) was measured. Thus, participants judged the brightness of not only the high-reflectance area (L_1) and the low-reflectance one (D_2) of the half-wave patterns, but also the uniform field, and compared them with those of Munsell achromatic paper.

The three participants were students at Hokkaido University and the author. They compared the brightness of the stimulus pattern with the brightness of Munsell achromatic paper (33 sheets of paper ranging from 1.5 to 9.5 at 0.25 brightness intervals) using the three cases (bright, same, and dark), and took the average of the upper and lower thresholds by the method of limits as the point of subjective equality. They repeated six sessions on different days.

3.2.2 Results and discussion

The experimental results are shown in Fig. 3.6. The measured values for the high-reflectance areas (L_1, solid circles) of G_1 in the wavelength width of 8' are all significantly darker than those for the uniform field (solid horizontal line). However, when the wavelength width is 24' or more, the brightness of the high-reflectance area (solid circles) changes systematically compared to that of the uniform field. In other words, as the reflectance changes from 40–12% to 40–24% and then to 40–36%, the brightness of the high-reflectance area (L_1, solid circles) is initially darker than that of the uniform field, but then becomes almost the same, and finally significantly brighter. In this connection, Walker (1978) showed that the brightness in the high luminance phase of a square wave pattern is brighter than that of a uniform luminance surface with the same luminance. Hamada (1984a, Experiment 1) reported

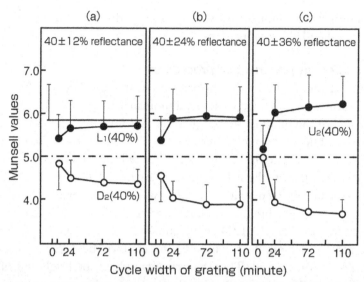

Fig. 3.6 Mean of Munsell brightness values as a function of wavelength width for a half-wave pattern (a–c). *Vertical bars* indicate 1SD. *(From Hamada, J., (1984a). Lightness decrease and increase in square-wave gratings.* Perception & Psychophysics, 35, 16–21. *(Springer Nature).)*

that the brightness of the high-reflectance area (L_1) with reflectance difference of 10% in a half-wave pattern was significantly lower than that of the uniform field with the same reflectance. Furthermore, Hamada (1983) reported a paradoxical decrease in brightness at a reflectance difference of 3%, as shown in Fig. 3.3. From these results, we can conclude that the brightness of the high-reflectance area is significantly lower than that of the uniform field when the reflectance difference is low, and conversely, it significantly increases when it is high. On the other hand, the brightness of the low-reflectance area (D_2, open circles) decreases as the reflectance increases from $40 + 12\%$ to $40 + 24\%$ to $40 + 36\%$, except for the 8′ wavelength range. This characteristic indicates that the excitation and inhibition increase as the reflectance difference increases.

3.2.2.1 Symmetry of brightness and the decrease in brightness levels

The brightness for the high-reflectance L_1 and low-reflectance D_2 with 40% reflectance show a symmetrical relationship for all reflectance differences (i.e., 12, 24, and 36%). Moreover, as shown in Fig. 3.6, the symmetry axes of the brightness of the three reflectance differences are consistent with the Munsell brightness value of about 5.0 (single-dotted lines). This result means that the brightness level of the entire half-wave pattern is lower than that of the uniform field with a brightness of 5.8, and the degree of decrease is about 0.8 in brightness.

3.2.2.2 Transition from brightness contrast to assimilation

In the half-wave patterns, there is a difference between L_1 (solid circles) and D_2 (open circles) with 40% reflectance in all patterns, where there is a brightness contrast except for the wavelength width of $8'$ in the $40 \pm 36\%$ condition. In the case, L_1 (solid circle) and D_2 (open circle) converge to the symmetry axis (single-dotted line) with a brightness of about 5.0, and brightness assimilation occurs.

3.2.3 Antagonistic process and the decrease in brightness levels in a five-level qualitative model

We would like to explain the brightness change of the half-wave patterns by the five-level qualitative model of the Craik-O'Brien illusion (see Fig. 2.10). In Fig. 3.5, a half-wave pattern G_1 (Fig. 3.5d) is created by reducing the reflectance of parts of the uniform field U_2 to a vertical grid pattern. Then, the neural response of L_1 is relatively stronger than that of U_2, as shown by the solid up arrow in Fig. 3.5d. This is because the inhibition from the gray areas is lost. The neural response at D_2 in Fig. 3.5e is weaker than at U_2, as indicated by the solid down arrow. This is because D_2 in the half-wave pattern G_2 receives inhibition from L_2, which has a higher reflectance than the uniform field U_2. For the same reason, if we measure the brightness of the low-reflectivity area D_1 of G_1, it should be darker than the uniform field U_1 due to the inhibition induced by the high-reflectivity areas. Also, if we measure the brightness of the high-reflectance area L_2 of G_2, it should be brighter than that of the uniform field U_3 due to the reduced inhibition from the low-reflectance area. This is confirmed by Hamada (1984a, Experiment 1).

However, in addition to the antagonistic process of the excitation and inhibition, a decrease in brightness levels occurs. Therefor, the brightness of the overall half-wave pattern decreases in different degrees, as shown in the dotted line with the down arrow (Fig. 3.5d and e). The antagonistic process in the first level and the decrease in brightness levels in the fifth level of this model can explain the brightness change of the half-wave patterns shown in Fig. 3.6 at least qualitatively, as well as the Craik-O'Brien illusion and simultaneous contrast of brightness. Thus, by adding luminance steps (edges) to a uniform field, first a decrease in brightness levels occurs, and then a brightness contrast occurs to emphasize the difference between light and dark, or a brightness assimilation occurs to reduce the difference, depending on the situation. The solid arrows (i.e., excitation and inhibition) and the dotted arrows (i.e., decrease in brightness levels) in Fig. 3.2 in the previous section are similar.

Fiorentini, Baumgartner, Magnussen, Schiller, and Thomas (1990) discussed the relationship between neurophysiological receptive fields and psychological phenomena such as brightness contrast, brightness assimilation, Mach bands, and Craik-O'Brien-Cornsweet illusion. In the future, the relationship between these psychological phenomena and neurophysiology will be further clarified.

3.3 Brightness contrast induction in separation distances

In the previous two sections, black and white photographic paper was rotated at high speed on a drum, and the apparent brightness of patterns consisting of low and high reflectance was compared with that of Munsell achromatic paper. Then, the brightness of the uniform field with the same reflectance as these patterns was measured to confirm the brightness contrast and the decrease in brightness levels. In this experiment, we separate the low- and high-luminance areas without adhering to each other using a computer screen and examine the induction of brightness contrast and the decrease in brightness levels by absolute judgments without comparison stimuli. In this section, Hamada, Ehrenstein, Müller, and Cavonius (1992) and Hamada and Ehrenstein (2008) will be reviewed.

3.3.1 Methods

3.3.1.1 Experimental apparatus and stimulus patterns

A computer-controlled CRT screen (Barco, Type HIREM) was used to present the stimuli: squares with a visual angle of 1° and three different separation distances (d) were presented on a light-free background as the induction (I) or control (C) conditions, as shown in Fig. 3.7. In the induction condition, the test and induction fields were presented to the left or right of a small fixation mark (3′ × 3′ in visual angle), and their distances were 0.05°, 1°, and 3° in visual angle. In the control condition, only the test field was presented to the left or right of the fixation mark. The presentation time was 5 s. The participant's head was fixed on a chin rest in a darkened room, and the screen was observed from a distance of 2 m with binocular free vision. The luminance of the test and induction fields ranged from 0.1 to

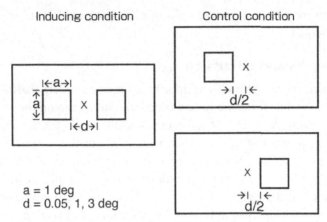

Fig. 3.7 Schematic diagram of stimulus presentation. *(From Hamada, J., Ehrenstein, W. H., (2008). Long-range effects in brightness induction: An absolute judgment approach. Gestalt Theory, 30, 61–69.)*

$10\,cd/m^2$, with 10 logarithmic units. Thus, luminance contrast in the induction condition ranged from 0.25 to 0.98, and there were 100 stimulus pairs (10×10). Luminance contrast was defined by the following Michelson formula: $(L_{max} - L_{min})/(L_{max} + L_{min})$.

3.3.1.2 Procedure

The participants were two students and a staff member at Dortmund University, and the author. Their task was to rate the brightness of the test field on an integer scale from 1 to 10. They were instructed to use all the integers. The left or right field was rated first, followed by the other field. What is rated here is the test field, and the other is the induction field. In the control condition, only the test field was presented. They were instructed to rate the stimuli verbally as soon as possible after presentation. After the dark adaptation, a few preliminary trials were conducted to become familiar with the full range of luminance levels. The order in which the test and induction fields were rated was counterbalanced in different sessions on different days.

In each separation distance condition, there were 100 stimuli: 10 equiluminant stimuli were presented 4 times each for a total of 40 stimuli, and 90 stimuli with different luminance presented 2 times each (180 stimuli in total). In the control condition, 10 stimuli were presented 5 times each (50 stimuli in total). The measurement order of the induction and control conditions was counterbalanced. Three conditions with different separation distances were repeated for two sessions each, for a total of six sessions for each participant.

3.3.2 Results and discussion

A 4 (participant) × 2 (stimulus position) × 2 (decision order) analysis of variance was conducted for the induction condition, including the three separate conditions. A significant difference was found only for the main effect of (participant) but not for the other main effects or the interaction. Similarly, a 4 (participant) × 2 (stimulus position) analysis of variance for the control condition showed a significant difference only in the main effect of (participant). In the induction condition, there were no significant differences between the left and right stimulus positions or between the preceding and following decision order. Since no significant differences were found in the interaction, the four participants were treated as random factors.

3.3.2.1 Brightness induction
The 90 stimuli, excluding 10 stimuli with the same luminance in the induction condition, were classified into two groups according to whether the test field was high luminous (H) or less luminous (L) than the induction field, and the difference in their ratings ($H - L$) was calculated. In the same way, the difference between the ratings in the corresponding control condition ($h - l$) was calculated. Then, $(H - L)/(h - l)$ is defined as the brightness induction. If the ratio is 1.0, it means that the brightness contrast is not induced, and the larger the ratio is, the stronger the brightness induction is. Fig. 3.8 shows the brightness induction as a function of luminance contrast for each separation condition. The brightness induction is large at the lowest luminance contrast and the minimum separation distance and approaches 1.0 at the maximum luminance contrast at all separation distances. As you can see, the closer the two fields are to each other and the lower the luminance contrast, the greater the brightness contrast.

3.3.2.2 The decrease in brightness levels
Fig. 3.9 shows the difference between inducing and control ratings plotted as a function of luminance contrast with negative (left side) or positive (right one) polarity. Here, scaled brightness is calculated analogously, taking brightness ratings instead of luminance. The scaled brightness values for the three separation distances are consistent at zero luminance contrast, but are reduced by 0.3 units. In other words, the decrease in brightness levels occur regardless of luminance contrast or separation distance. This result is consistent with Hamada (1984a),

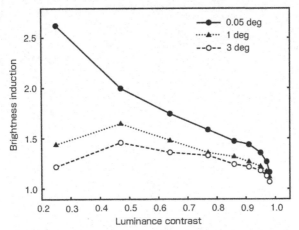

Fig. 3.8 Brightness induction as a function of luminance contrasts at three separation distances. *(From Hamada, J., Ehrenstein, W.H., (2008). Long-range effects in brightness induction: An absolute judgment approach.* Gestalt Theory, 30, 61–69.)

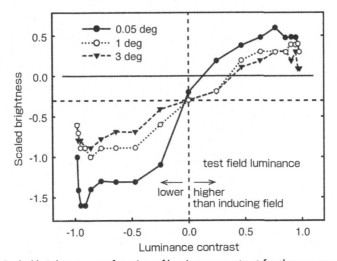

Fig. 3.9 Scaled brightness as a function of luminance contrast for three separation distances. *(From Hamada, J., Ehrenstein, W.H., (2008). Long-range effects in brightness induction: An absolute judgment approach.* Gestalt Theory, 30, 61–69.)

who found that the brightness of the entire half-wave pattern decreased to about 0.8 in Munsell value regardless of the difference in reflectance and cycle with of grating (the single–pointed lines of Fig. 3.6). Thus, the decrease in the brightness levels occurred universally regardless of the luminance difference or the degree of separation of regions, supporting the five-step qualitative model of Figs. 3.2 and 3.5.

CHAPTER FOUR

A three-level qualitative model for the Ehrenstein illusion

4.1 The Ehrenstein illusion

Fig. 4.1 shows a white background (a) and a black one (b) with 12 black and white lines radiating from each. In this illustration, though there is no luminance bump physically and objectively, psychologically and subjectively there appear to be raised diamond-shaped brightness steps. This phenomenon has been called illusory or subjective contours since the first description by Schumann (1900), Ehrenstein (1941, 1954), Kanizsa (1955, 1976), Petry and Meyer (1987), and others (Kennedy, 1979; Rock & Anson, 1979; Treisman, Cavanagh, Fischer, Ramachandran, & von der Heydt, 1990). In Fig. 4.1, there are only 12 lines, but a white or black diamond appears to float in front of the six lines. Whether this illusory diamond appears to be white or black, it depends on the contrast between the ground and the figure (i.e., the 12 lines). When the figure is lower in luminance than the ground (Fig. 4.1a: negative contrast), the illusory diamond appears to be white, while it appears to be black, when it is higher in luminance (Fig. 4.1b: positive contrast).

Kanizsa (1976), after making various figures, found that illusory contours always appear when there is something incomplete in the visual field, and that if these are supplemented by illusory contours, a complete and stable image is produced (Oyama, 2010). However, the existence of the corners and line ends of the figure is essential for this phenomenon to occur. Many of his examples of illusory contours have corners or line ends. In fact, Minguzzi (1987) and Sambin (1987) showed that the Ehrenstein illusion disappears when the tips of thick lines are rounded. Jory and Day (1979) showed that there was no significant difference between the sharpness of the Kanizsa and Ehrenstein illusions and the degree of lightness difference using a 10-point rating method, suggesting that the strength of illusory contours and lightness difference are closely related.

Psychophysics and Experimental Phenomenology of Pattern Cognition   Copyright © 2023 Elsevier Inc.
https://doi.org/10.1016/B978-0-323-95286-6.00004-1   All rights reserved.

(a)   (b)

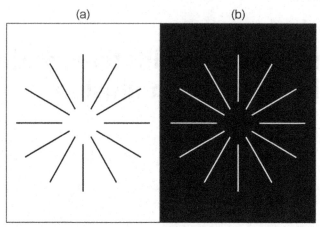

Fig. 4.1 Illusory contours (a and b). *(From Hamada, J. (2008). The excitation and the compound inhibition in brightness illusion. Tokyo: Kazama Press (Japanese text).)*

This chapter focuses on the Ehrenstein illusion in Fig. 4.2A and a, B and b (Ehrenstein, 1941; Jung, 1973). When black or white crosses are regularly arranged on a white background (A), a black background (a) or a gray background (B and b), where line segments are missing, clear white or black illusory disks appear and oblique gratings appear. Ehrenstein (1941) and Jung (1973) showed that this illusion disappears when a solid circle is drawn on the line ends of the disk. However, the illusion disappears when arcs of 30° are added instead of a circle as shown in the lower left of Fig. 4.2A and a, B and b. Similarly, Hamada (2020) pointed that the illusory disk disappears when four small circles are added to the four line ends, as shown in the lower left of this figure. However, placing these four small circles in the center of the upper right cross does not affect the illusion in any way. These imply that line ends play an important role in the generation of illusory contour lines. Here, the four circles in the lower left appear to be clearer and larger than those in the upper right. These phenomena are also seen in (B and b) with a gray background. Minguzzi (1987) reported that the Ehrenstein illusion disappears when two small dots are added to the ends of four thin lines.

Day and Jory (1978) called the Ehrenstein illusion the line contrast and showed that the lightness dissimilation (i.e., the Ehrenstein illusion) disappears when small T shapes are placed at the tip of the parallel lines. An example of this line contrast is shown in Fig. 4.3, where black lines are drawn on a white background. In the leftmost column, 12 black lines are arranged in a

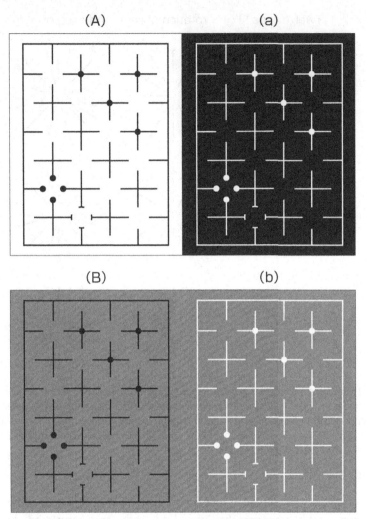

Fig. 4.2 The Ehrenstein illusion (A and a, B and b). *(Adapted from Jung, R. (1973). Visual perception and neurophysiology. In: R. Jung (Ed.),* Central processing of visual information, handbook of sensory physiology *(pp. 1–152), VII/3 A. Berlin: Springer-Verlag; Hamada, J. (2020).* Psychophysics of pattern cognition. *Tokyo: Kazama Press (Japanese text).)*

radial pattern with the line ends linearly along the sides of the regular polygon. Here instead of regular polygons, rounded contours and illusory planes appear. For example, the leftmost column in (a) appears to be a rounded white shape instead of an equilateral triangle. On the other hand, if the 12 lines are rotated by 15°, as shown in the center column, so that the line ends follow the sides of the regular polygon and the line ends are positioned at the vertices, an

Twelve lines   15° rotation of lines   Addition of lines

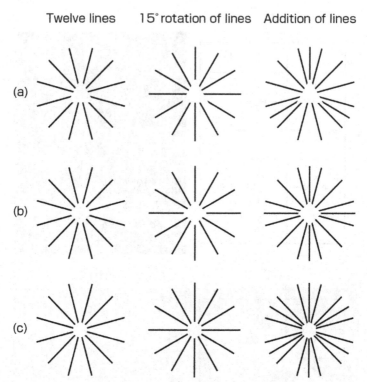

Fig. 4.3 Illusory contours without corners *(left columns)* and illusory contours with corners *(middle and right columns)* (a–c). *(From Hamada, J., & Nakahashi, T. (1995). Relationship between form and brightness in the Ehrenstein illusion. Perception, 24 (Supplement), 79; Hamada, J. (2008). The excitaion and the compound inhibition in brightness illusion. Tokyo: Kazama Press (Japanese text).)*

illusory regular polygon of white triangle (a), diamond (b), and hexagon (c) appears. This shows that the line ends are connected linearly (Fig. 4.1). Finally, when line segments are added to the vertices of the pattern in the left column, the white illusory regular polygon becomes clearer as shown in the right column. Similarly, when the black and white of these figures are reversed and white lines are drawn on a black background, illusory contours and black illusory planes appear (Hamada, 2008). This phenomenon indicates that the line ends must be placed at the vertices of the polygon in order to create an illusory polygon. In other words, if the line ends are placed linearly on sides other than the vertices, no illusory polygons will be formed, and the shape will be rounded. It is not enough to arrange the line ends in straight lines to form an illusory polygon, but it is necessary to place them at the vertices. This phenomenon indicates that the line ends play an important role in the generation of polygonal illusory contours.

4.1.1 Effects of contrast polarity, distance, and direction on the Ehrenstein illusion

In this experiment, we use the pattern shown in Fig. 4.4, which consists of eight black, white, or black-and-white lines arranged radially on a uniform gray field. When observing this Ehrenstein pattern, light or dark illusory disks are produced even though the reflectance of the central circular disk and the surrounding background field are equal. We will examine how the strength of this illusion depends on (1) the contrast polarity of the lines, (2) the distance between the line ends (i.e., the gap diameter), and (3) the direction of the black-and-white lines. We also examine the decrease in brightness levels in comparison with a uniform field. In this section, Hamada (1995), an extension of Hamada (1987), will be reviewed.

4.1.2 Method

4.1.2.1 Experimental apparatus and stimulus pattern

The front and side views of the apparatus are shown in Fig. 4.5. Eight halogen lamps (6 V, 20 W) uniformly illuminated test and comparison fields. The test and comparison fields were surrounded by black paper with a Munsell brightness value of N2.5 (6.2 c/m^2), which were 80 cm in length and width (36° in visual angle). The test and comparison fields were presented with a shutter for 3 s. There were 12 test fields with different combinations of black-and-white lines, distances between line ends (i.e., gap diameter), and two uniform fields as a control condition, for a total of 14

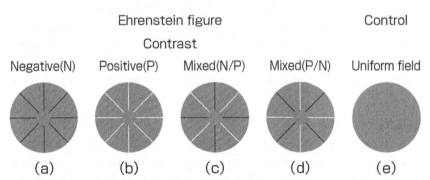

Fig. 4.4 An illustration of the Ehrenstein patterns (a–d) and uniform field (e) used. *(From Hamada, J. (1995). The Ehrenstein illusion: Effect of contrast polarity, gap size, and line orientation. Japanese Psychological Research, 37, 117–124.)*

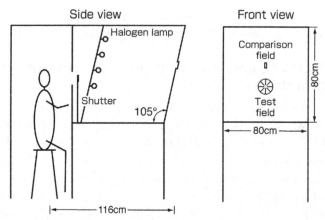

Fig. 4.5 Front and side views of the experimental apparatus. *(From Hamada, J. (2020). Psychophysics of pattern cognition. Tokyo: Kazama Press (Japanese text); adapted from Hamada, J. (1987). Overall brightness decrease in the Ehrenstein illusion induced for both contrast polarities. Perception & Psychophsics, 41, 67–72. (Springer Nature).)*

stimuli. Fig. 4.4 shows examples of four Ehrenstein patterns with eight black lines (a: negative contrast), eight white ones (b: positive contrast), four black vertical horizontal lines and four white sloping ones (c: mixed contrast), four white vertical horizontal lines and four black sloping ones (d: mixed contrast), and a uniform gray field (e: control condition). The reflectance of the black and white lines was 2% and 73%, respectively, and that of the uniform field was 39% (N6.7 in brightness value).

The width of the eight lines was 0.5 mm, and they were placed at 45° intervals. The lengths of the lines were 52.5, 44.5, and 36.5 mm, and the gap diameter were 16 (47′ in visual angle), 32 (1°34′), and 48 mm (2°22′). The diameter of the test field was 121 mm (6°). Thirty-three Munsell achromatic papers were used as comparison stimuli, with the value ranging from 1.5 to 9.5 at 0.25 intervals. The comparison stimulus (30′ wide × 105′ high) was placed directly above the test field at a visual angle of 5.72°. The participant's head was fixed on a chin rest, and the viewing distance was 116 cm.

4.1.2.2 Procedure

There were eight participants in the experiment: undergraduate students at Tokushima University and the author. They compared the brightness of the illusory disk in the center of the Ehrenstein pattern, the surrounding background field, and the uniform field with that of the comparison stimulus (Munsell achromatic paper) using the three cases (bright, same, and dark) by method of limits. The 14 patterns were presented in random order, and the order of measurement of the illusory disk and the background field was counterbalanced within each participant. After one practice session, each participant repeated six sessions on different days.

4.1.3 Result

The decrease in the brightness level of the background field. The experimental results are shown in Fig. 4.6. The mean value of the brightness matched to the uniform field is 6.29 and is indicated by the dotted horizontal line. The brightness of the background field in the black, white, and mixed line conditions were similar. According to the analysis of variance, there was

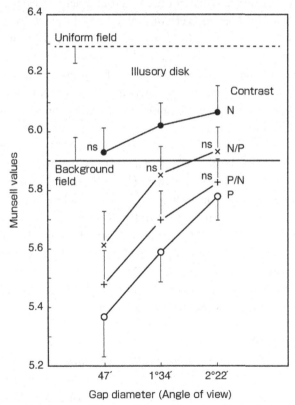

Fig. 4.6 Apparent brightness of illusory disks as a function of gap diameter (i.e., distance between line ends). Apparent brightness of the background field *(solid horizontal lines)* and the uniform field *(dotted lines)* were also shown. Vertical bars indicate 1SD. *(From Hamada, J. (1995). The Ehrenstein illusion: Effect of contrast polarity, gap size, and line orientation.* Japanese Psychological Research, 37, 117–124.)

no significant difference between the brightnesses matched to these 12 background fields, and the mean value of the brightness values was 5.90, which is shown by the solid horizontal line. The mean value of the background field ($M = 5.90$) is significantly darker than that of the uniform field ($M = 6.29$), which has the same reflectance. Thus, when black, white, or mixed lines are added to the uniform field, in all the brightness level of the background field decreases, causing the difference of 0.39 in brightness.

4.1.3.1 The Ehrenstein illusion

The Munsell brightness value matched to the illusory disk is shown in Fig. 4.6 as a function of the gap diameter. Analysis of variance was used to examine whether there was a significant difference between the brightness of the illusory disk and that of the background field for each pattern. As a result, significant differences were observed in eight pairs, except for four pairs indicated as ns. Here, there was no significant difference between the brightness of the illusory light disks (N) and that of the background field at the minimum distance (47' in visual angle) between the line ends, and the illusion was enhanced as the distance increased. On the contrary, the brightness of the dark illusory disk (P) caused by the white lines decreases as the distance between the line ends increases. In other words, the brightness is moving upward against the distance between the line ends, regardless of contrast polarity. The illusion of mixed lines (P/N and N/P) is intermediate between that of white lines (P) and that of black lines (N). That is, the brightness of the two illusory disks induced by the four white lines and the four black ones in the mixed lines (P/N and N/P) mutually cancel each other out. The brightness of the illusory disk is not the same for mixed lines (P/N), where the white lines are aligned horizontally and vertically and the black lines are tilted, and vice versa (N/P). This indicates that the direction of the white and black lines affects the amount of the illusion and produces an anisotropy of the brightness illusion.

4.1.4 Discussion

4.1.4.1 Effects of contrast polarity and gap diameter

Spillmann, Fuld, and Gerrits (1976) reported that the Ehrenstein illusion is stronger with positive contrast than with negative contrast at threshold. Furthermore, Spillmann, Fuld, and Neumeyer (1984) found the same effect above the threshold. The results of the present experiment at a moderate gap diameter (i.e., 1°34') are consistent with their results. However, as shown in Fig. 4.6, when the gap diameter is short (47'), the illusion is strong in positive contrast, but not in negative contrast. On the other hand, when the gap diameter is long (2°22′), the illusion tends to be stronger with negative contrast than with positive contrast. Thus, the strength of the illusion due to positive and negative contrast depends on the gap diameter. In the case of negative contrast, Fuld and O'Donnell (1984) confirmed Ehrenstein's (1941) report that the illusion increases as the gap diameter increases. This result is consistent with the present experiment. Thus, asymmetry appears in the Ehrenstein illusion of light and dark induced by negative and positive contrasts. Here, Fig. 4.6 shows that the brightness of the illusory disks tends to move upward as the gap diameter increases, approaching the uniform gray field. However, since the Ehrenstein pattern has luminance steps (i.e., edges), it is not likely to reach the brightness for the uniform field without a luminance step.

4.1.4.2 Decrease in brightness levels
In the case of black, white, and mixed lines, there was no significant difference in brightness between the background fields, and the brightness level decreased compared to the uniform field. The decrease in brightness levels is consistent with the results of the Craik-O'Brien-Cornsweet patterns (Figs. 2.4 and 2.9), the induced brightness contrast patterns (Fig. 3.3), the half-wave patterns (Fig. 3.6), and the brightness contrast in the separation distances (Fig. 3.9). This decrease in the brightness level is thought to be closely related to the Ehrenstein illusion.

4.1.5 Antagonistic processes, edge detection, and blocking of lateral spread in a three-level qualitative model
First, we consider the light Ehrenstein illusion in Fig. 4.4a. The illusory disk with black lines (N) are brighter than the background field. Then, the concept of lateral spread and its blocking was newly introduced, referring to the one-dimensional five-step qualitative model shown in Fig. 2.10. A three-level qualitative model for the two-dimensional Ehrenstein pattern is then proposed in Fig. 4.7. In Fig. 4.4a, in the lower level of cognitive system when a black line is added to a uniform field, as shown in Fig. 4.7, inhibition (−) of the black line is strengthened, while surrounding excitation (+) is relatively strengthened according to the decrease in luminance of the black line. In the middle level, edges are detected on both sides of the black line as shown by the dotted lines, and a circular edge connecting the tips of the eight lines is assumed to be detected. In addition, the excitation and inhibition induced in the lower level spread laterally, as indicated by

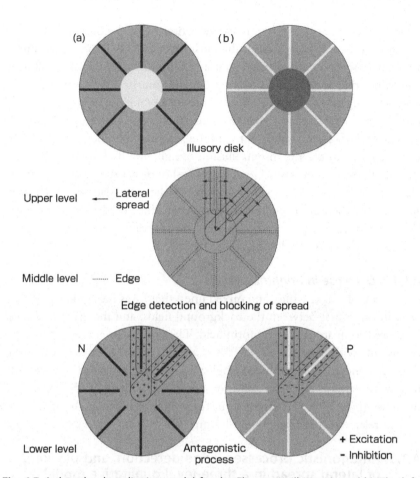

(a) (b)

Illusory disk

Upper level ← Lateral spread

Middle level ⋯⋯ Edge

Edge detection and blocking of spread

N   P

Lower level   Antagonistic process   + Excitation
                                                    − Inhibition

Fig. 4.7 A three-level qualitative model for the Ehrenstein illusion (a and b). The left (a) shows negative contrast (N) and the right (b) shows positive contrast (P), showing an antagonistic process *(lower level of the cognitive system)*, edge detection *(middle level)*, and blocking of lateral spread by edges *(upper level)*, and illusory disks. *(From Hamada, J. (2020).* Psychophysics of pattern cognition. *Tokyo: Kazama Press (Japanese text); adapted from Hamada, J. (1995). The Ehrenstein illusion: Effect of contrast polarity, gap size, and line orientation.* Japanese Psychological Research, 37, 117–124.)

the arrows in the upper level. However, because the lateral spread is blocked by the linear and circular edges, excitation and inhibition are averaged within the edges, causing a stronger decrease in brightness levels on the background field than on the circular disk. The light Ehrenstein illusion is produced when the brightness levels decrease due to edge detection and lateral spread, and the degree of decrease differs between the illusory disk and the background field. Incidentally, as a function similar to edge detection, lateral spread, and blocking of it, Gerrits and Vendrik (1970) postulated a filling-in process to explain the phenomena of brightness contrast and stabilized retinal images (See section 1.4.4) (Grossberg, 1983; Grossberg & Todorovic, 1988).

The basis for assuming circular edge detection in addition to straight line detection here is the behavior of goodness and simplicity for repetitive patterns in Part 3, Chapter 10, Experiment 1. In other words, the goodness and simplicity of the repetitive pattern consisting of circular motifs were specifically increased ($p4m$ in Fig. 10.5b). This suggests that there is a mechanism for detecting not only straight line but also circle in the cognitive system. In this connection, neurophysiologists Hubel and Wiesel (1965, 1979) have shown the existence of a mechanism for straight line detection in the brain. Therefore, since the goodness and simplicity of the repetitive pattern consisting of circular components increased specifically, it would be a probable assumption to assume the existence of a detection mechanism for circular components (bottom part of Fig. 10.4) as well as for linear components. Thus, Part 3 (symmetry cognition) and Part 1 (contour perception and brightness illusion) seem to be closely related.

A psychological example that supports the detection of straight lines and circular components is given here by Kanizsa (1955). He reported that increasing the number of equally spaced dots from 4 to 10 produced illusory regular polygonal contours when the number of dots was small, while circular illusory contour was produced when the number of dots was large (Koffka, 1931; Metzger, 1953). Furthermore, Day and Jory (1980) reported that adding eight dots at equal intervals to the surroundings of the eight lines in the two vertical and horizontal brackets [ ] of Koffka (1935) produced illusory contours such as square, diamond, and circle depending on the distance. These reports suggest that the cognitive system has a mechanism to detect the straight lines and circles.

The three-level qualitative model for the dark Ehrenstein illusion is also applicable to the white lines (P) in Fig. 4.4b. Here, when the white lines are added to the uniform field, the antagonistic process in the lower level of the cognitive system induces excitation (+) for the white lines and inhibition (−) for the surrounding field. In addition, at the middle level, linear and circular edges are detected. At an upper level, the excitation and inhibition undergo lateral spread as indicated by arrows but are blocked by linear and circular edges. The excitation and inhibition within the edges are averaged out, and the degree of decrease in the brightness levels is stronger in the illusory disk than in the background field, producing the dark Ehrenstein illusion.

The apparent brightness of the black-and-white (N/P) and white-and-black (P/N) illusory disks with mixed lines were different, and the latter was more illusory than the former. The brightness of the two illusory disks (c and d in Fig. 4.4) with four white and four black lines of different tilt angles was intermediate between that of the black and white disks with eight lines of the same color (a and b). This indicates that black-and-white (N/P) and white-and-black (P/N) mixed lines have a canceling effect on the brightness of the illusory disk. On the other hand, circular illusory contour also appears at the tips of the mixed lines in Fig. 4.4c and d, and the illusory contours appear regardless of the contrast polarity of the black-and-white and white-and-black mixed lines. Here, in Part 3, Chapter 8, Experiment 2, the similarity between the 21-dot standard and 13-dot comparison pattern pairs consisting of solid-and-open dots (heterogeneous condition) and solid-and-solid dots (homogeneous condition) was determined by configuration regardless of contrast polarity (Figs. 8.8 and 8.9). Thus, contrast polarity is not considered to be involved in the generation of configurations.

The brightness of the illusory disks induced by the Ehrenstein pattern with four black and four white lines cancels each other out, but as shown in Fig. 4.4c and d the illusory contours are clearly visible. This phenomenon indicates that the illusory contours and illusory disks are processed differently in the cognitive system. This view is consistent with the view of Prazdny (1983), who argued that simultaneous contrast of brightness is not the cause of illusory contours, based on the fact that illusory contours are produced whether 16 thick black lines are arranged in a circular pattern, or 8 black and white lines are arranged alternately. However, the present three-level qualitative model in Fig. 4.7 asserts that the illusory contours are generated first by edge detection, and then the illusory disk is generated to complete the Ehrenstein illusion. In other words, Hamada's qualitative model asserts that the Ehrenstein illusion is produced when linear and circular edges cause the decrease in brightness levels and the degree of decrease differs between the illusory disk and the background field. Thus, this model claims that illusory contour formation occurs first and brightness contrast occurs later.

According to this experiment, as the distance between the black line (N) ends increased, the brightness of the illusory light disks increased and the light Ehrenstein illusion was enhanced. However, with white lines (P), the brightness of the illusory dark disks increased as well, and the dark Ehrenstein illusion weakened (Fig. 4.6). The behavior of the light and dark

Ehrenstein illusions with increasing the distance between line ends is a subject of future study. In addition, the strength of the illusion changed when the lines were rotated by 45° in the black-and-white mixed line pattern. Therefore, the anisotropy of the brightness illusion depending on the direction of the lines should be investigated in the future. In addition, an asymmetry between dark and light was reported in the simultaneous contrast of brightness by Hamada (1983, 1984a) and in the Craik-O'Brien-Cornsweet illusion by Hamada (1982, 1985) where negative contrast caused a stronger illusion than positive. In contrast, in the Ehrenstein illusion, the positive contrast tended to be stronger than the negative contrast. The difference in the asymmetry of the dark and light Craik-O'Brien-Cornsweet illusion and the Ehrenstein illusion according to contrast polarity should be examined in the future.

Cohen and Grossberg (1984), Grossberg and Mingolla (1985, 1987), and Shapley, Caelli, Grossberg, Morgan, and Rentschler (1990) distinguish between two parallel contour detection processes (i.e., boundary contour and feature contour). The correspondence between the models and Hamada's model will require further experimental and theoretical investigation in the future. In addition, the three-level qualitative model for the Ehrenstein illusion needs to be reconfigured as a mathematical model. In other word, the illusion needs to be simulated by incorporating the detection of linear and circular edges, the blocking of lateral spread, the decrease in brightness levels, and the anisotropy of the brightness illusion. Furthermore, neurophysiological explanations of these psychological phenomena, as Spillmann and Werner (1990) and Zeki (1993) have attempted, are also awaited.

PART TWO

Negative time-order effect on weight sensation

CHAPTER FIVE

Excitation and inhibition in negative time-order effect

Since, the discovery of Gustav Theoder Fechner (1801–1887), the constant error in the relative judgments for two identical stimuli presented in succession, where the preceding first and the following second stimuli are regularly judged differently, has been called the time error. For example, in terms of weight sensation, an error in which the second stimulus is judged to be heavier than the first one is a negative time error (Woodworth & Schlosberg, 1954; Guilford, 1954). However, it seems inappropriate to call this regular discrepancy an error, since it does not occur by chance but by certain causes. In fact, Helson (1947, 1964) examined this discrepancy in relation to the level of adaptation determined not only by the specific stimulus being judged but also by the set of related stimuli. He referred to this discrepancy as the time-order effect when the stimulus presentation interval is less than about 3 s. So, we will use the term time-order effect instead of time error. In this chapter, Hamada (1990a) will be reviewed.

5.1 Examination on negative time-order effects

In the case of the weight sensation, the first hypothesis is represented by the trace sedimentation theory of Köhler (1923) and the assimilation theory of Lauenstein (1933). These hypotheses are that the memory trace of the preceding first stimulus is diminished by the passage of time or assimilation to the surrounding environment, and this is compared with the new impression of the following second stimulus, so that the first stimulus is judged to be lighter, resulting in a negative time-order effect (Guilford, 1954). The second hypothesis, represented by Helson's (1947, 1964) adaptation level theory, does not focus only on the traces of the first stimulus but also considers that negative time-order effects occur in relation to the judgment criteria based on the trace system formed by the entire series of stimuli preceding the first stimulus. The adaptation level is the stimulus that is judged as "medium" by the participants, and it is assumed that the adaptation level decreases in the situation of successive comparisons. The second stimulus is judged more heavily than the first stimulus because they judge the second stimulus based on the relational framework of the entire set of stimuli faced by them, that is, the adaptation level (Guilford, 1954).

The previously mentioned studies were based on relative judgments between two stimuli and not on absolute judgments of individual stimuli. However, the relative judgments between two stimuli should be considered as a comparison of individual absolute judgments made for the two stimuli. In the present experiment, we measured the two weight stimuli presented in succession by both relative and absolute judgments and compared the negative time-order effects in these judgments to examine the mechanism of their occurrence.

5.1.1 Method

5.1.1.1 Apparatus and procedure

The stimuli were lead in opaque plastic cans, 40 mm in diameter and 55 mm in height, and consisted of five weighted stimuli (94, 97, 100, 103, and 106 g) spaced at 3 g intervals. To reduce the burden on the participants, only 17 pairs of stimuli were used in the 5 × 5 matrix, which were located vertically, horizontally, and right ascension and declination diagonally. A feature of this stimulus structure is that there are pairs in which the first and second stimuli are the same (e.g., the first and second stimuli are both 100 g), and there are also pairs in which the first and second ones are exchanged (e.g., the first stimulus is 94 g and the second one is 106 g, and vice versa). A total of 10 participants, 9 undergraduate students at Tokushima University and the author, were alternately experimenters and participants. One of them did not lift weights to the sound of the metronome, so the data were not included in the analysis. The experiment was conducted collectively in pairs, with 10 participants at the same time, in a psychology laboratory training class.

The timing of stimulus elevation was controlled by a metronome, and the elevation time was about 1 s. Relative and absolute judgments were used to judge the paired stimuli. In the relative judgment, the second stimulus was judged in three cases to be "heavier", "the same", or "lighter" than the first stimulus, after the paired stimuli were dropped off. In the absolute judgments, the weights of the two individual stimuli were judged immediately by a seven-category rating after the end of the second stimulus, that is, "very light", "light", "somewhat light", "medium", "somewhat heavy", "heavy", and "very heavy", in the order from the first to the second stimulus. In addition, a single-judgment condition was also established as a control condition, in which participants made absolute judgments in seven categories after the end of the weighting of a single stimulus. The experimental procedure for this condition was the same as that for the absolute judgment condition, except that one stimulus was presented and rated. These seven categories were analyzed by assigning integers ranging from one to seven points. The interval between each trial was about 5 s or more.

The 3 and 1 s conditions in the relative and absolute judgment conditions were conducted. The 3 and 1 s absolute judgment conditions and the single judgment condition were administered separately. These three absolute judgment conditions constituted one session. The order of implementation of the 3 and 1 s conditions was counterbalanced both in the relative and absolute conditions. Thus, the experiment consisted of (relative and absolute judgment conditions) × (3 and 1 s conditions) + (single judgment condition) = 5 conditions. In the relative and absolute judgment conditions, 17 stimulus pairs were presented randomly, one at a time. In the single judgment condition, five stimuli were randomly presented two times each.

Three practice trials were conducted for each of the above five conditions before entering them. In addition, 10 practice judgments were made using single stimuli in order to determine the criteria for judgment before entering the absolute judgment session. In this way, one participant performed each of the five conditions one time, and then the participant and the experimenter took turns to perform the same experiment. Nine experiments were conducted every other week, and the data of the first week were not analyzed as practice trials. The number of judgments made by the nine participants was 72 for each stimulus pair (9 participants × 8 weeks) and 144 for each single stimulus (2 times × 9 participants × 8 weeks).

5.1.2 Results

5.1.2.1 Relative and absolute judgments

Fig. 5.1 shows the percentages of the 17 pairs of relative and absolute judgments in which the second stimulus was judged to be "heavier, H" and "lighter, L" than the first stimulus. The points (H,L) in the 3 s (large solid circles) and 1 s (large open circles) in relative judgment conditions are both located below the 45° diagonal through the origin. If there were no time-order effect, the points (H, L) would be plotted on the diagonal. Here, the value of H is higher than L, and the points (H, L) are located below the diagonal, so there is a negative time-order effect. The degree of time-order effect is defined as the distance between the point (H, L) and the diagonal, that is,

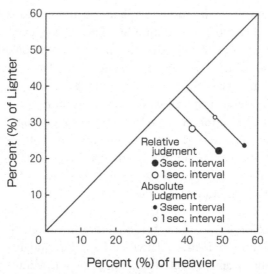

Percent (%) of Heavier

Fig. 5.1 Strength of the negative time-order effect. *(From Hamada, J. (1990a). Examination of negative time order effect based on relative and absolute judgments. Japanese Journal of Psycholomic Science, 9, 1–10. (Japnese text with English abstract and captions).)*

$TE = (L - H)/\sqrt{2}$. In the relative judgment, $TE = -19.0$ in the 3 s condition and $TE = -9.4$ in the 1 s one, and there is a significant difference between them. In other words, there is a stronger negative time-order effect in the 3 s condition than in the 1 s one.

Next, we examine the relationship between the seven category ratings for the first and second stimuli in the absolute judgment condition. If the second stimulus had a higher rating than the first one, it was classified as "heavier"; if the opposite was true, it was classified as "lighter"; and if the ratings were identical, they were classified as "the same". The ratios of "heavier, H" and "lighter, L" for the 17 stimulus pairs were then calculated, and the average ratio (%) of these values was calculated (see Fig. 5.1). Points (H, L) in absolute judgments are plotted for the 3 s (small solid circles) and 1 s conditions (small open circles). In the condition, since the number of categories was 7, the ratio of "the same" was lower than that in the relative judgment condition using the three cases, and the points (H, L) moved in the upper right direction on the diagonal. In the absolute judgment, $TE = -23.3$ in the 3 s condition and $TE = -12.2$ in the 1 s one, with a significant difference between them. There was a significant difference

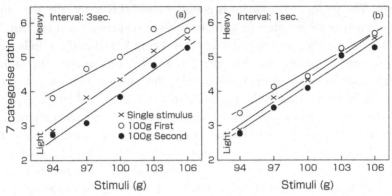

Fig. 5.2 Rating values for weight stimuli in absolute judgments. *(From Hamada, J. (1990a). Examination of negative time order effect based on relative and absolute judgments. Japanese Journal of Psycholomic Science, 9, 1–10. (Japnese text with English abstract and captions).)*

between the *TE* values in the absolute and relative judgment conditions in the 3 s condition, but not in the 1 s one.

Ratings for the first and second stimuli based on absolute judgments. Fig. 5.2a and b shows the ratings for the five first stimuli (open circles) when 100 g is the first stimulus, and conversely for the five first stimuli (solid circles) when 100 g is the second one, separately for the 3 and 1 s conditions, and the five ratings for single stimuli (×). The ratings for the single stimulus are in the middle of ones for the second and first stimuli. Here, the first stimulus was judged significantly lighter than the single one in both the 3 and 1 s conditions, while the second one was judged significantly heavier than it. The negative time-order effect was caused by the first stimulus becoming lighter and the second one becoming heavier than the single stimulus. In addition, the ratings for the first and second stimuli converged to those for the single stimuli in the 1 s condition than in the 3 s one.

5.1.3 Discussion

In addition to relative judgments, a new method of absolute judgments was introduced. In both methods, the negative time-order effect was stronger when the weight-interval between stimulus pairs was 3 than 1 s. Hayashi (1937) made relative judgments by varying the presentation intervals between the first stimulus (100 g) and the second one (88–104 g) in the range of 1.3 to 3.25 s. As a result, the frequency for the second stimulus of "heavier" increased as time elapsed, increasing the negative time-order effect. The present experiment is consistent with his result. On the other hand, the time-order effect in absolute judgments in the present experiment was caused by the preceding first stimulus being lighter and the following second one being heavier than the single one. Furthermore, the ratings for the first and second stimuli converged to those for the single stimuli when the weight-interval was reduced from 3 to 1 s. As described previously, this experiment reconfirmed the results of the conventional relative judgment of the time-order effect and found new findings based on absolute judgment. In the following, we will show that the conventional hypotheses cannot explain the negative time-order effect revealed in this experiment, and we will discuss the mechanism of this effect by means of the antagonistic process of excitation and inhibition and by means of disinhibition. First, we would like to examine Köhler's (1923) theory of trace sedimentation and Lauenstein's (1933) theory of assimilation.

5.1.3.1 Explanations by trace sedimentation and assimilation theories

According to the absolute judgments of the present experiment, the ratings for the first stimulus were lighter than those for the single ones and became lighter as time elapsed. This result for the first stimulus is consistent with the predictions of the trace sedimentation and assimilation theories, which postulate a decline in memory traces. However, these theories do not address the weight of the second stimulus and fail to account for the fact that the second one becomes heavier than the single one over time. Next, we would like to discuss Helson's adaptive level theory.

5.1.3.2 Application of the adaptation level theory

Helson (1947) asked participants to rate their relative weight sensations for stimuli ranging from 200 to 400 g in nine categories and found that the rating for stimuli judged to be "medium" was 249 g, lighter than the arithmetic mean of 300 g for the series stimuli. He attributed this result to the fact that the series stimuli as a whole reduced the adaptation level. The same trend was observed in the single stimulus series in the present experiment, where the stimulus that produced a "medium" judgment (corresponding to a rating of four points) was not 100 g but 98.3 g (the value interpolated by 5 × symbols in Fig. 5.2). Therefore this 1.7 g discrepancy in 3 g interval can be explained by a decrease in the adaptation level. On the other hand, the first stimulus was treated as an anchor stimulus in Helson's experiment, and participants did not judge its weight. Therefore, it is not possible to predict quantitatively the weight of both the first and second stimuli by directly applying this theory, but we would like to discuss it as follows. According to this theory, the adaptation level is the synergistic mean of the stimuli S_i ($i = 1$, 2, ..., n) according to Fechner's law (Guilford, 1954). In the present experiment, there were 10 and 34 stimuli (i.e., 17 pairs) in the single and absolute judgment conditions, respectively. The synergistic means of the two conditions as calculated to be 99.91 and 99.92 g, respectively, which are almost equal, and the adaptation level of the two conditions is the same. In the absolute judgment condition in the present experiment, the time-order effect also occurred, and the first and second stimuli of the same weight were judged lighter and heavier, respectively. Furthermore, when the presentation interval was shortened from 3 to 1 s, the ratings of the first and second stimuli were close to that of the single stimulus. Since the adaptation level theory treats the interstimulus interval and time-order effects as constants (Noguchi, 1964), it cannot predict these factors. Next, we would like to explain the negative time-order effects by disinhibition based on the antagonistic process of excitation and inhibition.

Explanation by disinhibition. As described in Part 1, Chapter 1, Békésy (1959, 1960) described the antagonistic process of excitation and inhibition in terms of neural units and showed that it works commonly in cutaneous sensation and vision. Ratliff (1965) explained the phenomenon of disinhibition by excitation and lateral inhibition in individual eyes of horseshoe crabs. On the other hand, Pavlov (1927) explained disinhibition on the basis of reinforcement and extinction in conditioned reflexes (Sokolov, 1963). An example of disinhibition here is the rapid secretion of saliva by the presentation of a new stimulus during the extinction phase of the conditioned reflex of salivation. This disinhibition means that the previously existing inhibition is released by the presentation of a new stimulus. In the following, the negative time-order effect is qualitatively explained by this disinhibition.

The disinhibition hypothesis explains the negative time-order effect when the weights of the first and second stimuli are equal as follows. First, we describe the excitation and inhibition induced by the single stimulus shown in Fig. 5.3a. A single stimulus induces a corresponding excitation (represented by a triangular distribution), at the same time, an inhibition is induced in response to it. We assume that the inhibition is weaker than the excitation but increases with time, and that a weight sensation is produced by the synthesis of excitation and inhibition. The increase in inhibition is indicated by the sloping solid line. Then, we assume that the inhibition, which intensifies with time, gradually decreases the weight sensation

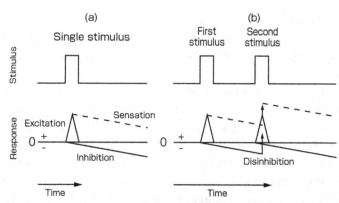

Fig. 5.3 Explanation of the negative time-order effect by the disinhibition hypothesis (a and b). + and −signs indicate excitation and inhibition, respectively. *(From Hamada, J. (1990a). Examination of negative time order effect based on relative and absolute judgments. Japanese Journal of Psycholomic Science, 9, 1–10. (Japnese text with English abstract and captions).)*

of a single stimulus (indicated by the dashed slope). However, in the single-judgment condition, the weight judgment is made immediately after the lifting of the weight, so the effect of inhibition is weak.

As shown in Fig. 5.3b, when the first stimulus is weighed, the excitation and inhibition are induced as in the case of a single stimulus, and the inhibition becomes stronger with time and the weight sensation gradually decreases. Thus, we do not think that the memory trace of the first stimulus simply fades, as in the trace sedimentation and assimilation theories, but that the weight of the first stimulus decreases as a result of active inhibition in the sensory impression. Then, when the second stimulus is raised, new excitation and inhibition are induced. At the same time, the inhibition induced by the first stimulus is released, and the reaction produces an opposite process of excitation (indicated by the up arrow in Fig. 5.3b) in proportion to the strength of the inhibition, which is added to the excitation of the second stimulus. As a result, the excitation to the second stimulus becomes higher than that to the first one. When the weight of the second stimulus ends, the added excitation is evaluated as the weight for the second stimulus, so the first stimulus is judged to be lighter and the second one heavier than the single stimulus.

A larger negative time-order effect occurs in the 3 than in the 1 s condition because the inhibition intensifies along the time course after the first stimulus. In addition, if the presentation interval between the first and second stimuli is sufficiently short, the induced inhibition becomes weaker and the weight sensation for them approaches that of a single stimulus. Using the concept of disinhibition in this way, we can at least qualitatively explain the convergence of the ratings of the first and second stimuli to the ratings of the single stimuli as the presentation interval is shortened.

PART THREE

Symmetry cognition

CHAPTER SIX

Rotational and reflectional transformations

6.1 Japanese family crests and group theory

Mach (1918) emphasized the role of transformations (reflection, rotation, translation, and dilatation) by mathematically representing geometric symmetry to the cognitive system and pointed out that reflection transformations are particularly easy to perceive among them (Bertamini, Silvanto, Norcia, Makin, & Wagemans, 2018). Thus, the geometric symmetry has played a central role in the study of shape perception. Symmetry in vision has been studied, especially in terms of its role in goodness, and its earliest claims were made by Gestalt psychologists. For example, Koffka (1935), based on Prägnanz's law introduced by Wertheimer (1880–1943), held that psychological organization is always as good as conditions allow, but the term goodness is a subjective judgment that is not defined. And he states that goodness includes regularity, symmetry, and simplicity. In this chapter, we discuss the relationship between geometric symmetry and goodness, as illustrated by the transformations of rotation and reflection.

Usually, Japanese family crests are drawn in a circular outline, and when special ones are added, they reach a few thousand, which is said to include most of the motif patterns in Japan. The ideal form of Japanese family crests is the simple geometric figure that has some symmetry (Fushimi, 1967a, 2013). In order to show the geometric symmetry in mathematics, eight examples of the family crests with rotational and reflectional symmetry are shown in Fig. 6.1.

The set of rotational transformations that do not have reflection axes and show no change in shape when rotated about the central axis of the family crest generates a cyclic group (C_n). These crests are invariant to n rotational transformations of $360°/n$ rotations, so the number of transformations is n. For example, in Fig. 6.1, C_1 shows invariance only for one rotation of $360°$,

Psychophysics and Experimental Phenomenology of Pattern Cognition
https://doi.org/10.1016/B978-0-323-95286-6.00006-5 Copyright © 2023 Elsevier Inc.

89

Order of symmetry group

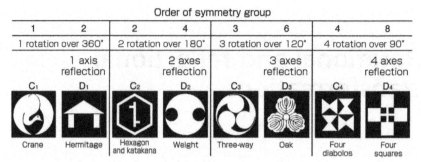

1	2	2	4	3	6	4	8
1 rotation over 360°		2 rotation over 180°		3 rotation over 120°		4 rotation over 90°	
1 axis reflection		2 axes reflection		3 axes reflection		4 axes reflection	
C_1	D_1	C_2	D_2	C_3	D_3	C_4	D_4
Crane	Hermitage	Hexagon and katakana	Weight	Three-way	Oak	Four diabolos	Four squares

Fig. 6.1 Eight examples of Japanese family crests and symmetry transformation groups. *(From Hamada, J., Amano, K., Fukuda, S.T., Uchiumi, C., Fukushi, K., & van der Helm. P.A. (2016). Group theoretical model of symmetry cognition. Acta Psychologica, 171, 128–137. https://doi.org/10.1016/j.actpsy.2016.10.002; adapted from Hamada, J., Uchiumi, C., Fukushi, K., & Amano, K. (2011b). Complexity and goodness of dot patterns depending upon symmetry groups. Japanese Psychological Review, 54, 138–152. (Japanese text with English abstract).)*

so the number of transformations is 1. C_4 is invariant to four rotations of 90° around the central axis, so the number of transformations is 4.

On the other hand, the set of reflectional transformations that show invariance when the front and back are reversed with respect to the n reflection axes passing through the center of the family crest, with no change in shape, and the set of rotational transformations that show invariance with respect to the n rotations described previously, generates a dihedral group (D_n). The number of transformations is $2n$ since these crests are invariant to n reflectional and n rotational transformations. For example, in Fig. 6.1, D_1 shows invariance for one reflection axis (vertical axis) and also invariant with respect to one rotation of 360°, so the total number of transformations is 2. D_4 is invariant to reversals of the four reflection axes (vertical, horizontal, and two diagonal) that pass through the center of the family crest and is also invariant to four rotations of 90° each, so the total number of transformations is 8.

Cyclic means that the family crest shows invariance by rotation around the central axis of the crest, while dihedral means two sides that show invariance by reversing front and back. The number of transformations is mathematically called the order of the group and is an indicator of the degree of geometric symmetry of the family crest. In the following, we will refer to the method of studying the relationship between physical factors such as geometric symmetry, which is defined objectively and mathematically, and symmetry cognition as the group theoretical approach. In addition to geometric symmetry, the family crests contain many different factors such as the history of the family and differences in power. In this study, we use abstract and simplified dot patterns instead of concrete family crests to examine the relationship between geometric symmetry and human symmetry cognition.

6.2 ESS and transformational structure theory

Psychological experiments have shown that rotational and reflectional transformations play an important role in symmetry cognition. Garner and Clement (1963) and Garner (1966, 1970, 1974) hypothesized that the goodness of the 5-dot pattern depicted in the 3×3 grid in Fig. 6.2 is not determined solely by the pattern in question, but also by its relationship to other patterns, especially similar patterns. Thus, they assumed that when a specific dot pattern is presented, the cognitive system will apply rotational and reflectional transformations to the pattern and guess the number of patterns that result. That is, they assumed that the cognitive system would guess the number of

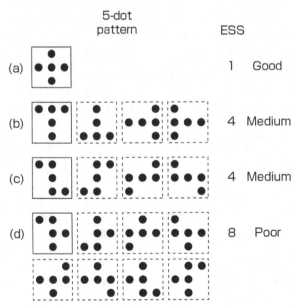

Fig. 6.2 Examples of 5-dot pattern and equivalent subset size (ESS). Transformations of rotation and reflection for the 5-dot pattern in solid grid produces the patterns shown in dotted grid (a–d). *(Adapted from Strother, L., & Kubovy, M. (2003). Perceived complexity and the grouping effect in band patterns.* Acta Psychologica, 114, 229–244.)

dot patterns in the solid and dotted grids in Fig. 6.2. In other words, it was assumed that the ESS (i.e., the equivalence subset size) would be estimated by applying four rotational transformations of 90° and reflectional transformations of the four symmetry axes to a 5-dot pattern in the solid grid. And the lower the ESS of the dot pattern, the higher the goodness. Their rating experiment showed that patterns with ESS of 1 were the best, patterns with ESS of 8 were the poorest, and patterns with ESS of 4 were in between them. Thus, it became clear that the figural goodness depends on ESS, which is determined by the rotational and reflectional transformations (Gyoba, 1995). Garner's theory, however, did not distinguish between rotational and reflectional transformations, assuming that pattern goodness was determined by ESS (Garner, 1974; Hochberg, 1971, 1978). Incidentally, when we look at the pattern in the solid grid in Fig. 6.2, even though the center column has three dots arranged in a straight line, moving the leftmost dot up in (a) results in the lowest goodness in (d) and moving the left and right dots up and down results in the medium goodness in (b and c). This result means that it is not the position of the dots, but its structure that determines its goodness. Next, we would like to explain Imai's (1977a) transformational structure theory, which clarifies the effect of the structure of a dot pattern on its goodness.

Imai, Ito, and Ito (1976a) conducted a seven-point rating experiment on the complementary 5- and 4-dot patterns in a 3×3 grid. Here, the 5-dot pattern in Fig. 6.3 and the 4 dots in the 4 blank cells are complementary patterns. The results are summarized in Fig. 6.3. The structure M_4 means that the pattern is invariant even if mirror-image transformation is applied. to the four symmetry axes. They added a vertical mirror-image structure M_V and a diagonal mirror-image structure M_D. They also added the structure R_4, which is invariant to four rotations in 90° increments, and the

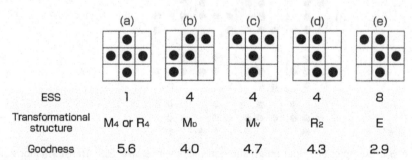

Fig. 6.3 ESS, transformational structures, and goodness ratings for the five patterns (a–e). *(Adapted from Imai, S. (1977). Various theories about the goodness of patterns. Japanese Psychological Review, 20, 258–272. (Japanese text with English abstract).)*

structure R_2, which is invariant to two rotations in 180° increments. On the other hand, M_4 or R_4 indicates that the pattern is invariant to either transformation M_4 or R_4. They focused on the invariance that the pattern does not change when these transformations are applied. And E is an empty transformational structure whose pattern does not show invariance for all transformations except 360° rotation. As shown in Fig. 6.3, the results of their experiment supported Garner's theory by increasing the goodness with decreasing the ESS. However, for the three patterns with ESS of 4 (b–d), M_V was significantly better than M_D and R_2, and ESS could not explain this result. Therefore, Imai (1977a, 1986, 1992) proposed the transformational structure theory, which states that these three types of patterns must be distinguished. In other words, the more invariant a pattern is to rotational and reflectional transformations, the better it is, not ESS it has. Thus, the pattern goodness is determined by its invariance to the transformational structure, and the goodness of M_V, M_D, and R_2 with ESS of 4 does not match because they have different transformational structures. Incidentally, Matsuda (1978), Otsuka (1984), and Gyoba, Seto, and Ichikawa (1985) measured the goodness of 5-dot patterns in a 3×3 grid and showed that the pattern goodness with ESS of 4 was not the same, confirming Imai's transformational structure theory (Ichikawa & Gyoba, 1984).

Matsuda (1978) conducted a rating experiment for the goodness of 192 patterns including four patterns Fig. 6.4 using integers from 1 to 7 points. The results showed that the pattern goodness followed Imai's transformational structure theory, and the four patterns in Fig. 6.4, which had an ESS of 8, had the poorest average rating of 2.6. In other words, goodness of four patterns with different configuration is uniformly poor regardless of the presence or absence of four open circles and the square frames. In this way, the pattern goodness in 3×3 grid is hardly affected by its configuration. However, as will be shown in Chapter 9, goodness in 9×9 and 19×19 grids

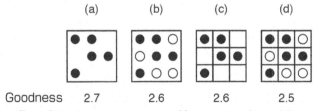

	(a)	(b)	(c)	(d)
Goodness	2.7	2.6	2.6	2.5

Fig. 6.4 The effect of the absence or presence of four open circles and the grid on goodness and complexity (a–d). *(Adapted from Matsuda, T. (1978). Judgments of pattern goodness and intra-configurational transformation structures: An examination of Imai's theory. Japanese Journal of Psychology, 49, 207–214. (Japanese text with English abstract).)*

is affected by differences in configuration. On the other hand, the pattern complexity is greatly influenced by the configuration. That is, when we observe these figures, we feel that (a) is simple and (d) is complex, while (b and c) are intermediate between them. The pattern goodness depends strongly on the transformational structure, while the complexity is affected by both the transformational structure and the configuration. Yodogawa (1980, 1982) also point out that goodness and complexity are not univocally related. For a review of symmetry, see Wagemans (1997) and Treder (2010), and for its neural processing, see Bertamini et al. (2018).

CHAPTER SEVEN

Goodness and complexity of dot patterns in a hexagonal grid

7.1 Dependence on group order and linearity in nonfilled patterns (Experiment 1)

As shown in the previous chapter, rotational and reflectional transformations are involved in the goodness of dot patterns, but only C_1, C_2, D_1, and D_4 patterns can be created with 5 and 4 dots in a 3 × 3 grid. Therefore, in this chapter, the dot patterns C_1, C_2, and C_3, which generate cyclic group, and the dot patterns D_1, D_2, and D_3,[a] which generate dihedral group are used in a 19-cell regular hexagonal grid. In this section, Hamada and Ishihara (1988, Experiment 2) will be reviewed.

7.1.1 Methods

7.1.1.1 Stimulus patterns and procedures

All 62 of the 9-dot nonfilled patterns used are shown in Fig. 7.1. They were presented by a slide projector (Kodak Model B-2) on a transmissive screen with a diameter of 17 cm and an observation distance of 1 m. The stimulus patterns were presented for 10 s.

The participants were 18 undergraduate students at Tokushima University who participated in the experiment individually. They rated goodness (or complexity) and complexity (or goodness) over two different days. Their task was to rate goodness or complexity on a seven-point integer scale ranging from 1 (poorest or simplest) to 7 (best or most complex). Participants were instructed to give verbal ratings as soon as possible after the stimulus presentation. They were not informed about the criteria of goodness and complexity and were asked to rate them according to their own criteria. Prior to the

[a] After Professor Toru Ishihara proposed the D_3 pattern with three reflection axes, the author suggested a regular hexagonal grid, and Prof. Ishihara counted all the D_n and C_n patterns ($n = 1, 2, 3$) based on Pólya's fundamental theorem concerning combinatorial mathematics (Liu, 1968). Later, the author created specific patterns and found that the goodness and complexity of dot patterns are determined by the order of cyclic and dihedral groups.

Psychophysics and Experimental Phenomenology of Pattern Cognition   Copyright © 2023 Elsevier Inc.
https://doi.org/10.1016/B978-0-323-95286-6.00007-7   All rights reserved.

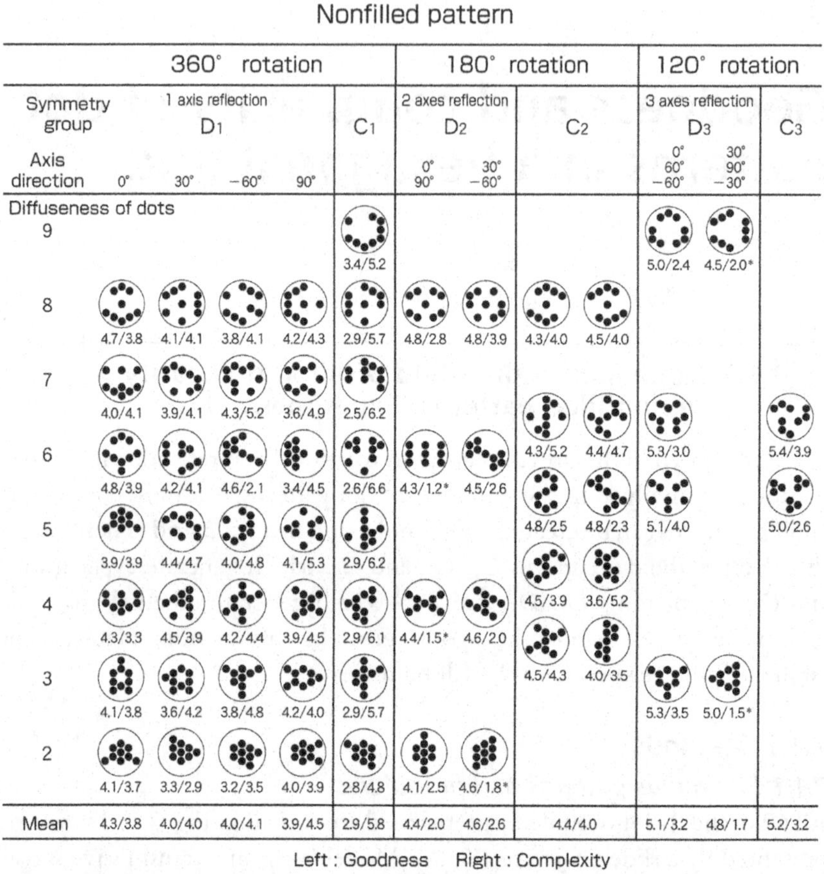

Nonfilled pattern

Diffuseness of dots	360° rotation — 1 axis reflection D1 — 0°	D1 30°	D1 -60°	D1 90°	C1	180° rotation — 2 axes reflection D2 — 0°/90°	D2 30°/-60°	C2	120° rotation — 3 axes reflection D3 — 0°/60°/-60°	D3 30°/90°/-30°	C3
9					3.4/5.2				5.0/2.4	4.5/2.0*	
8	4.7/3.8	4.1/4.1	3.8/4.1	4.2/4.3	2.9/5.7	4.8/2.8	4.8/3.9	4.3/4.0 4.5/4.0			
7	4.0/4.1	3.9/4.1	4.3/5.2	3.6/4.9	2.5/6.2						
6	4.8/3.9	4.2/4.1	4.6/2.1	3.4/4.5	2.6/6.6	4.3/1.2*	4.5/2.6	4.3/5.2 4.4/4.7	5.3/3.0		5.4/3.9
5	3.9/3.9	4.4/4.7	4.0/4.8	4.1/5.3	2.9/6.2			4.8/2.5 4.8/2.3	5.1/4.0		5.0/2.6
4	4.3/3.3	4.5/3.9	4.2/4.4	3.9/4.5	2.9/6.1	4.4/1.5*	4.6/2.0	4.5/3.9 3.6/5.2			
3	4.1/3.8	3.6/4.2	3.8/4.8	4.2/4.0	2.9/5.7			4.5/4.3 4.0/3.5	5.3/3.5	5.0/1.5*	
2	4.1/3.7	3.3/2.9	3.2/3.5	4.0/3.9	2.8/4.8	4.1/2.5	4.6/1.8*				
Mean	4.3/3.8	4.0/4.0	4.0/4.1	3.9/4.5	2.9/5.8	4.4/2.0	4.6/2.6	4.4/4.0	5.1/3.2	4.8/1.7	5.2/3.2

Left : Goodness   Right : Complexity

Fig. 7.1 Nine-dot nonfilled patterns in a hexagonal grid, and average values of goodness and complexity. *(From Hamada, J., & Ishihara, T. (1988). Complexity and goodness of dot patterns varying in symmetry. Psychological Research, 50, 155–161. (Springer Nature).)*

experiment, they randomly observed each of the solid 62 dot patterns printed on thick white cards to get a general outline of the patterns. They then repeated three sessions of rating the goodness (or complexity) of the 62 patterns presented in random order in each day's experiment. The first of these sessions was regarded as practice, and the average of the data from the second and third sessions was analyzed.

7.1.2 Results and discussion

The average ratings of goodness and complexity for the cyclic group C_n and the dihedral group D_n patterns ($n = 1, 2, 3$) and for the direction of the axis's direction are shown in Fig. 7.1. From the values in this figure, the mean values for the cyclic and dihedral groups are calculated and are shown in Fig. 7.2. The average rating is indicated by an open circle for the cyclic group and a solid circle for the dihedral group. Goodness is indicated by solid curves and complexity by a dotted one.

7.1.2.1 Goodness

In Fig. 7.2, the goodness increases with the order of the cyclic and dihedral groups separately: the means for D_2 and C_2 ($M = 4.5$ and 4.4) and for D_3 and C_3 ($M = 5.0$ and 5.2) are both nearly equal. Also, C_2 ($M = 4.4$), whose order is 2, is better than D_1 ($M = 4.0$) with the same order. Thus, the goodness of the cyclic group C_n and the dihedral group D_n are separate ($n = 1, 2, 3$), and two curves fit, increasing monotonically with the order of the group.

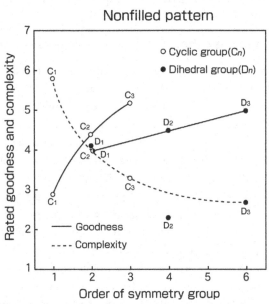

Fig. 7.2 Dependence of goodness and complexity on the group order for 9-dot nonfilled dot patterns in a hexagonal grid. *(From Hamada, J., & Ishihara, T. (1988). Complexity and goodness of dot patterns varying in symmetry. Psychological Research, 50, 155–161. (Springer Nature).)*

7.1.2.2 Complexity

The complexity is the same for the cyclic group C_n and the dihedral group D_n ($n = 1$, 2, 3), with a curve that decreases monotonically with the group order. The D_2 pattern, however, deviates from this curve and is simpler than the other patterns. This is, because among the eight D_2 patterns in Fig. 7.1, the three patterns marked with * symbol are composed of straight lines. The mean value of complexity for these three linear patterns is ($M = 1.5$), which is very simple, while that of goodness is ($M = 4.4$), which is a medium value. The two linear patterns marked with * symbol in D_3 are also simple and have moderate goodness.

As described previously, there is a difference in the dependence of goodness and complexity on the group order. The complexity of dot patterns composed of straight lines is specifically low, while the goodness is hardly affected by them. These results imply that the goodness and complexity of the 9-dot nonfilled patterns arranged in a hexagonal grid are different cognitive judgments and are processed differently. Incidentally, Yodogawa (1980, 1982) reported that the goodness of a two-dimensional pattern is determined by the overall characteristics of the pattern, while the complexity is determined by both the overall and partial characteristics.

7.2 General method for free-viewing tasks with cards

In all experiments conducted at Tokushima University on the two-dimensional dot patterns reported later, participants freely observed dot patterns printed in solid and/or open circles on a thick white paper at a reading distance. Garner and Clement (1963) measured goodness using dot patterns printed on cards, and Imai et al. (1976a) conducted a goodness rating experiment using cards by the free-viewing tasks, which does not control the direction of the cards and the distance of observation, so this experimental phenomenological method will be adopted in these studies. In the case of rating goodness, complexity, disjointedness (the inverse of unifiedness), and regularity for dot patterns within a square grid, cards printed with four orientations (0°, 90°, 180°, and 270°) were distributed to each of the four sets of participants. However, since they were not control the orientation of the cards and the observation distance, we treated them as random factors and did not analyze them. Hamada and Ishihara (1988, Experiment 2), who presented a pattern from a projector and fixed the face with a chin rest, and Hamada et al. (2016, Experiment 2), who used cards as described in the next section, agreed not only on the dependence of goodness and complexity on the group order but also on that on the relationship between D_1 and C_2 patterns with the same group order. So the reliability of the free-viewing tasks is high.

The participants in the experiments were students who were taking a psychology class and participated as different groups throughout the experiments, with no overlap. They were assigned a brief analysis and discussion of their data at the end of the experiment. It took about 90 min for the instructing, experiment, and report writing. Participants rated the goodness, complexity, disjointedness (the inverse of unifiedness), or regularity of individual patterns and the similarity of pattern pairs on a nine- or seven-point integer scale. The higher the integer, the higher the cognitive judgments. The participants were not taught the criteria for these cognitive judgments, and it was made clear to them by verbally reading the distributed instructions that they were free to set their own criteria. They read through all the cards in random order before starting the experiment to get a general outline of the patterns. The cards were then thoroughly shuffled at the beginning of each experimental session. They were conducted two or three times, and the first session was used for setting up the criteria and for practice trials, and not analyzed. They wrote the pattern number and rating for each pattern on a response sheet at their own pace. The pattern number was a small random three-digit number printed in the center of the lowest part of the card. Statistical tests were conducted at a significance level of less than 5%.

7.3 Group order, contrast polarity, and collinearity in filled patterns (Experiment 2)

Using 5-dot patterns in a 3×3 grid, Garner and Clement (1963), Matsuda (1978), and Otsuka (1984) showed that linear arrangement of dots enhances goodness. However, Hamada and Ishihara (1988) showed that the complexity of patterns with linearity in a regular hexagonal grid was singularly low, while there was little effect on goodness. On the other hand, as mentioned previously, Matsuda (1978) showed that there was no significant difference in goodness between 5-dot solid nonfilled patterns with four blank cells in a 3×3 grid and 9-dot solid-open filled patterns (see Fig. 6.4). Therefore Hamada (1988a) devised filled patterns consisting of 19 open-solid dots in a hexagonal grid to study the effects of contrast polarity and collinearity on goodness and complexity. In this section, Hamada et al. (2016, Experiment 2), an extension of Hamada et al. (2013, Experiment 2), will be reviewed.

7.3.1 Methods

7.3.1.1 Stimulus patterns

We used D_n and C_n filled patterns ($n = 1$, 2, 3) with 19 open-solid dots arranged in a hexagonal grid, as shown in Fig. 7.3. Patterns were classified into collinear filled and noncollinear filled patterns. Since C_3 collinear filled patterns cannot be created in this grid, 5 collinear filled patterns and 12 non-collinear filled patterns were used by self-selection. Although only the basic patterns are shown here, the open-solid reversal patterns are also used. The directions of the two dot patterns, which were rotated by 60° each, were used as random factors. The open-solid dot pattern was printed on a thick white card (65 mm long × 62 mm wide). The diameter of each dot was 7 mm and the distance between the centers of adjacent dots was 10 mm.

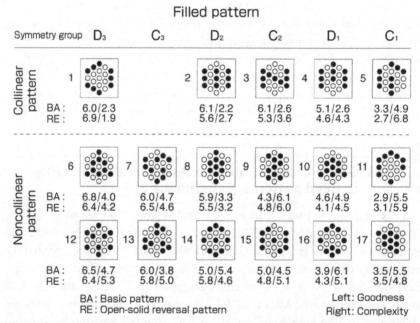

Fig. 7.3 Basic patterns in a hexagonal grid and mean ratings of goodness and complexity. Open-solid reversal patterns were also used. *(From Hamada, J., Uchiumi, C., Fukushi, K., & Amano, K. (2013). Goodness and complexity of compound and filled patterns depending upon a hierarchy of perception.* Japanese Journal of Psychonomic Science, *31, 123–134. (Japanese text with English abstract and captions); Hamada, J., Amano, K., Fukuda, S.T., Uchiumi, C., Fukushi, K., & van der Helm, P.A. (2016). Group theoretical model of symmetry cognition.* Acta Psychologica, *171, 128–137. https://doi.org/10.1016/j.actpsy. 2016.10.002)*

7.3.1.2 Participants and procedures

The participants were 144 undergraduate students at Tokushima University. Half of the students (72) rated goodness and the other half rated complexity. The number of cards distributed to them was (17 (basic pattern) + 17 (reversed pattern)) × 2 (pattern direction) = 68, and they were rated on a nine-point integer scale to determine goodness or complexity. Two sessions were repeated and only the ratings of the second session were analyzed.

7.3.2 Results and discussion

Fig. 7.4A and a shows the mean ratings of goodness, and Fig. 7.4B and b shows the mean ratings of complexity. Panels (A) and (B) are the results for the collinear filled patterns, and panels (a) and (b) are the results for

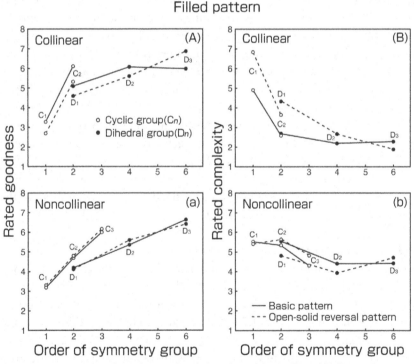

Fig. 7.4 Mean ratings of goodness (A and a) and complexity (B and b) for 19-dot open-solid filled patterns in a hexagonal grid. *(From Hamada, J., Uchiumi, C., Fukushi, K., & Amano, K. (2013). Goodness and complexity of compound and filled patterns depending upon a hierarchy of perception.* Japanese Journal of Psychonomic Science, 31, 123–134. *(Japanese text with English abstract and captions).)*

the noncollinear filled patterns. The basic patterns are shown as solid lines, and the open-solid reversal patterns are shown as dotted lines.

7.3.2.1 Goodness

The dependence of goodness on group order is similar between the collinear filled patterns (A of Fig. 7.4) and the noncollinear filled patterns (a). Comparing C_2 and D_1, which have the same order of 2, C_2 is $M = 5.4$ and D_1 is $M = 4.6$ for the basic pattern. Similarly, in the open-solid reversal pattern, C_2 is $M = 5.0$ and D_1 is $M = 4.4$. Here C_2 is significantly better than D_1 for both patterns.

In the left side of Fig. 7.3, when two C_3s, three C_2s, and three C_1s are included, there is no significant difference between the goodness of the basic and the open-solid reversal patterns ($M = 4.6$ and 4.6). Similarly, when a total of nine D_ns are included ($n = 1, 2, 3$), there is no significant difference in the goodness of the basic and the open-solid patterns ($M = 5.5$ and 5.5). In other words, there is no significant difference in goodness between the basic and the open-solid reversal patterns, and contrast polarity has no effect on goodness. On the other hand, when the basic and open-solid reversal patterns were averaged, the collinear pattern, which included two C_2s and two C_1s for a total of four ($M = 4.4$), was significantly better than the noncollinear pattern, which included four C_2s and four C_1s for a total of eight ($M = 4.0$). There is no significant difference in the goodness of the collinear pattern ($M = 5.7$), which includes a total of six D_ns of two each, and the noncollinear pattern ($M = 5.4$), which includes a total of 12 D_ns of four each ($n = 1, 2, 3$). In other words, the goodness was significantly higher for the collinear filled C_n patterns ($n = 1, 2$) than for the noncollinear filled C_n patterns, indicating the effect of collinearity, but not for the D_n patterns ($n = 1, 2, 3$).

7.3.2.2 Complexity

In the right side of Fig. 7.4, the dependence of the complexity on the group order is different between the collinear and the noncollinear filled patterns. In Fig. 7.4B and b, the basic patterns are significantly simpler than the open-solid reversal patterns ($M = 4.7$ and 5.2) when two C_3s and three C_2s and C_1s are included, for a total of eight. However, when a total of nine D_n patterns of three each are included ($n = 1, 2, 3$), there is no significant difference in the complexity of the basic and open-solid reversal patterns ($M = 3.9$ and 4.0). In other words, contrast polarity has an effect on the complexity of C_n patterns, whereas it has no effect on the complexity of D_n patterns ($n = 1, 2, 3$). On the other hand, the collinear filled pattern involving a total of four

C_2 and C_1 of two each is significantly simpler than the noncollinear filled pattern involving a total of eight C_2 and C_1 of four each ($M = 4.5$ and 5.4). Similarly, the collinear filled pattern with a total of six D_n each ($M = 2.7$) is significantly simpler than the noncollinear filled pattern with a total of 12 D_n each ($M = 4.6$). In other words, there was a significant difference in complexity between the collinear and noncollinear filled patterns common to C_n and D_n, and collinearity had a significant impact for complexity. Incidentally, this is similar to D_2 and D_3 with linearity in the 9-dot nonfilled patterns, which were significantly simpler than the other patterns in the hexagonal grid (Fig. 7.1).

7.3.3 Dependence of goodness and complexity on group order

The mean values of goodness and complexity as a function of the group order are shown in Fig. 7.5, including all the basic and reversal patterns as

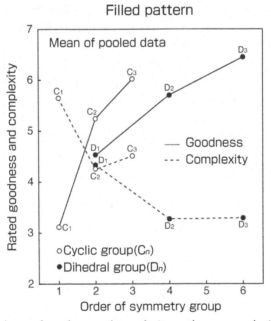

Fig. 7.5 Dependence of goodness and complexity on the group order in 19-dot open-solid filled patterns in a hexagonal grid. *(From Hamada, J., Amano, K., Fukuda, S.T., Uchiumi, C., Fukushi, K., & van der Helm, P.A. (2016). Group theoretical model of symmetry cognition. Acta Psychologica, 171, 128–137. https://doi.org/10.1016/j.actpsy.2016.10.002)*

well as the collinear and noncollinear filled patterns in Fig. 7.4. For goodness, the cyclic group C_n and the dihedral group D_n are separated and two curves apply, while for complexity, they are congruent and one curve applies ($n = 1, 2, 3$), except for C_3. The C_3 pattern is deviatingly complex because there is no collinear filled pattern. Here, C_2 was better than D_1 with the same order 2, but they matched in complexity. Thus, for goodness and complexity, the dependence of the 9-dot nonfilled patterns (Experiment 1) and the 19-dot filled patterns (Experiment 2) in the hexagonal grid on the group order is consistent (Figs. 7.2 and 7.5). In other words, the goodness monotonically increases with respect to the group order according to two curves, distinguishing the cyclic and dihedral group patterns, while the complexity monotonically decreases according to one curve without distinguishing them. The results of Experiments 1 and 2 of this chapter show that the weighting (effect) on group order is higher for C_n than for D_n for the goodness of the 9-dot nonfilled and 19-dot filled patterns ($n = 1, 2, 3$) in the hexagonal grid, but the same for the complexity. This means that the goodness and simplicity (the inverse of complexity) of the dot pattern in the hexagonal grid are both specified by the group theory and increase monotonically with the group order. However, the goodness is affected by the presence or absence of the reflection axes (i.e., D_n or C_n) and two curves apply, while the simplicity is not affected by the presence or absence of the reflection axes and one curve applies. This means that the reflection axes are not cognized in the simplicity judgment for dot patterns in a hexagonal grid, while it is cognized in the goodness one. As will be discussed in detailed in later two chapters, the cognitive system has a former stage in which the reflection axes are not recognized and a latter stage in which they are recognized.

CHAPTER EIGHT

Cognitive judgments and group theoretical model for dot patterns in a square grid

8.1 Goodness and complexity for open-solid 21-dot patterns (Experiment 1)

Goodness was not affected by contrast polarity in the filled patterns in a hexagonal grid in Experiment 2 of the previous chapter. Complexity was also not affected by contrast polarity in D_n patterns but was affected in C_n ($n = 1$, 2, 3). In this experiment, we investigate the effects of group order and contrast polarity on the goodness and complexity of 21-dot open and/or solid compound patterns in a square grid in heterogeneous and homogeneous conditions.

Hamada, Uchiumi, Fukushi, and Amano (2011a) created the 21-dot compound patterns illustrated in Fig. 8.1. Here, in the second line of open-solid polarity, 21-dot compound pattern is drawn by a 13-dot prototype pattern consisting of open dots in a 5×5 grid and an 8-dot prototype pattern consisting of solid dots in a 4×4 grid are superimposed on each other with the centers of the grids coinciding. The open-open polarity in the first line is the result of changing these eight solid dots to open ones. Similarly, in the third line of the solid-open polarity, 21-dot compound pattern is drawn by a 13-dot prototype pattern consisting of solid dots is superimposed on an 8-dot prototype one consisting of open ones. These eight open dots are changed to solid in the fourth line, results in solid-solid polarity. In this experiment, these 21-dot compound patterns are used. In this section, Hamada et al. (2016, Experiment 1), which extended Hamada et al. (2013), will be reviewed.

8.1.1 Stimulus patterns

8.1.1.1 Prototype patterns

The 8-dot and 13-dot prototype patterns were open and/or solid dots, drawn in 4×4 and 5×5 grids (top row and leftmost column in Fig. 8.2).

Psychophysics and Experimental Phenomenology of Pattern Cognition
https://doi.org/10.1016/B978-0-323-95286-6.00008-9
105

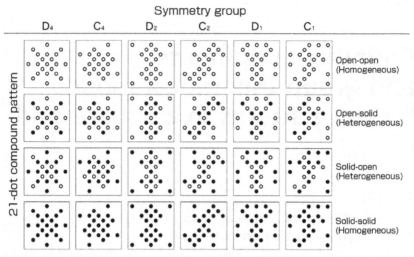

Fig. 8.1 Examples of 21-dot compound patterns with different polarities of open or solid dots in a square grid. *(From Hamada, J. (2020). Psychophysics of pattern cognition. Tokyo: Kazama Press (Japanese text).)*

Four dots were placed in the central four cells in the 8-dot prototype D_n pattern, and five dots were placed in a straight line in the central column in the 13-dot prototype D_n pattern ($n = 1, 2, 4$). On the other hand, the C_n prototype pattern was created based on the D_n prototype pattern as follows: For the 4×4 and 5×5 grids, all the dots located at the outermost periphery for D_n patterns were moved one cell clockwise to create the C_n ones. For example, as shown in the top row and in the leftmost column of Fig. 8.2, if we move all dots at the outermost periphery of the 8 and 13-dot D_4 patterns, we get C_4 patterns that look like windmill patterns. In the same way, the C_2 prototype patterns were created from the 8-dot and 13-dot D_2 prototype patterns, and the C_1 prototype patterns were created from the D_1 prototype patterns. In this way, the D_n and C_n prototype patterns were made to correspond to each other. The 8- and 13-dot prototype patterns were not used in this experiment.

8.1.1.2 21-dot compound patterns

As shown in Fig. 8.1, we have an open–open polarity and a solid–solid polarity, which we call collectively the homogeneous condition. The open–solid polarity and the solid-open polarity are called the heterogeneous conditions. Fig. 8.2 shows nine examples of 21-dot compound patterns in four quadrants: two homogeneous conditions (first and third quadrants) and two

Solid and/or open dots pattern

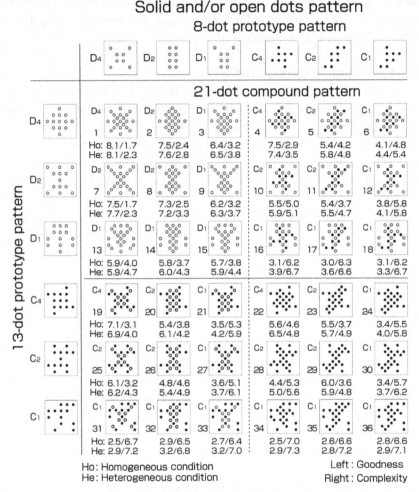

Fig. 8.2 The configuration of the 8- and 13-dot prototype patterns, the 21-dot compound patterns, and the rated values for goodness and complexity for the 21-dot patterns. (From Hamada, J., Uchiumi, C., Fukushi, K., & Amano, K. (2013). Goodness and complexity of compound and filled patterns depending upon a hierarchy of perception. Japanese Journal of Psychonomic Science, 31, 123–134. (Japanese text with English abstract and captions); Hamada, J., Amano, K., Fukuda, S.T., Uchiumi, C., Fukushi, K., & van der Helm, P.A. (2016). Group theoretical model of symmetry cognition. Acta Psychologica, 171, 128–137. https://doi.org/10.1016/j.actpsy.2016.10.002)

heterogeneous conditions (second and fourth quadrants). The contrast polarity was different for these four conditions, but the structure of the 21-dot compound pattern (i.e., dihedrals and cyclic groups) and the configuration of the dot patterns were the same. The solid and open dot patterns were printed on thick white cards (70 mm long × 66 mm wide). The diameter of each dot was 4 mm, and the distance between the centers of adjacent dots in the prototype pattern was 10 mm.

8.1.1.3 Participants and procedures

A total of 208 undergraduate students at Tokushima University were randomly assigned to 104 groups, each of which was rated for goodness or complexity. Half of them (52 students, a set of A) used a total of 72 patterns, 36 of which were homogeneous compound patterns with an open-open polarity and 36 of which were heterogeneous ones with an open-solid polarity. The other half (a set of B) used a total of 72 patterns, consisting of 36 homogeneous compound patterns with a solid-solid polarity and 36 heterogeneous compound patterns with a solid-open polarity. The 18 examples for sets A and B are shown in the top and bottom panels of Fig. 8.2, respectively. They were rated on a 9-point integer scale to determine goodness or complexity. The experiment was repeated for two sessions, and only the second ratings were analyzed.

8.1.2 Results

The ratings for sets of A and B were similar, with no significant difference in either goodness or complexity between the 72 pairs of compound patterns, and Pearson's correlation coefficient was $r = .943$ for goodness and $r = .980$ for complexity, both highly significant correlations. Therefore, the data from sets of A and B are combined for analysis. The mean ratings of goodness and complexity by the 104 participants are shown in Fig. 8.2 for the homogeneous and heterogeneous conditions.

8.1.2.1 Effect of group order on goodness and complexity

Fig. 8.3 shows the mean ratings of goodness (solid lines) and complexity (dotted lines) for the C_n compound pattern (open symbols), and for the D_n one (solid symbols) ($n = 1, 2, 4$). The mean values of goodness and complexity as a function of group order are shown for the homogeneous condition (circles) and the heterogeneous condition (diamonds). The numerical values of the 21-dot compound patterns are categorized by C_n and D_n patterns, and the average of 15, 9, and 3 rated values for C_1, C_2, and C_4 patterns, respectively, and 5, 3, and 1 rated values for D_1, D_2, and D_4 patterns, respectively, are shown in the figure.

Correlation between goodness and complexity. In Fig. 8.3, Pearson's correlation coefficient between goodness and complexity for six

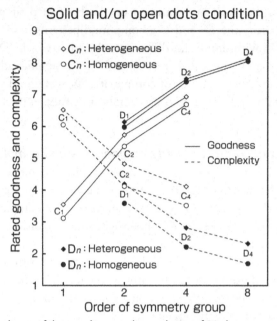

Fig. 8.3 Dependence of the goodness and complexity of 21-dot compound patterns in the square grid on the group order. *(From Hamada, J., Uchiumi, C., Fukushi, K., & Amano, K. (2013). Goodness and complexity of compound and filled patterns depending upon a hierarchy of perception.* Japanese Journal of Psychonomic Science, 31, 123–134. *(Japanese text with English abstract and captions); Hamada, J., Amano, K., Fukuda, S.T., Uchiumi, C., Fukushi, K., & van der Helm, P.A. (2016). Group theoretical model of symmetry cognition.* Acta Psychologica, 171, 128–137. https://doi.org/10.1016/j.actpsy.2016.10.002)*

homogeneous and six heterogeneous conditions, 12 each in total, was $r = -.943$, indicating a high, negative, and significant correlation.

8.1.2.2 Dependence of C_n and D_n compound patterns (n = 1, 2, 4) on the group order

In Fig. 8.3, there were significant differences in both goodness and complexity among the C_1, C_2, and C_4 patterns, with goodness increasing and complexity decreasing as the group order increased. Similarly, there was a significant difference in both goodness and complexity among D_1, D_2, and D_4 patterns, with goodness increasing and complexity decreasing as the group order increased.

8.1.2.3 C_{2n} and D_n compound patterns (n = 1, 2) with the same order

Because the ratings for the homogeneous and heterogeneous conditions in the 21-dot D_n and C_n compound patterns ($n = 1, 2, 4$) showed qualitatively similar trends, they will be examined on the basis of their pooled mean values. Comparing the D_n and C_{2n} compound patterns ($n = 1$, 2), D_n was better than C_{2n} with significant differences. In other words, D_1 was significantly better than C_2 ($M = 6.1$ and 5.6) and D_2 was significantly better than C_4 ($M = 7.5$ and 6.8). In terms of complexity, D_1 was significantly simpler than C_2 ($M = 3.9$ and 4.5) and D_2 was significantly simpler than C_4 ($M = 2.5$ and 3.8).

8.1.2.4 Effect of contrast polarity on goodness and complexity

D_n compound patterns ($n = 1$, 2, 4). In Fig. 8.3, for goodness, there was no significant difference between the compound patterns of the homogeneous and heterogeneous conditions. On the other hand, the complexity was significantly more complex in the heterogeneous condition than in the homogeneous one.

C_n compound pattern ($n = 1$, 2, 4). The compound pattern for the heterogeneous condition was significantly better than that for the homogeneous one. In addition, the heterogeneous condition was significantly more complex than the homogeneous one.

8.1.3 Discussion

8.1.3.1 Effect of contrast polarity

As shown in Experiment 2 of the previous chapter, for the filled pattern in the hexagonal grid (Fig. 7.4), there was no significant difference in the goodness of the D_n patterns ($n = 1$, 2, 3) between the basic and the open–solid reversal patterns, indicating that contrast polarity was not functioning effectively. Similarly, for the 21-dot compound pattern in Fig. 8.3 of this experiment, there was no significant difference in the goodness of the D_n patterns ($n = 1, 2, 4$) between the homogeneous and heterogeneous conditions. Wenderoth (1996) reported that the reaction time required to detect the symmetry of D_1 patterns consisting of black/white dots on a gray background does not differ between patterns in which all dots are black and patterns in which the right half is black, and the left half is white (or vice versa). This result is consistent with Tyler and Hardage's (1996) finding that contrast polarity does not work effectively in detecting mirror symmetry. Therefore, their experimental results are a corroboration that the contrast polarity is not involved in the goodness of D_n patterns ($n = 1, 2, 3, 4$) in Experiment 2 (Fig. 7.4 in Chapter 7) and Experiment 1 (Fig. 8.3 in this chapter). On the other hand, in Experiment 2 of the previous chapter, the contrast polarity for goodness did not work effectively for the cyclic group C_n patterns

($n = 1$, 2, 3) in the regular hexagonal grid (Fig. 7.4). However, in this experiment (Fig. 8.3), the C_n patterns in the heterogeneous condition ($n = 1$, 2, 4) were better than those in the homogeneous condition. Thus, the goodness of the C_n pattern is affected by the difference between regular hexagonal and square grids and by the difference in contrast polarity.

In terms of complexity, there was no significant difference between the basic D_n patterns ($n = 1$, 2, 3) and the open–solid reversal ones, but there was significant difference in the C_n patterns between them in the hexagonal grid (Fig. 7.4), whereas in the square grid, the D_n patterns ($n = 1$, 2, 4) in the heterogeneous condition were more complex than those in the homogeneous condition (Fig. 8.3). In other words, for D_n patterns ($n = 1$, 2, 3, 4), the effect of contrast polarity on complexity was affected by the differences in the grids. However, for the C_n pattern, the contrast polarity was effective on the complexity regardless of the differences in the grids.

8.1.3.2 Group order and two-stage group-theoretic serial processing model

In both goodness and simplicity (the inverse of complexity) for the 21-dot pattern in the square grid, the cyclic group C_{2n} and the dihedral group D_n are distinguished, and the weighting (effect) on group order is higher for D_n than for C_{2n} ($n = 1$, 2). This is in contrast to the 9-dot nonfilled and 19-dot filled patterns in the hexagonal grid described above (Figs. 7.2 and 7.5). In other words, the goodness of the 9- and 19-dot patterns in the hexagonal grid, where the weighting for group order was higher for C_2 than for D_1 with the same order, was contrary to the 21-dot pattern in the square grid. In contrast, the weighting of simplicity to group order was the same for C_2 and D_1 in the hexagonal grid. Thus, the difference between the square and hexagonal grids causes a large difference in goodness and simplicity. The results for goodness are consistent with Palmer (1991), who drew 9-dot and 10-dot patterns in a 5×5 grid.

Fig. 8.4 shows the two-stage group-theoretic serial processing model for goodness and simplicity in hexagonal and square grids. The goodness and simplicity of dot patterns in these grids are monotonically increasing functions of group order as specified by group theory. The model then assumes that goodness and simplicity are processed hierarchically from a former stage in which the presence or absence of the reflectional axes is not distinguished to a latter stage in which it is distinguished. In other words, the former stage is unable to cognize the reflection axes, but the latter stage cognizes them. In the hexagonal grid, goodness is processed in the latter stage where the cyclic

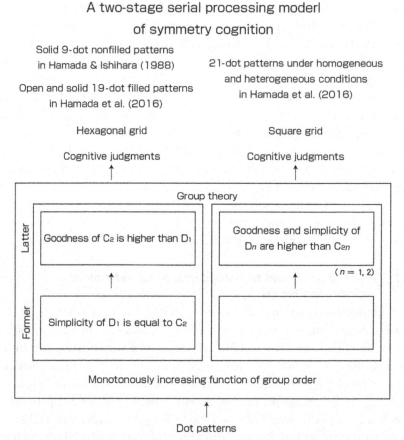

A two-stage serial processing moderl
of symmetry cognition

Fig. 8.4 A two-stage group-theoretic serial processing model for the goodness and simplicity of dot patterns in hexagonal and square grids. The differences in the grids are apparent. *(Adapted from Hamada, J. (2020). Psychophysics of pattern cognition. Tokyo: Kazama Press (Japanese text).)*

group C_2 and the dihedral group D_1 are distinguished, whereas simplicity is processed in the former stage where they are not distinguished. This means that goodness in the hexagonal grid bypasses the former stage and is processed in the latter stage. However, in the square grid, both goodness and simplicity bypass the former stage and are processed in the latter stage. Next, we will discuss Palmer's transformational model and van der Helm's holographic model in comparison to Hamada et al.'s two–stage group-theoretic serial processing model.

8.1.4 Transformation model, holographic model, and two-stage group-theoretic serial processing model

van der Helm and Leeuwenberg (1996) and van der Helm (2014) compare Palmer's (1982, 1983) transformational model with van der Helm's holographic model. The former deals with pattern cognition, whereas the latter is concerned with pattern perception. Pattern cognition deals with the goodness and complexity of dot patterns themselves, which are rated under a free-viewing task with no time limit (e.g., Garner & Clement, 1963; Imai, Ito, & Ito, 1976a; Hamada & Ishihara, 1988; Hamada et al., 2016). Pattern perception, on the other hand, measures the reaction time and accuracy required to detect symmetry (e.g., Bruce & Morgan, 1975; Wenderoth & Welsh, 1998), and patterns that are detected faster and more accurately are considered good. We will not discuss complexity but only goodness.

According to van der Helm, Palmer's transformation model, shown in Fig. 8.5, assumes a three-dimensional space and asks whether a five-dot random pattern on the left side can be matched to the right side by the transformations. His model assumes that the cognitive system judges symmetry by applying a 180° mirroring transformation and repetition by translational transformation. In the transformation model, both symmetry and repetition are represented by the block structure in the solid boxes, so his model expects them to be equally good.

As shown in Fig. 8.6, in the holographic model of van der Helm, symmetry has a point structure, and repetition has a block structure. According to this model, goodness is determined by the weight of evidence (W), that is, $W = E/n$, where E is the number of arcs and n is the number of dots. Then, in (a), $W = 5/10 = 0.50$, and in (b), $W = 1/10 = 0.10$. Therefore, unlike the transformation model, which assumes that symmetry and repetition are equal, the holographic model predicts that on goodness, symmetry is better than

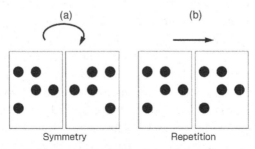

Fig. 8.5 The two types of patterns handled by Palmer's transformation model (a and b).

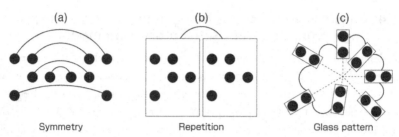

Fig. 8.6 The three types of patterns targeted by van der Helm's holographic model (a–c).

repetition, which explains the basic phenomenon of goodness (e.g., Bruce and Morgan, 1975). Furthermore, the holographic model explains the goodness of the Glass pattern (Glass, 1969; Glass & Pérez, 1973) with a dipole structure as follows: for example, seven dipoles of two dots have 14 dots and connected by 7 arcs, resulting in $W = 6/14 = 0.43$. Thus, symmetry and Glass patterns are approximately equal in goodness. Here, Palmer's transformational model and Hamada et al.'s two-stage group-theoretic serial processing model cannot handle Glass patterns. On the other hand, Palmer (1991) and Hamada et al. (2016) showed that dot patterns with n reflection axes in a square grid are better than those that show invariance to only n rotations ($n = 1, 2, 4$). Conversely, this is opposite for the hexagonal grid of Hamada and Ishihara (1988) and Hamada et al. (2016) (see Figs. 7.2 and 7.5). However, the holographic model considers that the dot patterns that show invariance to n rotations as repetitive patterns in polar coordinates.

As mentioned above, the difference between Palmer's transformational model and van der Helm's holographic model is that the former captures aspects of pattern cognition with no limit on presentation time, whereas the latter captures pattern perception in brief presentations of about 500 ms or less (Hamada et al., 2016). Incidentally, the mental rotation experiments by Shepard and Metzler (1971) and Cooper and Shepard (1984) can be said to capture the aspect of pattern cognition as they reported that it takes about 1 to 5 s to mentally rotate a three-dimensional line drawing.

If we restrict the discussion to the goodness of D_n patterns with reflection axes ($n = 1, 2, 3, 4$), the transformational model predicts that the goodness increases as the number of reflection axes increases from 1 to 2, 3, and 4. However, the holographic model predicts that patterns with two reflection axes will be better than those with one, patterns with three reflection axes will be poorer than that with two, and patterns with four reflection axes will be better than that with two. The two-stage group-theoretic serial processing model predicts that the goodness of patterns with one, two, and three reflection axes in a hexagonal grid (Fig. 7.5) and one, two, and four reflection axes in a square grid (Fig. 8.3) is a monotonically increasing function of the number of reflection axes, consistent with the predictions of the transformational model. However, the holographic model predicts that the goodness of the D_2 pattern is higher than that of D_3, which is not consistent with the transformational model and the two-stage group-theoretic serial processing model. Wenderoth and Welsh (1998) measured the time required to detect the reflection axes from dot patterns with one, two, three, and four axes and reported that the time for patterns with two and three reflection axes was equal, whereas it was faster than patterns with one axis and slower than patterns with four axes. This result is contrary to the transformation model and closer to the prediction of the holographic model because the reaction times for patterns with two and three axes are equal (van der Helm, 2011).

The goodness of the 19-dot pattern with two reflection axes in a hexagonal grid (D_2: $M = 5.9$) is clearly lower than that of the 21-dot pattern with two reflection axes in a square grid (D_2: $M = 7.5$) in a 9-point rating by Hamada et al. (2016). The transformational and holographic models cannot explain the phenomenon. However, the two-stage group theoretic serial processing model of Hamada et al. is consistent because of the distinction between grids. Thus, the difference in grids has an effect on the goodness.

van der Helm and Leeuwenberg (1996) used a circular grid, Hamada and Ishihara (1988, Experiment 2) and Hamada et al. (2016, Experiment 2) used a regular hexagonal grid, and Palmer (1991) and Hamada et al. (2016, Experiment 1) use a square grid. The 9-dot nonfilled and 19-dot collinear filled patterns in the hexagonal grid do not have a C_3 pattern, and the 21-dot compound pattern in the 9×9 grid cannot create D_3 and C_3 patterns. However, van der Helm's circular grid can create any regular polygon. These differences in grids cause the differences in goodness.

Although the transformational model and the holographic model deal only with goodness, it can be concluded that the two-stage group-theoretic serial processing model of Hamada et al. is highly versatile, being applicable not only to goodness (i.e., poorness) and complexity (i.e., simplicity) (Hamada & Ishihara, 1988; Hamada, 1996; Hamada et al., 2016) but also to the disjointedness (i.e., unifiedness) shown in Figs. 9.11 and 9.12 (Hamada et al., 2021). Next, we discuss similarity.

8.2 Similarity for nonfilled pattern pairs with numerosity (8-, 13-, 21-dot) and contrast polarity (Experiment 2)

In this Experiment 2, 21-dot compound patterns from Experiment 1, which were used to study the goodness and complexity of patterns, will be used as standard patterns, whereas 8- and 13-dot prototype patterns will be used as comparison ones (Fig. 8.2), and their similarity to each other will be studied. The numerosity (the number of dots) and open-solid contrast polarity are also examined. The pattern pairs used in this experiment are different in the number of dots and have no possibility of mutual transformation and have an empty transformational structure E (see Figs. 6.3 and 11.7).

In Experiment 1 of the previous section, no significant difference was found between conditions A and B, in terms of both goodness and complexity, and a high correlation was obtained between these conditions. Therefore, in this experiment, we will study the effect of group order and the numerosity (8, 13, and 21 dots), contrast polarity, and configuration on similarity for two-dimensional dot pattern pairs only for the heterogeneous condition with an open-solid polarity and the homogeneous condition with a solid-solid polarity. In this section, Hamada (2020) will be reviewed.

8.2.1 Method

8.2.1.1 Stimulus patterns

Examples of the 21-dot standard and 8- or 13-dot comparison pattern pairs used are shown in Fig. 8.7. The conditions were divided into two conditions: heterogeneous (A and a) and homogeneous (B and b). The 21-dot standard pattern was superimposed by the 8- and 13-dot prototype patterns. In the homogeneous condition, all open dots in the heterogeneous

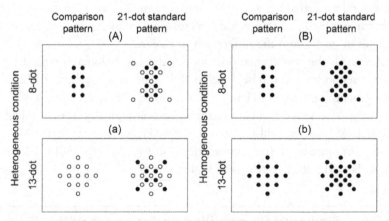

Fig. 8.7 Examples of comparison and 21-dot standard pattern pairs in a square grid (A and a, B and b). *(From Hamada, J. (2020). Psychophysics of pattern cognition. Tokyo: Kazama Press (Japanese text).)*

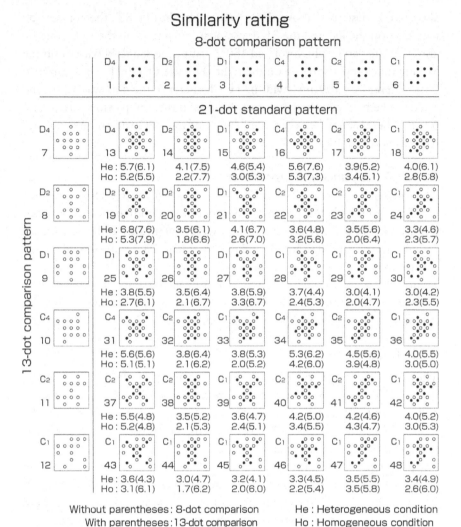

Fig. 8.8 Similarity rating values for 21-dot and 8-dot pattern pairs, and 21-dot and 13-dot ones. *(From Hamada, J. (2020). Psychophysics of pattern cognition. Tokyo: Kazama Press (Japanese text).)*

condition were changed to solid dots (B and b). The top row of Fig. 8.8 shows the 8–dot comparison patterns (numbers 1 to 6), and the leftmost column shows the 13–dot comparison patterns (numbers 7 to 12). Then, the 21–dot standard pattern (numbers 13 to 48) is shown at the intersection of the row and the column. Although only the heterogeneous condition is illustrated in Fig. 8.8, pattern pairs for the homogeneous condition were also used, as described above (Fig. 8.7B and b). In Fig. 8.7, the comparison pattern is on the left and the 21-dot standard pattern is on the right, but we also used the cards, which rotated 180°, that is, the standard pattern on the left and the comparison one on the right. The size of a thick white card was 53 mm (length) × 100 mm (width). The diameter of the dots was 3 mm, and the distance between the centers of the dots in the comparison pattern was 6 mm. The distance between the centers of the comparison and standard patterns was 50 mm.

8.2.1.2 Participants and procedures

The participants were 92 students at Tokushima University. They were randomly assigned to heterogeneous (46 students) and homogeneous (46) conditions. Half of the 46 participants (23) were given cards with the standard pattern printed on the right side and the other half (23) on the left side. Each participant used 36 cards with 8-dot comparison patterns and 36 cards with 13-dot patterns for a total of 72 cards. They judged the similarity of the pattern pairs on a 9-point integer scale. The experiment was repeated for two sessions, and only the second ratings were analyzed.

8.2.2 Results

The means of the similarity ratings were not significantly different between the right and left 21-dot standard patterns. Therefore, based on those averages, we will analyze the data separately for the heterogeneous condition and for the homogeneous one. In Fig. 8.8, apart from the heterogeneous and homogeneous conditions, the rated values for the 21-dot standard and 8-dot comparison pattern pairs are shown without parentheses (left side), and the rated values for the 13-dot comparison pattern pair are shown in parentheses (right side). Based on this, Fig. 8.9 shows the similarity between the 21-dot standard and comparison pattern pairs as a function of the group order of the standard patterns for the heterogeneous (solid line) and homogeneous (dotted line) conditions. In addition, 8-dot is marked with a circle and 13-dot is marked with a diamond. Note that in this section, n in C_n and D_n means 1, 2, and 4.

8.2.2.1 Effects of numerosity, contrast polarity, and group order

We showed the 21-dot standard pattern and the paired 13-dot or 8-dot comparison patterns and their means of them in Fig. 8.8. For the effect of numerosity (8, 13, and 21 dots), the mean similarity in the heterogeneous condition is significantly higher for 13-dot ($M = 5.4$) than for 8-dot ($M = 4.1$) and in the homogeneous condition also significantly higher for 13-dot ($M = 5.8$) than for 8-dot ($M = 3.0$). On the other hand, for contrast

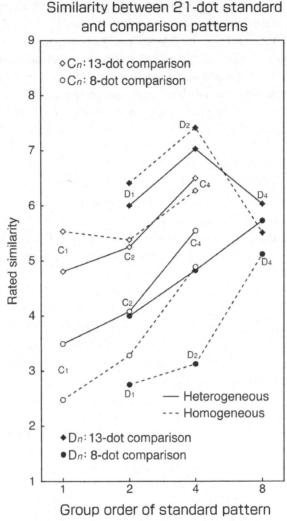

Fig. 8.9 Similarity rating values for 21-dot standard and comparison pattern pairs. *(From Hamada, J. (2020). Psychophysics of pattern cognition. Tokyo: Kazama Press (Japanese text).)*

polarity, in the 13-dot comparison pattern paired with the 21-dot standard pattern, the similarity between the heterogeneous ($M = 5.4$) and homogeneous ($M = 5.8$) conditions is not significant. However, for the 8-dot comparison pattern, the heterogeneous condition ($M = 4.1$) was significantly higher than the homogeneous one ($M = 3.0$).

The number of 21-dot standard patterns in Fig. 8.8 is 9 for D_n and 27 for C_n. Therefore, the mean of their similarity was compared. In the heterogeneous condition, the similarity of the 8-dot comparison pattern to the 21-dot standard pattern was significantly higher for D_n ($M = 4.4$) than for C_n ($M = 3.9$), and for the 13-dot comparison pattern, D_n ($M = 6.4$) was significantly higher than C_n ($M = 5.1$). On the other hand, in the homogeneous condition, the difference between D_n ($M = 3.1$) and C_n ($M = 3.0$) for the 21-dot standard and 8-dot comparison pattern pairs is not significant, whereas D_n ($M = 6.6$) is significantly higher than C_n ($M = 5.5$) for the 13-dot comparison pattern pair.

8.2.2.2 Effect of group order
As can be seen in Fig. 8.9, the dependence of the similarity on the group order is similar in the heterogeneous and homogeneous conditions, so we included these rated values. Then, the similarity between the 13-dot comparison and 21-dot standard pattern pair is as follows: D_1, D_2, and D_4 are ($M = 6.2$, 7.2, and 5.8, respectively), with a significance not only between D_1 and D_2 but also between D_2 and D_4 and no significance between D_1 and D_4. Similarly, C_1, C_2, and C_4 have ($M = 5.2$, 5.3, and 6.3, respectively), which is not significant between C_1 and C_2 but significant not only between C_1 and C_4 but also C_2 and C_4. Here, the similarity of the 8-dot comparison and 21-dot standard pattern pair is as follows: D_1 and D_2 and D_4 are ($M = 3.4$, 4.0, and 5.4, respectively), and all between them are significant. Also, C_1, C_2, and C_4 are all significant at ($M = 3.0$, 3.7, and 5.2, respectively).

8.2.2.3 Effect of configuration
In Fig. 8.8, if we look at the row numbered 7, we can see that the ratings of the heterogeneous and homogeneous conditions are similar. When these conditions are pooled, the similarity between the 21-dot standard D_4 pattern (number 13) paired with the 8-dot comparison (number 1) and that with the 13-dot comparison (number 7) is not significant ($M = 5.4$ and 5.8). Therefore, we removed D_4 and counted the number of dots that protruded from the diamond-shaped frame of number 7. Numbers 14 and 16 are 0, number 18 is 1, and numbers 15 and 17 are 2. The mean rating values were ($M = 7.5$) for 0, ($M = 6.0$) for 1, and ($M = 5.3$) for 2, all of which were significantly different from each other.

8.2.3 Discussion
8.2.3.1 Effect of numerosity
In common with the heterogeneous and homogeneous conditions, the similarity of the 21-dot standard pattern paired with the 13-dot comparison

was significantly higher than that with the 8-dot comparison pattern. This indicates that the smaller the difference in the number of dots with the 21-dot standard patterns, the higher the similarity.

8.2.3.2 Effect of contrast polarity

In the 21-dot standard and 13-dot comparison pattern pairs, contrast polarity did not work effectively and the similarity between the heterogeneous and homogeneous conditions was not significant (13-dot D_n comparison patterns in Fig. 8.9). In the 21-dot standard and 13-dot comparison pattern pairs in the heterogeneous condition (e.g., Fig. 8.7a), the 13 dots are both open dots. Therefore, the 8 solid dots, which are fewer in number, are ignored and the 13 open dots, which have the same configuration, are compared prominently, so the similarity is high. On the other hand, in the homogeneous condition, the difference in the number of dots between the 21-dot standard and the 13-dot comparison pattern is small, so the similarity is high. As a result, there is no significant difference in the similarity of these pattern pairs between the heterogeneous and homogeneous conditions.

In the 21-dot standard and 8-dot comparison pattern pairs, the heterogeneous conditions were significantly higher than the homogeneous conditions. Thus, contrast polarity was effective in the 21-dot standard and 8-dot comparison pattern pairs in the heterogeneous condition (e.g., Fig. 8.7A). This is because in the 21-dot standard pattern, the 13 open dots with the largest number of dots become the "ground", and the 8 solid dots become the "figure". Therefore, the solid dots of the 21-dot standard pattern stand out and are directly compared to the solid dots of the 8-dot comparison pattern, so the similarity is relatively high (Rubin, 1921; Imai et al., 1976a; Matsuda, 1978). However, in the homogeneous condition, the similarity between the 21-dot standard and the 8-dot comparison pattern pair is low because of the large difference in the number of dots. As a result, there is a significant difference in the similarity between the 21-dot standard and 8-dot comparison pattern pairs for the heterogeneous and homogeneous conditions.

8.2.3.3 Comparison between 9 pairs of D_n and 27 pairs of C_n

Comparing the 9 pairs of dihedral groups D_n and the 27 pairs of cyclic groups C_n, D_n had significantly higher similarity than C_n in the 21-dot standard and 13-dot comparison pattern pairs, in common with the heterogeneous and homogeneous conditions. This is because the group order of D_n is twice that of C_n. Also, in the heterogeneous condition, D_n was significantly higher than

C_n in the 21-dot standard and 8-dot comparison pattern pairs because the order of D_n is twice that of C_n. On the other hand, there was no significant difference between D_n and C_n for the 8-dot comparison pattern paired with the 21-dot pattern in the homogeneous condition. However, the similarity increased monotonically and significantly with group order for both D_n and C_n (Fig. 8.9). Therefore, the similarity between the 21-dot standard and the 8-dot comparison pattern pairs, even in the homogeneous condition, is dictated by group theory.

8.2.3.4 Effect of configuration

As shown in Fig. 8.9, regardless of homogeneous and heterogeneous conditions, the dependence of the similarity on the group order is the same for the 8-dot C_n and D_n, and the 13-dot C_n. However, the similarity of D_n with 13 dots is not determined by the group order and contrast polarity but by the configuration, as shown below. That is, in Fig. 8.8, the ratings for the heterogeneous and homogeneous conditions are similar in the row numbered 7 (i.e., 13-dot D_n comparison pattern in Fig. 8.9). Also, there was no significant difference in the similarity not only of the 21-dot D_4 standard pattern of number 13 paired with the 8-dot D_4 of number 1 but also that paired with the 13-dot D_4 of number 7. This 21-dot standard pattern with number 13 is radial-shaped. Also, number 1 of the 8-dot comparison pattern is ×-shaped, and number 7 of the 13-dot comparison pattern is diamond-shaped. These are all D_4 and very different in configuration. Therefore, the similarity between the two pattern pairs is relatively low and not significant. On the other hand, for the 21-dot standard pattern in the number 7 row, if we remove this D_4, the similarity decreases significantly as the number of dots that protrude from the diamond-shaped frame increases. This shows that the diamond-shaped frame of number 7 plays an important role. Furthermore, the configuration of the D_2 comparison pattern in number 8 consists of one vertical and two diagonal lines for a total of three straight line components. This is the same for the D_2 of number 19, and the D_2 of number 20 is similar to it. Also, the D_2 standard pattern, number 14, has no dots that extend beyond the diamond-shaped frame. Therefore, the similarity between the D_2 standard and comparison patterns in Fig. 8.9 is the highest. As a result, the similarity between the 21-dot standard and 13-dot comparison pattern pairs, in common to both the heterogeneous and homogeneous conditions, is affected by the configuration of the dot patterns, resulting in an inverted V-shape with respect to group order in Fig. 8.9.

CHAPTER NINE

A three-stage serial processing model based on spatial filter and group theory for cognitive judgments

9.1 Goodness and complexity for 21-dot patterns in original and expanded conditions (Experiment 1)

In this Experiment 1, we study the effect of cyclic and dihedral group order on goodness and complexity for two types of 21-dot patterns (i.e., the original and expanded patterns) that exhibit the same invariance to rotational and reflectional transformations but have different configurations. Wertheimer (1923) pointed out the factor of proximity as an effect of grouping. If this factor works effectively, then in a pattern consisting of multiple dots, nearby dots should be grouped together, while distant dots should be seen separately. van der Helm and Leeuwenberg (1996) found that for 6-dot random patterns, increasing the degree of grouping by translation increases the goodness. Therefore, the effects of grouping on the goodness and complexity of 21-dot patterns are also examined. In this section, Hamada et al. (2017) will be reviewed.

9.1.1 Method

9.1.1.1 Stimulus patterns

In Experiment 1 in the previous chapter, 21-dot D_n and C_n compound patterns ($n = 1, 2, 4$) were used and 8-dot and 13-dot prototype patterns were not used (see Fig. 8.2).

The dot patterns in the original conditions are shown in Fig. 9.1 for D_n and C_n patterns ($n = 1, 2, 4$). As in Fig. 8.2 in the previous chapter, the 8-dot D_n prototype pattern is in a 4×4 grid, with 4 dots in each of the four central cells. The 13-dot D_n prototype pattern was created by placing five dots in the center column of cells in a 5×5 grid. The C_n prototype pattern was then

Psychophysics and Experimental Phenomenology of Pattern Cognition
https://doi.org/10.1016/B978-0-323-95286-6.00009-0
123

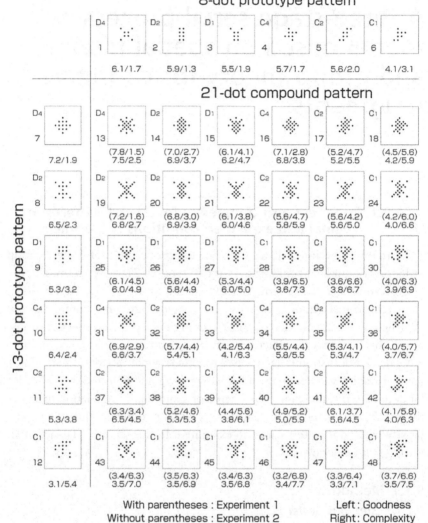

Fig. 9.1 Goodness *(left side)* and complexity *(right side)* in the original condition of Experiment 1 (in parentheses) and of Experiment 2 (without parentheses). *(From Hamada, J., Nabeta, T., Fukuda, S.T., Uchiumi, C., Fukushi, K., & Amano, K. (2017). Goodness and complexity of dot patterns in a matrix framework based on a group theoretical model. Japanese Journal of Psychonomic Science, 36, 30–39. (Japanese text with English abstract and figure captions). https://doi.org/10.14947/pshchono.36.4; Hamada, J., Fukuda, S.T., Uchiumi, C., Fukushi, K., & Amano, K. (2019). Effects of dot number and symmetry group order on goodness and complexity of dot patterns in a group theoretical approach. Japanese Journal of Psychonomic Science, 37, 153–162. (Japanese text with English abstract and figure captions). https://doi.org/10.14947/psychono.37.22)*

created by moving all the dots at the outermost periphery of the square grid of the D_n prototype pattern by one cell in a clockwise direction. The 21-dot original pattern was drawn in a 9×9 grid by superimposing two prototype patterns with the centers of the two grids aligned. Therefore, the dot size of the 21-dot compound patterns in Fig. 8.2 where the contrast polarity was examined, was different from that of the original pattern (Fig. 9.1), but the configuration was the same.

For the 8-dot prototype pattern in the expanded condition, the 4×4 grid was enlarged to a 10×10 grid, so the distance between dots was tripled. 13-dot D_n prototype pattern was the same as that in the original pattern in the 5×5 grid. For the C_n prototype pattern, all dots located at the outermost periphery of the square grid of the D_n prototype pattern were moved clockwise. In other words, for the 8-dot pattern, three cells in the grid were moved clockwise; for the 13-dot pattern, one cell in it was moved clockwise. The 21-dot compound patterns were drawn in a 19×19 grid by superimposing the two prototype patterns with the centers of the two grids coinciding.

The solid dot pattern was printed on a thick white card (70 mm long $\times$ 66 mm wide) with a dot diameter of 2 mm. The distance between the centers of the dots in the prototype pattern was 5 mm, and only the expanded 8-dot prototype pattern was 15 mm.

9.1.1.2 Procedure
The participants were 104 undergraduate students at Tokushima University, and they were randomly divided into 52 students for judging goodness and 52 students for judging complexity. The 21-dot compound pattern distributed to each participant consisted of 36 original patterns and 36 expanded ones, for a total of 72 patterns. Goodness or complexity was rated on a 9-point integer scale. Two sessions were repeated in the experiment, and only the rated values of the second session were analyzed.

9.1.2 Results and discussion
The mean ratings of goodness and complexity for the 21-dot compound patterns in the original and expanded conditions are shown in parentheses in Figs. 9.1 and 9.2. In these figures, the left side is goodness and the right side is complexity. Based on these results, Fig. 9.3 shows the mean ratings of goodness (solid line) and complexity (dotted line) as a function of group order.

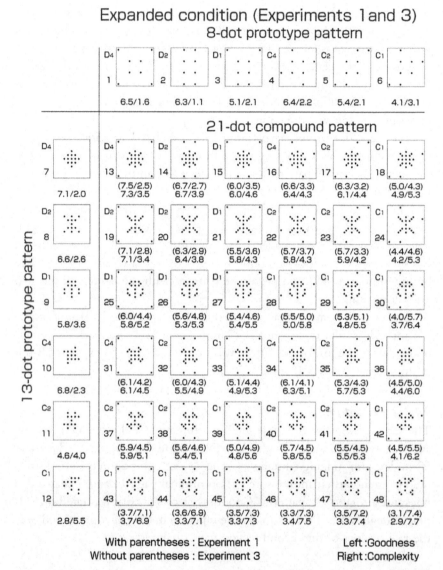

Fig. 9.2 Goodness *(left side)* and complexity *(right side)* in the expanded condition of Experiment 1 (in parentheses) and of Experiment 3 (without parentheses). *(From Hamada, J., Nabeta, T., Fukuda, S.T., Uchiumi, C., Fukushi, K., & Amano, K. (2017). Goodness and complexity of dot patterns in a matrix framework based on a group theoretical model. Japanese Journal of Psychonomic Science, 36, 30–39. (Japanese text with English abstract and figure captions). https://doi.org/10.14947/pshchono.36.4; Hamada, J., Fukuda, S.T., Uchiumi, C., Fukushi, K., & Amano, K. (2019). Effects of dot number and symmetry group order on goodness and complexity of dot patterns in a group theoretical approach. Japanese Journal of Psychonomic Science, 37, 153–162. (Japanese text with English abstract and figure captions). https://doi.org/10.14947/psychono.37.22)*

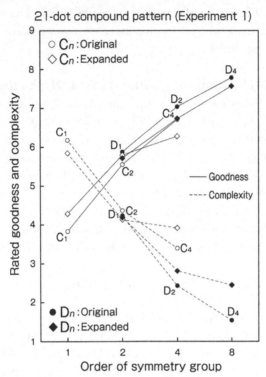

Fig. 9.3 Mean ratings of goodness and complexity of 21-dot compound patterns in original and expanded conditions. *(From Hamada, J., Nabeta, T., Fukuda, S.T., Uchiumi, C., Fukushi, K., & Amano, K. (2017). Goodness and complexity of dot patterns in a matrix framework based on a group theoretical model. Japanese Journal of Psychonomic Science, 36, 30–39. (Japanese text with English abstract and figure captions). https://doi.org/10.14947/pshchono.36.4)*

9.1.2.1 21-dot compound patterns in original and expanded conditions

Pearson's correlation coefficient between goodness and complexity in the 72 original and expanded conditions showed a significant high negative correlation ($r = -.955$). On the other hand, Figs. 9.1 and 9.2 in parentheses show that there is no significant difference between the goodness and complexity in the original and expanded conditions, so the difference in configuration has no effect on goodness and complexity. When we pooled the C_n and D_n patterns ($n = 1, 2, 4$), the mean values of the 36 patterns in total for goodness were $M = 5.1$ and 5.3 in the original and expanded conditions, respectively, and $M = 4.8$ and 4.7 for complexityin in Fig. 9.3. There was no significant difference between C_2 and C_4 in the complexity in the expanded conditions shown in Fig. 9.3, but significant differences were found in all others, with both goodness increasing and complexity decreasing monotonically as a function of group order.

9.1.2.2 C_{2n} and D_n compound patterns (n = 1, 2) with the same order

When the goodness ratings of group order 2 and 4 in the original pattern were pooled and averaged, C_{2n} and D_n ($M = 5.8$ and 6.3) were significantly different. However, in the expanded pattern, C_{2n} and D_n ($M = 5.9$ and 6.1) were not significantly different. The fact that the relationship between C_{2n} and D_n, where the order is the same, is different between the original and expanded patterns means that the goodness is affected by the difference in configuration. On the other hand, in terms of complexity, C_{2n} and D_n were ($M = 4.1$ and 3.6) in the original pattern and were ($M = 4.1$ and 3.7) in the expanded one, both of which were significantly different.

9.1.2.3 Grouping in 21-dot compound patterns in the expanded condition

The configuration of the 17 dots in the center of each row of the 21-dot expanded compound patterns (Fig. 9.2) drawn in a 19 × 19 grid is the same, and they are grouped and separated from the outermost four dots. Therefore, for the values in parentheses in Fig. 9.2, we calculated the average values for the goodness and complexity of the six patterns in each column to verify the effect of the outermost four dots. Then, the goodness is $M = 6.1$, 5.6, and 5.1 for D_4, D_2, and D_1, respectively, and likewise $M = 5.5$, 5.3, and 4.3 for C_4, C_2, and C_1, respectively. In terms of complexity, D_4, D_2, and D_1 have $M = 4.3$, 4.4, and 4.7, respectively, and C_4, C_2, and C_1 have $M = 4.7$, 4.6, and 5.4, respectively. That is, their values change in the order of their alignment, with goodness going down and complexity going up. Thus, the distant outermost 4-dot pattern is defined by the dihedral and cyclic groups while influencing the goodness and complexity of the 21-dot compound patterns. Incidentally, the same results were obtained for the 21-dot expanded compound patterns in Experiment 3, which will be shown later (figures without parentheses in Fig. 9.2).

9.2 Goodness and complexity for 8-, 13-, and 21-dot patterns in original condition (Experiment 2)

Imai, Ito, and Ito (1976a) showed that there was no difference in the goodness of complementary patterns with 4 and 5 dots in a 3 × 3 grid.

Hamada and Ishihara (1988, Experiment 1) showed that when the number of dots was increased from 4 to 5 and then to 8 in the 3×3 and 4×4 grids, the goodness of the D_1 pattern increased. On the other hand, van der Helm and Leeuwenberg (1996) found that increasing the number of dots from 12 through 24 to 96 in the D_1 patterns did not change the goodness. Thus, the effect of the numerosity (number of dots) on goodness has not been determined and seem to be few studies reporting that on complexity. Therefore, in this Experiment 2, we examine the effect of the numerosity (8, 13, and 21 dots) on goodness and complexity and its dependence on group order. In this section, Hamada et al. (2019, Experiment 1) will be reviewed.

9.2.1 Stimulus pattern and procedure

The stimulus pattern used is shown in Fig. 9.1, which was printed in black in the center of a thick white card (70 mm long × 66 mm wide). In addition to the 21-dot compound pattern for the original condition of Experiment 1 in the previous section, the 8- and 13-dot prototype patterns were used in this experiment 2. We used a total of 48 cards: six 8-dot and six 13-dot prototype patterns, and 36 21-dot compound patterns. The diameter of the dots in the prototype patterns was 2 mm and the distance between the centers was 5 mm.

The participants were 104 undergraduate students at Tokushima University, who were randomly assigned to 52 students for judging goodness and 52 ones for judging complexity. Goodness and complexity were rated on a 9-point integer scale. In the experiment, two sessions were repeated and only the second rating was analyzed.

9.2.2 Results and discussion

Pearson's correlation coefficients between goodness and complexity in Fig. 9.1 (without parentheses) were $r = -.955$ for 8-dot pattern 6 pairs, $r = -.982$ for 13-dot pattern 6 pairs, and $r = -.949$ for 21-dot pattern 36 pairs, all significant.

9.2.2.1 Effect of the numerosity

According to the average of the pooled C_n and D_n patterns ($n = 1, 2, 4$), the goodness of the 8-, 13-, and 21-dot patterns is ($M = 5.5$, 5.6, and 5.1, respectively). On the other hand, the complexity of them ($M = 2.0$, 3.2, and 5.5, respectively) increased monotonically as the number of dots increased.

9.2.2.2 Dependence on group order and a linear pattern

Fig. 9.4 shows that there is no significant difference in goodness between C_2 and C_4, between D_1 and D_2, and between D_2 and D_4 of the 8 dots, but they increase with group order. Thus, goodness is generally increasing on group order. Complexity is generally descending on group order for the 21-dot and 13-dot patterns. However, on 8-dot patterns (i.e., square symbols) there is no significant difference in complexity between D_1 and D_4, and D_2 is significantly lower than D_4 with high geometric symmetry and does not descend monotonically on group order. Hamada and Ishihara (1988, Experiment 2) and Hamada et al. (2016, Experiment 2) used dot patterns in a hexagonal grid, and Hamada et al. (2016, Experiment 1) and Hamada et al. (2017) used 21-dot patterns in a square grid. They found that

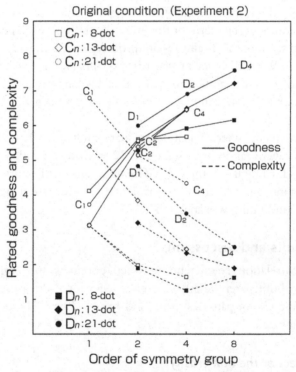

Fig. 9.4 Dependence of the goodness and complexity of 8-, 13-, and 21-dot patterns on the group order, and the effect of the number of dots in the original condition. *(From Hamada, J., Fukuda, S.T., Uchiumi, C., Fukushi, K., & Amano, K. (2019). Effects of dot number and symmetry group order on goodness and complexity of dot patterns in a group theoretical approach. Japanese Journal of Psychonomic Science, 37, 153–162. (Japanese text with English abstract and figure captions). https://doi.org/10.14947/psychono.37.22)*

goodness increased monotonically with respect to group order, and complexity decreased monotonically. In this Experiment 2 of this chapter, the dependence on group order was reconfirmed for the original patterns with 8, 13, and 21 dots, except for one case. One example of this is that the complexity for the 8-dot D_n pattern ($n = 1, 2, 4$; orders are 2, 4, 8) is V-shaped with respect to the order, and the D_2 linear pattern is significantly lower than D_4. The specific decrease in complexity for the D_2 linear pattern in the square grid in the present experiment is consistent with that in the hexagonal grid in Hamada and Ishihara (1988, Experiment 2). In other words, the D_2 linear pattern in Fig. 7.1 had the lowest complexity (M = 1.2) and medium goodness. This is reconfirmed in the next section and shows the effect of an anisotropic space filter on complexity.

9.2.2.3 C_{2n} and D_n patterns (n = 1, 2) with the same order

For C_{2n} and D_n patterns with the same order, the average values of C_2 and C_4 and those of D_1 and D_2 are shown for each number of dots below. Then, the goodness is ($M = 5.6$ and 5.7) for 8 dots and ($M = 5.9$ and 5.9) for 13 dots, both of which are not significant, but ($M = 5.7$ and 6.3) for 21 dots, which is significant. In terms of goodness, the mean values of the pooled dots were significantly different with C_{2n} at $M = 5.7$ and D_n at $M = 6.1$. On the other hand, the complexity was not significant for 8 dots ($M = 1.8$ and 1.6), but for 13 dots ($M = 3.1$ and 2.8) and for 21 dots ($M = 5.0$ and 4.3), both of which were significantly different. In terms of complexity, the mean values of the pooled dots were significant for C_{2n} at $M = 5.0$ and D_n at $M = 3.6$.

9.3 Goodness and complexity for 8-, 13-, and 21-dot patterns in expanded condition (Experiment 3)

In Experiment 2 (the original condition) of the previous section, it was shown that the goodness and complexity increased and decreased as a function of group order, respectively, with the exception that the complexity of the 8-dot D_2 linear pattern was significantly lower than that of the D_4 pattern. Therefore, we will check whether the same phenomenon occurs for the expanded patterns in this Experiment 3, and also examine the relationship between C_{2n} and D_n patterns ($n = 1, 2$) and the effect of the numerosity (8, 13, and 21 dots). In this section, Hamada et al. (2019, Experiment 2) will be reviewed.

Stimulus patterns and procedures. The stimulus pattern used was printed in black in the center of a thick white card (70 mm long × 66 mm wide), as in Experiments 2. As shown in Fig. 9.2, the distance between the dots of the 8-dot prototype patterns was increased to three times that of Experiment 2 (i.e., the original condition), and the 13-dot prototype one was the same as in Experiment 2. The 21-dot compound pattern was drawn on a 19 × 19 grid by superimposing the 8- and 13-dot prototype ones with their centers coinciding. The stimulus pattern consisted of 6 cards with 8-dot and 6 cards with 13-dot prototype patterns, and 36 cards with 21-dot compound patterns, for a total of 48 cards. The distance between the centers of the dots was 5 mm for the 13-dot prototype pattern, the same as in Experiment 2, while it was 15 mm for the 8-dot extended prototype pattern.

The participants were 104 undergraduate students at Tokushima University, who were randomly assigned to 52 students for judging goodness and 52 ones for judging complexity. Goodness or complexity was rated on a 9-point integer scale. Two sessions were repeated and only the second rating was analyzed.

9.3.1 Results

Pearson's correlation coefficient between goodness and complexity in Fig. 9.2 (without parentheses) was $r = -.836$ for 6 cards of 8-dot patterns, $r = -.987$ for 6 cards of 13-dot ones, and $r = -.946$ for 36 cards of 21-dot ones, all significant.

9.3.1.1 Effect of the numerosity

According to the average values including C_n and D_n patterns ($n = 1, 2, 4$), the goodness of the 8-, 13-, and 21-dot patterns is ($M = 5.6, 5.6$, and 5.2, respectively). The complexity of the 8-, 13-, and 21-dot patterns is ($M = 2.0, 3.3$, and 5.3, respectively), increasing monotonically as the number of dots increases.

9.3.1.2 Dependence on the group order

According to Fig. 9.5, as the order increases, the goodness increases, but the complexity decreases except for one case. This one case is that the 8-dot D_2 linear pattern in the expanded condition is significantly simpler than the D_4 pattern, as well as the original condition.

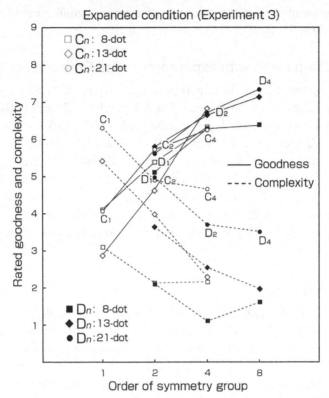

Fig. 9.5 Mean ratings of goodness and complexity for 8- and 13-dot prototype patterns, and 21-dot compound patterns in the expanded condition. *(From Hamada, J., Fukuda, S. T., Uchiumi, C., Fukushi, K., & Amano, K. (2019). Effects of dot number and symmetry group order on goodness and complexity of dot patterns in a group theoretical approach. Japanese Journal of Psychonomic Science, 37, 153–162. (Japanese text with English abstract and figure captions). https://doi.org/10.14947/psychono.37.22)*

9.3.1.3 C_{2n} and D_n patterns (n = 1, 2) with the same order

For the C_{2n} and D_n patterns with the same order, the mean values of C_2 and C_4 and those of D_1 and D_2 showed no significant difference in goodness for 8-dots ($M = 5.9$ and 5.7), significant for 13-dots ($M = 5.7$ and 6.2), and no significant difference for 21-dots ($M = 5.9$ and 6.0). Here, the means including the number of dots were not significant for C_{2n} at $M = 5.9$ and for D_n at $M = 6.0$. This result is different from the significant difference in the goodness between C_{2n} and D_n in the original condition. On the other hand, there was a significant difference in complexity for 8-dot ($M = 2.1$ and 1.6) and 21-dot ($M = 4.8$ and 4.5), but not for 13-dot ($M = 3.1$ and 3.1).

Here, the means including the number of dot were significant at $M = 4.3$ for C_{2n} and $M = 3.8$ for D_n.

9.3.2 Comparison with Experiment 1 and Experiments 2 and 3

Comparing the averages of Experiment 1, consisting of 21 dots only, with the 21-dot patterns of Experiments 2 and 3, in which 12 cards of the 8- and 13-dot patterns were added, the goodness is $M = 5.1$ and 5.1 in the original condition (Experiments 1 and 2) and $M = 5.3$ and 5.2 in the expanded one (Experiments 1 and 3). There is no significant difference between them. In contrast, the complexity in the original condition is ($M = 4.8$ and 5.5) and that in the expanded one is ($M = 4.7$ and 5.3). Thus, the complex in Experiments 2 and 3 adding 12 cards of the 8- and 13-dot patterns to 21-dot patterns were significantly higher than that in Experiment 1 of the only 21-dot ones.

9.3.3 Discussion

9.3.3.1 C_{2n} and D_n patterns (n = 1, 2) with the same order

Averages including 8-, 13-, and 21-dot showed that there was a significant difference in goodness between C_{2n} and D_n in the original condition, but not in the expanded one. This result indicates that the goodness is affected by the difference in configuration between the original and the expanded conditions, since the group order was fixed. Referring to these results with Experiment 1, in which only the 21-dot patterns were used, implies that the goodness in the original condition is distinguished by C_{2n} and D_n regardless of the presence or absence of the 8- and 13-dot patterns, whereas they are not distinguished in the expanded one. In terms of complexity, D_n was significantly simpler than C_{2n} in both original and expanded condition. This indicates that goodness and complexity are processed differently in the cognitive system.

9.3.3.2 Dependence on a spatial filter and group order

Hamada and Ishihara (1988) drew solid 9-dot nonfilled patterns in a regular hexagonal grid, and showed that among the 62 patterns, the complexity of the D_2 linear pattern (see Fig. 7.1) with three parallel straight lines consisting of three dots was the lowest at $M = 1.2$ by using a 7-point rating method, while the goodness was moderate at $M = 4.3$. In addition, Hamada (1996) devised $8 \times 9 = 72$-dot repetitive patterns in 16×16 grid. Here, nine 8-dot D_2 motifs in a 4×4 grid were arranged, three in each of the vertical, and horizontal directions (see Fig. 10.3). And among the 320 repetitive patterns, it is reported that the 16 repetitive patterns (*pmm*: D_{2vh} in Fig. 10.3) with 8-dot D_2 linear components as motifs have the lowest complexity but medium goodness (see Experiment 1 in the next chapter). Next, we consider the D_2 pattern with this linear component.

In Experiments 1, 2, and 3 in this chapter, the goodness of the 21-dot pattern in square grids increased monotonically with group order, and the complexity decreased monotonically (Figs. 9.3, 9.4, and 9.5). However, there was a notable exception for complexity. In other words, the complexity of the 8-dot D_n patterns ($n = 1, 2, 4$) was V-shaped with respect to the group order and D_2 was significantly lower than D_4, which had a higher order and higher geometric symmetry, in common with the original and expanded conditions. That is, the complexity of the 8-dot D_2 linear pattern was uniquely decreased.

Hamada (1976a, 1976b, 1984b) simulated the phenomenon of a border contrast in brightness by convolution-integrating the luminance distribution with a difference of two Gaussians (DOG), assuming isotropy (see Fig. 1.17 in Part 1). Replacing this isotropy with two-dimensional anisotropy, Dakin and Watt (1994) and Dakin and Herbert (1998) show that symmetry axis detection is performed by an anisotropic spatial filter. In other words, Dakin et al. pointed out the possibility that a low-resolution spatial filter with an approximate 2:1 ratio of directional long and short sides is applied in the lower stage of pattern cognition. Applying this idea, the D_2 linear pattern singularly yields a distinct single vertical rod (0°, 180°) or horizontal rod (90°, 270°) output from the longitudinal and transverse spatial filters that cannot be obtained with anything other than a D_2 linear pattern. This anisotropic spatial filter contributes to the reduction of the specific complexity of the D_2 linear pattern. Note that the generality of the direction of this spatial filter is not lost when considering all directions but does not contribute to the goodness judgment. As described above, the border contrast based on DOG and the complexity of the D_2 linear pattern are closely related.

9.3.3.3 *Effect of numerosity on goodness and complexity*
According to the averages in the original and expanded conditions (Experiments 2 and 3), the number of dots (8, 13, and 21) had no consistent effect on goodness. That is, goodness is 8-dot ($M = 5.6$), 13-dot ($M = 5.6$), and 21-dot ($M = 5.1$), with the former being insignificant and the latter being significant (see also the next section). This result is not consistent with Hamada and Ishihara's (1988) 7-point rating, where goodness is almost equal

for four dots ($M = 3.0$), five dots ($M = 3.3$), and eight dots ($M = 3.4$) in the average of D_1 patterns in the 3×3 and 4×4 grids. Therefore, the goodness does not show a consistent effect for increasing number of dots.

In terms of complexity, averaging over the original and expanded conditions (Experiments 2 and 3), there are all significant differences between the 8-dot ($M = 2.1$), 13-dot ($M = 3.3$), and 21-dot ($M = 5.4$) patterns, with complexity increasing monotonically with the number of dots. Palumbo, Ogden, Makin, and Bertamini (2014) reported that complexity increases with the number of elements in a checkerboard-like arrangement of patterns consisting of black and white square elements. Oliva, Mack, Shrestha, and Peeper (2004) also showed that complexity increases as the diversity in everyday objects such as furniture and wall surfaces in a room increases. Thus, it is concluded that the complexity increases monotonically as the numeriosity (8, 13, and 21 dots) increases.

9.3.3.4 Dot number contrast in complexity

When the results of Experiment 1, in which the number of dots was fixed at 21, were compared with the 21-dot patterns of Experiments 2 and 3, in which 8-, 13-, and 21-dot patterns were mixed, the goodness was not significant in both the original and the expanded conditions. On the other hand, the complexity in both the original and extended conditions was significantly more complex in Experiments 2 and 3, in which 12 8- and 13-dot patterns were added, than in Experiment 1, in which they were not. In other words, the addition of a total of 12 simple 8- and 13-dot patterns increased the complexity of the 36 21-dot patterns. This phenomenon occurs for complexity due to the difference in the number of patterns between 36 and 48. We name this the dot number contrast of complexity, analogous to the simultaneous brightness contrast (see Chapter 3 in Part 1). Therefore, when 6 13-dot patterns are added to 6 8-dot and 36 21-dot patterns, the complexity of 8-dot patterns is considered to become low and that of 21-dot patterns to become high.

9.3.4 A three-stage serial processing model of goodness and simplicity

Hamada et al. (2016, Experiment 1) found that for 21-dot compound patterns in a square grid, both goodness and simplicity (the inverse of complexity) are determined in the latter stage where C_{2n} and D_n ($n = 1, 2$) are distinguished, and proposed a two-stage group-theoretic serial processing model for goodness and simplicity in Fig. 8.4. We improve this model to a serial processing model with three stages. In the original and expanded conditions, Hamada et al. (2017) used a 21-dot pattern and Hamada et al. (2019) used mixed 8-, 13, and 21-dot patterns and reported goodness and simplicity. There, only the simplicity of the 8-dot D_2 linear pattern did not obey the group theory. Therefore, we maintain and improve the basic concept of Hamada's (2020) three-stage model proposed for goodness and simplicity, and propose the three-stage serial processing model in Fig. 9.6 by adding an anisotropic spatial filter to the lower stage of the two-stage

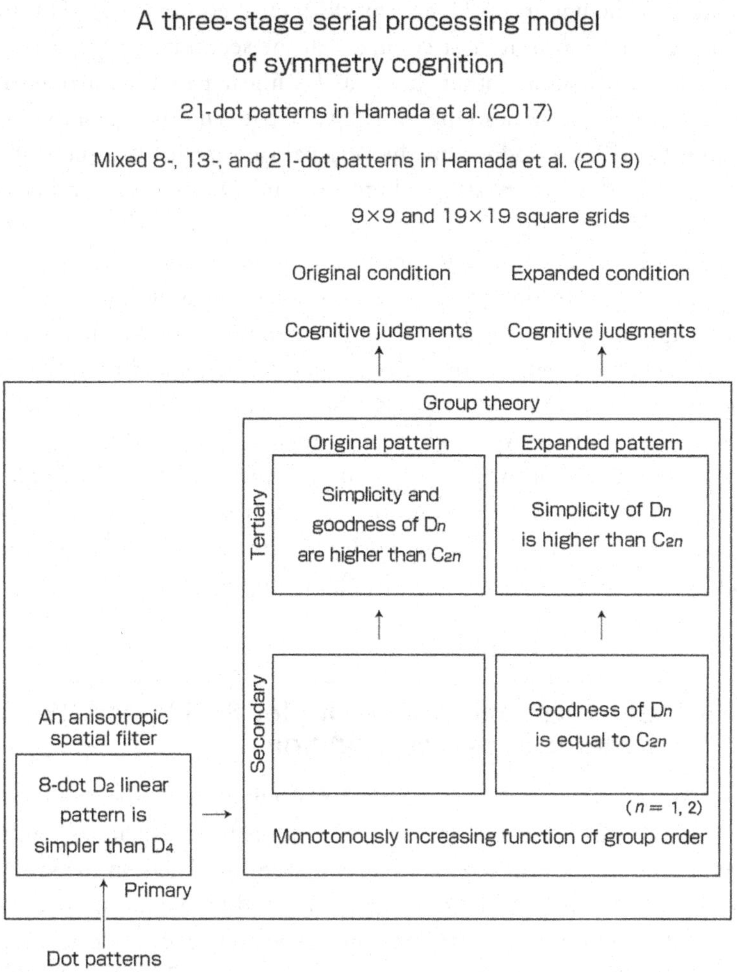

A three-stage serial processing model
of symmetry cognition

21-dot patterns in Hamada et al. (2017)

Mixed 8-, 13-, and 21-dot patterns in Hamada et al. (2019)

9×9 and 19×19 square grids

Original condition	Expanded condition
Cognitive judgments	Cognitive judgments
↑	↑

Group theory		
	Original pattern	Expanded pattern
Tertiary	Simplicity and goodness of D_n are higher than C_{2n}	Simplicity of D_n is higher than C_{2n}
	↑	↑
Secondary		Goodness of D_n is equal to C_{2n}
		$(n = 1, 2)$
	Monotonously increasing function of group order	

An anisotropic spatial filter

8-dot D_2 linear pattern is simpler than D_4 →

↑ Primary

Dot patterns

Fig. 9.6 A three-stage serial processing model for goodness and simplicity by a spatial filter and group theory. *(Adapted from Hamada, J. (2020). Psychophysics of pattern cognition. Tokyo: Kazama Press (Japanese text).)*

group-theoretic serial processing model. The spatial filter processes the simplicity for the D_2 linear pattern and raises it specifically. This implies that the D_2 linear pattern is the first special pattern to be processed in the primary stage. However, the goodness for this pattern bypasses the spatial filter in the primary stage and is processed according to group theory. Here, the goodness of the D_2 linear pattern must bypass this filter in order to be processed in the higher stage. Then, patterns other than the D_2 linear pattern undergo group theoretical processing and the goodness in the expanded condition is determined in the secondary stage where the cyclic group C_{2n} and the dihedral group D_n are not distinguished ($n = 1, 2$). This means that the reflection axes are not cognized in the secondary stage. However, the simplicity of pattern other than the D_2 linear pattern not only in the expanded condition but also the simplicity of pattern other than the D_2 linear pattern and the goodness in the original one bypass this stage and are determined in the tertiary stage where C_{2n} and D_n are distinguished. This means that the reflection axes are cognized in this stage. It is common to see that goodness and simplicity according to group theory rise monotonically with respect to the group order. As described above, these two cognitive judgments are processed in series through the secondary to the tertiary stages that follow group theory after processing or bypassing in the anisotropic spatial filter of the primary stage. Since they are processed in different places of the cognitive system, differences appear in each judgment. The difference in goodness for the patterns with the same order (i.e., C_{2n} and D_n) in original and the expanded conditions is due to that in configuration, since the group order was fixed. The simplicity also decreased with the increase in the number of dots and is affected by the configuration.

9.4 Goodness and complexity for 8-, 13-, and 21-dot patterns in cluster condition

In this section, we explain the cluster condition using the 13-dot prototype patterns, which are different from the original and expanded conditions (Experiments 2 and 3) in the previous two sections. Then, in the same 9 × 9 grid as in the original condition, we created 8- and 13-dot prototype patterns, and 21-dot compound patterns to study the dependence of goodness and complexity on the group order and the numerosity (8, 13, and 21 dots). The effect of the anisotropic spatial filter on the complexity of the D_2 linear pattern is also discussed. In this section, a part of Hamada (2020) will be reviewed.

9.4.1 Stimulus patterns and procedures

Dot patterns in the cluster condition were created as follows: 8–dot prototype patterns were drawn in a 4 × 4 grid (top row of Fig. 9.7) and 13–dot prototype patterns were drawn in a 5 × 5 grid (leftmost column). 8–dot prototype patterns (numbers 1 to 6) were the same as the original condition. However, the 13–dot prototype patterns (numbers 7 to 12) differed from the original condition in that nine dots were placed densely in a 3 × 3 square located in the center of the 5 × 5 grid for the all-prototype patterns. The C_n

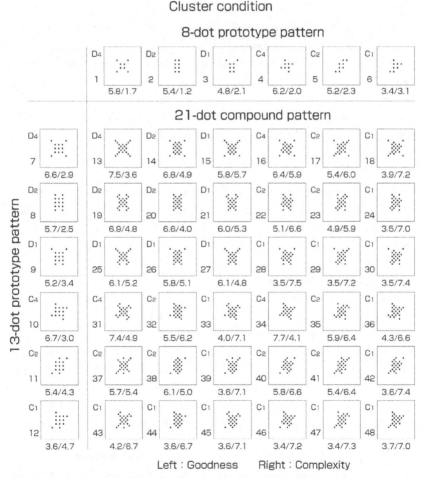

Left : Goodness   Right : Complexity

Fig. 9.7 Average ratings of goodness and complexity for 8- and 13-dot prototype patterns, and 21-dot compound patterns in the cluster condition. *(From Hamada, J. (2020). Psychophysics of pattern cognition. Tokyo: Kazama Press (Japanese text).)*

prototype patterns ($n = 1, 2, 4$) were created based on the D_n prototype patterns by moving the outermost four dots of the 8- and 13-dot prototype patterns by one cell in a clockwise direction. For example, the four dots located at the outermost four dots of the 8- and 13-dot D_4 prototype patterns were moved one cell clockwise to create the C_4 prototype patterns of the windmill patterns. In this way, D_n and C_n prototype patterns were made to correspond. The 21-dot compound pattern was created in a 9×9 grid by aligning the centers of the 4×4 and 5×5 grids for the prototype patterns and superimposing them. The size of the stimulus pattern was (43×40 mm), the diameter of the dot was 2 mm, the same as in Experiments 1, 2, and 3, and the distance between the centers was 5 mm.

The participants of the experiment were 104 students at Tokushima University, who were randomly divided into two groups: 52 students for judging goodness and 52 ones for judging complexity. The stimulus patterns consisted of six 8- and six 13-dot prototype patterns, and 36 21-dot compound patterns, for a total of 48 cards. Goodness or complexity was rated on a 9-point integer scale. Three sessions were repeated and the average ratings of the second and third sessions were analyzed.

9.4.2 Results

Pearson's correlation coefficient between goodness and complexity in Fig. 9.7 is $r = -.745$ for 6 pairs of 8-dot, and $r = -.783$ for 6 pairs of 13-dot, both of which are not significant. However, the correlation coefficient was significant at $r = -.924$ for the 36 pairs of 21-dot.

9.4.2.1 Dependence on group order

Fig. 9.8 shows that goodness increases with group order regardless of the C_n and D_n patterns ($n = 1, 2, 4$). Complexity is generally decreasing with group order, but is significantly lower for the D_2 linear pattern numbered 2 ($M = 1.2$) than D_4 numbered 1 ($M = 1.7$) of 8-dot as well as for that numbered 8 ($M = 2.5$) of 13-dot than D_4 numbered 7 ($M = 2.9$). In addition, among the three D_2 patterns in the 21-dot compound patterns in Fig. 9.7, the complexity of the linear pattern with two parallel edges numbered 20 is significantly lower than that of the patterns numbered 14 and 19.

9.4.2.2 C_{2n} and D_n patterns (n = 1, 2) with the same order

For C_{2n} and D_n patterns with the same order, the mean values of C_2 and C_4 and those of D_1 and D_2 were calculated for each number of dots. Then, 8-dot of goodness were significant at ($M = 5.7$ and 5.1), 13-dot was significant

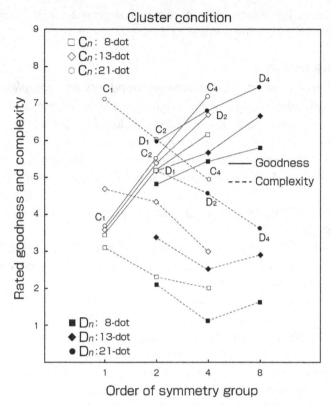

Fig. 9.8 Average ratings of goodness and complexity for 8- and 13-dot prototype patterns, and 21-dot compound patterns in cluster condition. *(From Hamada, J. (2020). Psychophysics of pattern cognition. Tokyo: Kazama Press (Japanese text).)*

at ($M = 6.0$ and 5.4), and 21–dot was significant at ($M = 5.9$ and 6.3) all, but the mean value with the number of dots included was not significant at ($M = 5.9$ and 5.9). There is no significant difference in goodness, which is the same as in the expanded condition. On the other hand, the complexity of the 8–dot was ($M = 2.1$ and 1.6), the 13–dot was ($M = 3.6$ and 2.9), and the 21–dot was ($M = 5.8$ and 5.0), all significant. Similarly, the means with the number of dots pooled were significant at ($M = 5.1$ and 4.1).

9.4.2.3 Effect of the numerosity
When C_n and D_n patterns ($n = 1, 2, 4$) are included, the mean values of goodness are ($M = 5.1$ and 5.5 and 5.1) for 8-, 13-, and 21-dot patterns, respectively. Complexity for the 8-, 13-, and 21-dot patterns is ($M =$

2.1, 3.4, and 6.1), respectively and, as in Experiments 2 and 3, increases significantly with increasing number of dots.

9.4.3 Discussion

9.4.3.1 Correlation coefficient between goodness and complexity

According to the average of the original condition (Experiment 2), the expanded condition (Experiment 3), and the cluster condition, the Pearson's correlation coefficient between goodness and complexity is $r = -.879$ for the 8-dot, $r = -.981$ for the 13-dot, and $r = -.979$ for the 21-dot, all significant. This result shows that goodness and complexity are interrelated.

9.4.3.2 Specific decrease in complexity of patterns with two parallel edges

The complexity of the D_2 patterns numbered 2, 8, and 20 in Fig. 9.7 was specifically decreased. The common graphic feature of these three patterns is that they have two parallel edges. Incidentally, in Fig. 9.8, the complexity of the 8- and 13-dot D_4 patterns decreased specifically, but that of the 21-dot D_4 pattern is lower than that of the D_2 pattern. Therefore, these results imply that the complexity of the D_2 pattern with two parallel edges is decreasing and not that of the D_4 pattern is increasing. This leads us to conclude that the complexity of the 8-dot D_2 patterns in Figs. 9.4 and 9.5 is also specifically decreasing, and not that of the D_4 ones is increasing.

9.4.3.3 C_{2n} and D_n patterns (n = 1, 2) with the same order

For the cluster condition, there was no significant difference in goodness for C_{2n} and D_n patterns with the same order, but there was a significant difference in complexity. This result was the same as for the expanded condition (Experiments 1 and 3). On the other hand, in the original condition (Experiments 1 and 2), there was a significant difference between C_{2n} and D_n for both goodness and complexity, which is different from the cluster and expansion conditions. These results indicate that goodness and complexity are being processed differently.

9.4.3.4 Effects of the numerosity on goodness and complexity

When the original, expanded, and cluster conditions are included, goodness is $M = 5.4$ for 8 dots, $M = 5.6$ for 13 dots, and $M = 5.1$ for 21 dots, showing no consistent effect for the number of dots. However, complexity increases with the number of dots with $M = 2.0$ for 8 dots, $M = 3.3$ for 13 dots, and $M = 5.6$ for 21 dots, showing consistent effect on the numerosity.

9.4.4 A three-stage serial processing model for goodness and simplicity in cluster condition

9.4.4.1 Effect of a spatial filter and the dependence on group order

In the original and expanded conditions (Experiments 1, 2, and 3) and the cluster condition, goodness increased monotonically with group order (Figs. 9.3, 9.4, 9.5, and 9.8). Complexity, however, was generally and monotonically decreasing with group order, with one notable exception. In other words, the complexity of all 8-dot D_n patterns ($n = 1, 2, 4$) was V-shaped with respect to group order, and the D_2 linear pattern was significantly lower than D_4, which had a higher order and higher geometric symmetry. In the cluster condition, the complexity of the 13-dot D_2 linear pattern was also significantly lower than that of D_4. In addition, among the three 21-dot D_2 patterns in the cluster condition, the linear pattern (number 20) was significantly simpler than the other two D_2 ones (numbers 14 and 19). Thus, the complexity of the linear pattern was singularly decreased. However, this phenomenon does not occur in goodness.

When comparing C_{2n} and D_n patterns ($n = 1, 2$) with the same order in the cluster condition, there was no significant difference between them in goodness and a significant difference in complexity. The behavior in this cluster condition is the same as that in the expanded condition as described above. On the other hand, in the original condition, both goodness and simplicity were significantly higher for D_n than for C_{2n}. Thus, there was a significant difference between C_{2n} and D_n in terms of goodness in the original condition, while there was no significant difference in the expanded and clustered conditions, indicating that goodness is affected by differences in the configuration of the dot patterns because group order is fixed.

Based on the above discussion and the model in Fig. 9.6, a three-stage serial processing model with an anisotropic spatial filter and group theory for the cluster condition is shown in Fig. 9.9. Here, the simplicity (the inverse of complexity) of the 8- and 13-dot D_2 linear patterns is significantly higher than that of D_4 pattern. Also, the simplicity of the linear pattern numbered 20 in Fig. 9.7 is the highest among the three 21-dot D_2 patterns. This specific increase in simplicity is due to the effect of the anisotropic spatial filter in the primary stage of the cognitive system. The three patterns numbered 2, 8, and 20 with the D_2 linear pattern in Fig. 9.7 share a common graphic feature: they have two parallel edges. Then, in this primary stage, the D_2 linear pattern is cognized for simplicity.

Next, not only the simplicity for dot patterns other than the D_2 linear pattern, but also the goodness for all dot patterns follows from group theory.

A three-stage serial processing model
of symmetry cognition

Mixed 8-, 13-, and 21-dot patterns in Hamada (2020)

9×9 square grid

Cluster condition

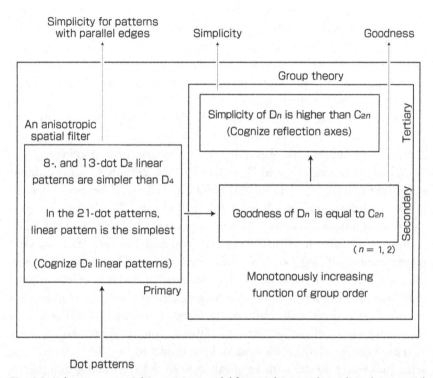

Fig. 9.9 A three-stage serial processing model for goodness and simplicity by a spatial filter and group theory in the cluster condition. *(Adapted from Hamada, J. (2020). Psychophysics of pattern cognition. Tokyo: Kazama Press (Japanese text).)*

In other words, the goodness of the dot pattern bypasses this primary stage and is determined at the secondary stage, while the simplicity of the dot pattern other than the D_2 linear pattern bypasses the secondary stage and is determined at the tertiary stage. In the secondary stage, the cyclic and dihedral groups are not distinguished, and the reflection axes are not cognized; however, in the tertiary stage, these groups are distinguished, and the reflection axes are cognized. The fact that C_{2n} and D_n ($n = 1, 2$) are not distinguished indicates that the reflection axes are not cognized, whereas the fact that they are distinguished means that the reflection axes are cognized. Thus, goodness and simplicity are processed serially, and goodness is determined by the secondary stage, bypassing the anisotropic space filter, while the simplicity for dot patterns other than the D_2 linear pattern is determined by the tertiary stage, bypassing the primary and secondary stages (see also Fig. 9.6).

9.5 Disjointedness (the inverse of unifiedness) for 8-, 13-, and 21-dot patterns in original condition

Gyoba, Seto, and Ichikawa (1985) applied the semantic differential method of Osgood, Suci, and Tannenbaum (1957) to 5-dot patterns in a 3×3 grid and showed that among nine morphological brevity factors including simplicity (simple-complex) and goodness (good-poor), unifiedness (unified-disjointed) had the highest factor loadings, followed by regularity (regular-irregular). Moreover, they reported that the ratings of unifiedness, regularity, and simplicity had a very high correlation with Matsuda's (1978) goodness. On the other hand, the correlations between the goodness ratings of Gyoba et al. and Matsuda were not relatively high. As for goodness, Gyoba et al. attributed this difference to the fact that the former is a composite judgment involving not only morphological brevity factor but also evaluative and activity factors in Osgood's (1957) terms, while the latter is mainly determined by morphological brevity factors.

Wertheimer (1923) called the cohesion of elements with each other as grouping. And he explained the cohesion of closely located dots by the factor of proximity. Here, the grouping of closely located dots is called unifiedness (the inverse of disjointedness). In this section, we use the patterns in the 9×9 grid to study the dependence of disjointness and regularity on group order and numerosity (8, 13, and 21 dots). However, regularity did not have a consistent effect on group order and mumerosity, so only the experimental data for it are shown in Appendix (Fig. 9.A.1). Goodness, simplicity, and unifiedness is then examined in a three-stage serial processing model of previous section. We measure the disjointness of the original patterns consisting of 8-, 13-, and 21-dot patterns used in the original conditions of the section 4–2 of this chapter. Then, the dependence of these cognitive judgments on the group order, the effect of a spatial filter, and the numerosity will be clarified. In this section, Hamada et al. (2021) will be reviewed.

9.5.1 Stimulus patterns and procedure

All the dot patterns used are shown in Fig. 9.10. They are all the same as in Fig. 9.1. In this experiment, we used 8-dot prototype patterns (numbers 1 to 6), 13-dot prototype patterns (numbers 7 to 12), and 21-dot compound

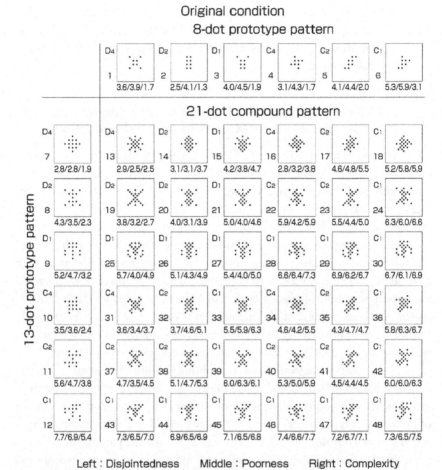

Left : Disjointedness   Middle : Poorness   Right : Complexity

Fig. 9.10 Average ratings of disjointedness for 8- and 13-dot prototype patterns, and 21-dot compound patterns in original condition. Based on Hamada et al. (2019) for poorness and complexity. *(From Hamada, J., Uchiumi, C., Sato, Y., Fukuda, T.S., Fukushi, K., & Amano, K. (2021). Examining disjointedness of dot patterns based on a three-stage serial processing model of symmetry cognition.* Journal of Human Science, Faculty of Integrated Arts and Sciences, Tokushima University, 29, 1–14. *(Japanese text with English abstract and captions). https://repo.lib.tokushima-u.ac.jp/116654)*

patterns (numbers 13 to 48). Fifty-two undergraduate students at Tokushima University participated in the experiment. They were given 48 stimulus patterns: six 8- and six 13-dot prototype patterns, and 36 21-dot compound patterns. They were rated by a 9-point integer scale (1 being the most unified and 9 being the most disjointed). The rating was repeated in three self-paced sessions with free-viewing tasks, and the results were analyzed based on the average of the second and third sessions.

9.5.2 Results and discussion

Fig. 9.10 shows the poorness (the inverse of goodness, i.e., the value obtained by subtracting the goodness rating from 10 in order to align the poorness from 1 to 9) and complexity obtained by Hamada et al. (2019, Experiment 1), along with the average rating of disjointedness, separately for the D_n and C_n patterns ($n = 1, 2, 4$). The mean ratings of the three types of cognitive judgments are shown in Fig. 9.11 as a function of group order. On the vertical axis of this

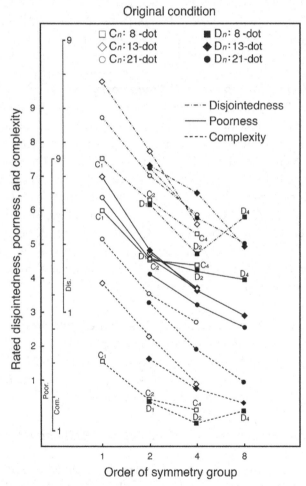

Fig. 9.11 Disjointedness, poorness, and complexity as a function of group order. *(From Hamada, J., Uchiumi, C., Sato, Y., Fukuda, T.S., Fukushi, K., & Amano, K. (2021). Examining disjointedness of dot patterns based on a three-stage serial processing model of symmetry cognition.* Journal of Human Science, Faculty of Integrated Arts and Sciences, Tokushima University, 29, 1–14. *(Japanese text with English abstract and captions). https://repo.lib. tokushima-u.ac.jp/116654)*

figure, disjointedness is shifted upward by 2.0 units, and complexity is shifted downward by 1.5 units, based on poorness.

In Fig. 9.10, Pearson's correlation coefficients were calculated in comparison with the data in the original conditions of Hamada et al. (2019, Experiment 1), and the correlation coefficients between disjointedness and poorness were ($r = .843$, $P < .05$) for 6 pairs of 8-dot patterns, ($r = .975$, $P < .01$) for 6 pairs of 13-dot patterns, and ($r = .886$, $P < .001$) for 36 pairs of 21-dot patterns. Similarly, the correlation coefficient between disjointedness and complexity was ($r = .956$, $P < .01$) for 6 pairs of 8-dot patterns, ($r = .972$, $P < .01$) for 6 pairs of 13-dot patterns, and ($r = .921$, $P < .001$) for 36 pairs of 21-dot patterns. All of the above correlation coefficients were significant.

9.5.2.1 Effects of group order and numerosity

As shown in Fig. 9.11, disjointedness, poorness, and complexity are monotonically decreasing with group order. However, both disjointedness and complexity are significantly lower for the 8-dot D_2 linear pattern than for D_4 pattern, which has the highest geometric symmetry. On disjointedness and complexity, there is no significant difference between D_1 and D_4. About numerosity, the mean values of disjointedness including C_n and D_n are 8-dot ($M = 3.8$), 13-dot ($M = 4.8$) and 21-dot ($M = 5.3$). Here, there is no significant difference between the 13- and 21-dots, and the 8-dot is significantly lower than them. The results are different in that an increase in the number of dots monotonically increases the complexity and that it does not have a consistent effect on the poorness (see Fig. 9.4).

9.5.2.2 C_{2n} and D_n patterns (n = 1, 2) with the same order

When the 8- and 13- and 21-dot are shown as pooled means, disjointedness is not significantly different between C_{2n} ($M = 4.4$) and D_n ($M = 4.4$), which is different from the fact that poorness and complexity were significant in the original condition in section 4–2 of this chapter.

9.5.2.3 A comparison between Gyoba et al. (1985) and Hamada et al. (2021)

According to Hamada et al. (2021), poorness is specified by group theory, complexity and disjointedness follow not only group theory but also a spatial filter, and regularity is not affected by group theory and numerosity (8, 13, and 21 dots) (see Fig. 9.A.1 in Appendix). On the other hand, the disjointedness, regularity and complexity of Gyoba et al. (1985) showed a high correlation with the goodness of Matsuda (1978), while the goodness of Gyoba et al. and Matsuda showed only a significant but moderate correlation. The difference between Gyoba et al. and Hamada et al. in the four types of cognitive judgments can be attributed to the fact that the former used only 5-dot patterns in a 3×3 grid, while the latter used patterns with different configurations and numerosity in a 9×9 grid. Specifically, the 5-dot patterns of Gyoba et al. are limited to C_1, C_2, D_1, and D_4, while the 8-, 13-, and 21-dot C_n and D_n patterns ($n = 1$, 2, 4) of Hamada et al. cover the entire symmetry that can be generated in a 9×9 grid.

If we take the 21-dot patterns in the line with number 7 in Fig. 9.10, the figure numbers with low disjointedness is 13, 14, and 16. These patterns are radial and rhombic in configuration, and they are coherent and have graphic features not found in the other 21-dot patterns. This corresponds to the similarity to pattern pairs (Figs. 8.8 and 8.9).

9.5.3 Three-stage serial processing model of symmetry cognition

In addition to goodness and simplicity (the inverse of complexity), Hamada et al. (2021) added unifeiedness (the inverse of disjointedness) to the three-stage serial processing model, as shown in Fig. 9.12. This model consists not only of the primary stage following an anisotropic spatial filter, but also of the secondary and tertiary stages following group theory. Thus, the three cognitive judgments are processed serially through the three stages. C_{2n} and D_n patterns ($n = 1$, 2) are not distinguished in this secondary stage, but they are distinguished in the tertiary stage. It is common that the three cognitive judgments according to group theory monotonically increase with respect to group order. However, unifiedeness and simplicity for 8-dot D_2 linear pattern are handled in the primary stage, where an anisotropic spatial filter is applied, and the two cognitive decisions are made here. The three types of cognitive judgments for other pattern bypass this primary stage, and sends to the secondary stage where the unifiedness judgment except for 8-dot D_2 linear pattern is decided. Then, the simplicity of patterns other than the 8-dot D_2 linear pattern and the goodness of all patterns bypass the secondary stage, and are processed in the tertiary stage, and where the two cognitive decisions are made here. Thus, the three types of cognitive judgments differ because they are processed at different stages. On the other hand, as the numerosity (8, 13, and 21 dots) increases, simplicity decreases monotonically, but there is no significant difference between 13- and 21-dot in unifiedness, and 8-dot is the highest. And numerosity does not have a consistent effect on goodness.

In terms of two-dimensional dot patterns, Imai's (1977a) transformational structure theory, Palmer's (1982, 1983) transformation model, and van der

A three-stage serial processing model
of symmetry cognition

Mixed 8-, 13-, and 21-dot patterns in Hamada et al. (2019, 2021)

9×9 square grid

Original condition

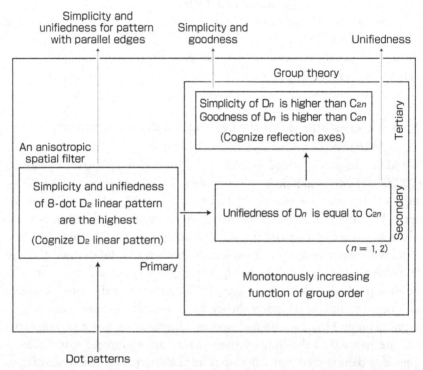

Fig. 9.12 A three-stage serial processing model for goodness, simplicity, and unifiedness by a spatial filter and group theory in the original condition. *(Adapted from Hamada, J., Uchiumi, C., Sato, Y., Fukuda, T.S., Fukushi, K., & Amano, K. (2021). Examining disjointedness of dot patterns based on a three-stage serial processing model of symmetry cognition.* Journal of Human Science, Faculty of Integrated Arts and Sciences, Tokushima University, 29, 1–14. *(Japanese text with English abstract and captions). https://repo.lib. tokushima-u.ac.jp/116654)*

Helm's (2014) holographic model focus only on goodness, and Imai, Ito, and Ito (1976b) on goodness and complexity (simplicity) for one–dimensional ellipse patterns, while Hamada et al.'s (2021) three–stage serial processing model for two–dimensional dot patterns can handle goodness, simplicity, and unifiedness and is highly versatile.

Appendix

According to Gyoba et al. (1985), the factor loadings of regularity are also high. However, the regularity ratings obtained with different 52 participants and using the same method and procedures as in the present experiment did not show consistent effects on group order and numerosity (8, 13, and 21 dots), so only the experimental data are shown in Fig. 9. A.1. A factor analysis was conducted for the regularity, but the results could not be interpreted. At present, the processing mechanism for regularity is unknown.

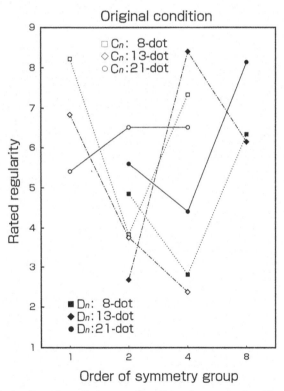

Fig. 9.A.1 Rated value of regularity as a function of group order. *(From Hamada, J., Uchiumi, C., Sato, Y., Fukuda, T.S., Fukushi, K., & Amano, K. (2021). Examining disjointedness of dot patterns based on a three-stage serial processing model of symmetry cognition.* Journal of Human Science, Faculty of Integrated Arts and Sciences, Tokushima University, 29, 1–14. *(Japanese text with English abstract and captions).* https://repo.lib.tokushima-u.ac.jp/116654)

CHAPTER TEN

Cognitive judgments for repetitive patterns

The geometric symmetry of a two-dimensional planar pattern is shown by its invariance to rotational and reflectional transformations. Also, by introducing translation and glide-reflection, we can create repetitive patterns by moving a motif along a straight line at equal intervals.[a] As shown in Fig. 10.1a, the 8-dot random motif on the left side can be inverted to form a D_1 pattern with one reflection axis. On the other hand, if it is moved linearly in the plane, it becomes a translation pattern (b), and if it is moved linearly and flipped over, it becomes a glide-reflection pattern (c). Translational and glide-reflectional transformations are sufficient to create repetitive patterns, and there are only 17 groups of planar repetitive patterns (Weyl, 1952; Coxeter, 1965; Fushimi, 1967b, 2013; Ledermann & Vajda, 1985). Translational transformations have been studied by Mach (1918), Bruce and Morgan (1975), Hamada (1996), Bertamini (2010), and Bertamini and Makin (2014). Glide-reflectional transformations have also been examined by Hamada (1996) for goodness, complexity, and similarity and by Strother and Kubovy (2003) for complexity.

10.1 Motifs

As shown in Fig. 10.2, all four cells in the center of a 4×4 grid are filled with solid dots, and the other four solid dots are placed around the four cells. These 8-dot patterns are called concentrated motifs. In addition, a diffused motif with eight solid dots in the blank cells of the concentrated motif was created. These motifs are complementary and have the same geometric symmetry but different configurations. In Fig. 10.2, to distinguish the direction of the reflectional axes for the motif of the dihedral group, the vertical and horizontal axis is denoted by the subscript vh and the diagonal axis is denoted by the subscript d. D_4, D_{2vh}, and D_{2d} are limited to these in

---

[a]Professor Toru Ishihara pointed out that repetitive patterns can be generated by the translation and the glide-reflection into a motif, and the author created specific repetitive patterns.

Psychophysics and Experimental Phenomenology of Pattern Cognition   Copyright © 2023 Elsevier Inc.
https://doi.org/10.1016/B978-0-323-95286-6.00010-7

(a)
(b)
(c)
D1
p1
pg
Reflection
Translation
Glide-reflection

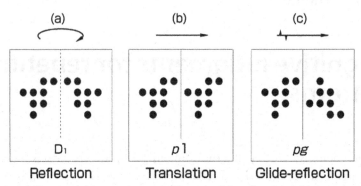

Fig. 10.1 Reflectional (a), translational (b), and glide-reflectional (c) patterns. *(From Hamada, J. (2020).* Psychophysics of pattern cognition. *Tokyo: Kazama Press (Japanese text).)*

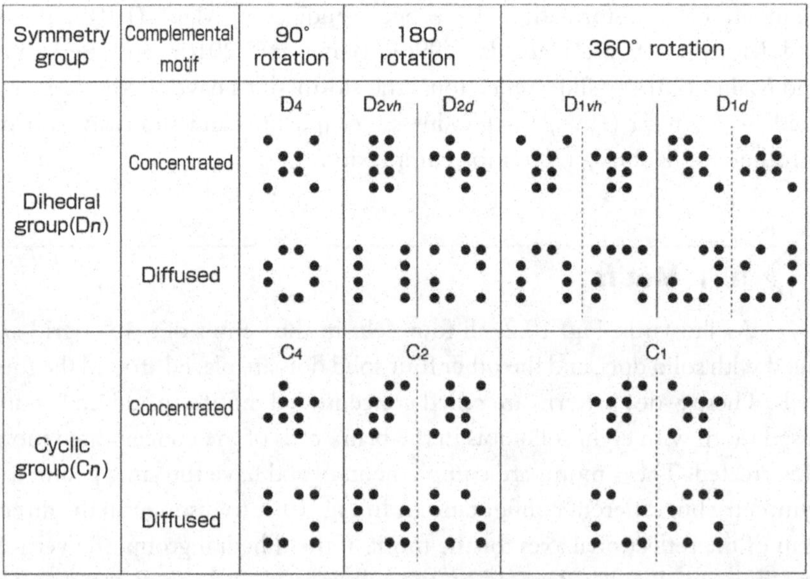

Symmetry group
Complemental motif
90° rotation
180° rotation
360° rotation
D4
D2vh
D2d
D1vh
D1d
Concentrated
Dihedral group(Dn)
Diffused
C4
C2
C1
Concentrated
Cyclic group(Cn)
Diffused

Fig. 10.2 The motifs used to create the repetitive patterns. *(From Hamada, J. (1996). Symmetry and pattern cognition: The general effect of glide-reflection and selective effect of inclination upon pattern cognition.* Japanese Psychological Review, 39, *338–360. (Japanese text with English abstract and figures).)*

Fig. 10.2, but there are several motifs for the others, so two motifs were employed by self-selection as indicated by the dotted line in Fig. 10.2.

10.2 Repetitive patterns

Fig. 10.3 shows 26 different repetitive patterns with nine motifs in a 3×3 arrangement with two cells spaced apart, and Hermann–Morgan's symbols. The symbols of repetitive patterns are shown on the left, and these for the dihedral group D_n and cyclic group C_n of the motifs ($n = 1, 2, 4$) are shown on the right. In the repetitive pattern symbol, g indicates the

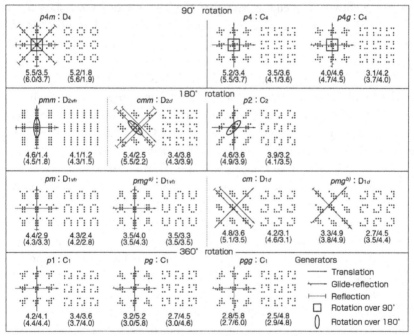

Without parentheses: Upright pattern   Left: Goodness
With parentheses: Oblique pattern   Right: Complexity

Fig. 10.3 Twenty-six examples of repetitive patterns, and their average ratings for goodness *(left side)* and complexity *(right side)*. The top row shows the mean ratings for upright patterns, and the bottom row shows those for oblique patterns. *(From Hamada, J. (1993). Goodness and complexity ratings of repetitive patterns formed by wallpaper groups. Journal of Human Science, Faculty of Integrated Arts and Sciences, Tokushima University, 1, 39–51. (Japanese text with English abstract and captions); Hamada, J. (1996). Symmetry and pattern cognition: The general effect of glide-reflection and selective effect of inclination upon pattern cognition. Japanese Psychological Review, 39, 338–360. (Japanese text with English abstract and figures).)*

glide-reflectional transformation, m indicates the reflectional transformation, and c means that the reflectional and glide-reflection axes run parallel. All others are marked with p. 4, 2, and 1 mean that the repetitive pattern is invariant when rotated 90°, 180°, and 360°, respectively. Thus, the repetitive pattern is represented by six transformations (i.e., translation, glide-reflection, reflection, and 90°, 180°, and 360° rotations).

In Fig. 10.3, the repetitive patterns consisting of the concentrated and diffused motifs are shown on the left and right sides, respectively. The generators are superimposed only on the concentrated repetitive pattern but are not on the diffused one. The translation has an axis with an arrow, the glide-reflection has an axis with two alternate arrow feathers, the reflection has an H-shaped axis, the 90° rotation is shown as a square, and the 180° rotation is shown as an ellipse; however, the 360° rotation is not shown with these markings. The geometric symmetry of Fig. 10.3 is now divided into repetitive patterns that show invariance when rotated by 90°, 180°, and 360°.

First, we describe a repetitive pattern that is invariant to a 90° rotation marked with a square. $p4m$ is generated by translating a D_4 motif in two directions, horizontally, and vertically on the reflection axes. $p4$ or $p4g$ is generated by translating or glide-reflecting a C_4 motif in two directions, horizontally and vertically. $p4m$ has four reflection axes, and $p4g$ has two glide-reflection axes; however, $p4$ has none of these axes.

Next, we describe a repetitive pattern that is invariant to a 180° rotation marked with an ellipse. pmm is generated by translating the D_{2vh} motif on two reflection axes. A glide-reflection on the D_{2d} motif parallel to the two reflection axes produces a cmm. Translating the C_2 motif in two directions, horizontally and vertically, produces $p2$. pmm has two reflection axes, and cmm has two reflection axes and glide-reflection axes parallel to it. $p2$ has none of these axes.

Finally, we describe the repetitive patterns listed in the bottom two rows, which are invariant only to 360° rotation. For the D_{1vh} motif, translation in two directions, horizontally and vertically, produces pm, whereas translation on the reflection axis and glide-reflection in the direction orthogonal to the reflection axis produces pmg[a]. On the other hand, glide-reflection on the D_{1d} motif parallel to the reflection axis and translation in the direction orthogonal to the reflection axis produces cm. When the D_{1d} motif is translated on the reflection axis and the glide-reflection is applied in the direction orthogonal to it, pmg[b] is generated. Translating the C_1 motif in two directions, horizontally and vertically, yields $p1$, translating in one direction and glide-reflecting in the orthogonal direction yields *pg*, and glide-reflecting in two directions yield *pgg*. *pm* has one reflection axis, *pmg*[a), b)] has one reflection axis and an orthogonal glide-reflection axis, and *cm* has one reflection axis and a parallel glide-reflection axis. *p*1, *pg*, and *pgg* have zero, one, and two glide-reflection axes, respectively.

Under the constraint of placing three motifs each in the vertical and horizontal directions, leaving two cells blank in the 16 × 16 grid, only 12 types of repetitive patterns (*p4m*, *pmm*, *cmm*, *pm*, *pmg*, *cm*, *p4*, *p4g*, *p2*, *p*1, *pg*, and *pgg*) can be generated, and *p3*, *p6*, *p3m*1, *p31m*, and *p6m* cannot be generated, although the details are omitted (for details, see Ledermann & Vajda, 1985).

10.3 Goodness and complexity (Experiment 1)

In this section, the goodness and complexity of Hamada's (1993; 1996, Experiment 1) repetitive patterns in Fig. 10.3 will be reviewed.

10.3.1 Stimulus patterns and procedures

The motifs are the 8-dot patterns in a 4 × 4 grid shown in Fig. 10.2. The repetitive patterns created from these motifs are referred to as the concentrated and diffused patterns. *p4m*, *pmm*, *cmm*, *p4*, and *p4g* in Fig. 10.3 were rated by all participants. On the other hand, because there were multiple *pm*, *pmg*[a)], *pmg*[b)], *cm*, *p2*, *p*1, *pg*, and *pgg*, two each were selected by self-selection as appropriate, and they were rated by different participants. To further examine the anisotropy of symmetry cognition, upright and 45° oblique patterns were prepared, as illustrated in Fig. 10.4. The total number of repetitive patterns used was 320, which consisted of [6 (repetitive patterns generated from D_4, C_4, D_2, and C_2 motifs) + 7 (repetitive patterns generated from other motifs)×2 (type)]×2 (concentrated and diffused patterns)×2 (upright and oblique patterns)×4 (observation direction). In order to equalize the combinations of repetitive patterns, a total of 52 cards were distributed to the participants, that is, 13 cards with concentrated patterns, 13 cards with diffused ones, 13 cards with upright ones, and 13 cards with oblique ones. The repetitive patterns were printed on thick white cards (65 length × 60 width mm) with 72-dots arranged in a 16 × 16 imaginary grid of 34 mm in length and width.

One hundred and forty-four undergraduate students at Tokushima University participated in the experiment, and half (72 students) were randomly assigned to goodness and the other half to complexity. They rated the goodness or complexity of the repetitive patterns on a 7-point integer scale. These

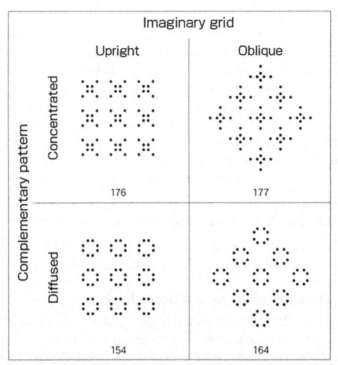

Fig. 10.4 Complementary repetitive patterns and imaginary grid directions. *p4m* repetitive patterns generated from the D_4 motif are shown. *(From Hamada, J. (1996). Symmetry and pattern cognition: The general effect of glide-reflection and selective effect of inclination upon pattern cognition.* Japanese Psychological Review, 39, 338–360. *(Japanese text with English abstract and figures).)*

72 participants were randomly divided into 36 participants, each rating two different repetitive patterns, and then into four groups (9 students each) with different observation directions (0°, 90°, 180°, and 270°). The results were analyzed based on the mean of the two different repetitive patterns and that of the four observation directions. Three sessions were repeated, and the mean values of the second and third sessions were analyzed.

10.3.2 Results and discussion

10.3.2.1 Concentrated and diffused repetitive patterns

Fig. 10.5a and b shows the mean ratings for the concentrated and diffused repetitive patterns, with goodness as the horizontal axis and complexity as

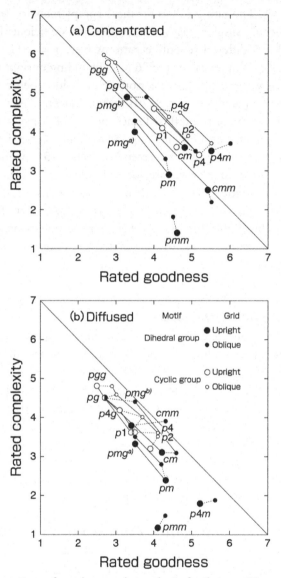

Fig. 10.5 Mean ratings of goodness and complexity for the repetitive patterns of concentrated (a) and diffused (b). *(From Hamada, J. (1996). Symmetry and pattern cognition: The general effect of glide-reflection and selective effect of inclination upon pattern cognition. Japanese Psychological Review, 39, 338–360. (Japanese text with English abstract and figures).)*

the vertical axis. The rating values for these complementary repetitive patterns are generally similar. Pearson's correlation coefficients between the concentrated and diffused repetitive patterns were $r = .811$ for goodness and $r = .785$ for complexity for the 26 pairs including upright and oblique, both of which were significant. Pearson's correlation coefficient between goodness and complexity was $r = -.701$ for the concentrated repetitive patterns and $r = -.798$ for the diffused ones, both significant.

In Fig. 10.5a, most of the values of goodness and complexity of the concentrated repetitive patterns are located above the 45° inclined diagonal, whereas those of diffused ones are located below it in (b). Goodness is higher for concentration ($M = 4.4$) than for diffusion ($M = 3.8$). Similarly, complexity is higher for concentration ($M = 3.8$) than for diffusion ($M = 3.4$). This result means that between complementary repetitive patterns with the same geometric symmetry but different configurations, the good repetitive pattern is more complex, indicating the effect of configuration.

10.3.2.2 Universal effect of glide-reflection
As shown in the solid lines in Fig. 10.5, when translation is replaced with glide-reflection, the goodness decreases and the complexity increases almost parallel to the 45° diagonal. In other words, when we change from pm to pmg[a], cm to pmg[b], p4 to p4g, and p1 to pgg via pg, the goodness decreases and the complexity increases. For example, although pm and pmg[a] are both repetitive patterns with D_{1vh} as the motif, the goodness and complexity ratings are very different. Thus, the difference in these ratings is significant depending on whether the same motif is translation or glide-reflection. In summary, replacing translation with glide-reflection universally results in a decrease in goodness and an increase in complexity.

10.3.2.3 Anisotropy of symmetry cognition with a 45° inclination
As shown by the dotted line in Fig. 10.5, there are many cases in which tilting the upright (large circles) by 45° (small circles) increases one of the goodness and complexity and leave the other unchanged. In contrast to the universal effect between translation and glide-reflection, the effect of 45° inclination was selective for goodness and complexity and showed anisotropy of symmetry cognition.

10.3.2.4 Comparison of glide-reflection and 45° inclination
In Fig. 10.5, the extent of the effect of glide-reflection on goodness and complexity is indicated by the length of the solid line, and that of the effect

of 45° inclination is indicated by the length of the dotted line. When we include the concentrated and diffused repetitive patterns, the mean distance between the solid lines for (pm:$pmg^{a)}$), (cm:$pmg^{b)}$), ($p4$:$p4g$), ($p1$:pg), and (pg:pgg) was $M = 1.21$. On the other hand, the dotted line distance between them had an average value of $M = 0.45$. Therefore, the effect of glide-reflection on goodness and complexity is clearly stronger than the effect of 45° inclination.

10.3.2.5 Effects of linear and circular motifs on complexity and goodness

The effect of linear patterns on goodness has been reported (Garner & Clement, 1963; Matsuda, 1978), and the effect on complexity has also been pointed out (Otsuka, 1984; Ichikawa, 1985). For example, according to Hamada and Ishihara (1988), a 9-dot D_2 linear pattern in a hexagonal grid strongly reduced complexity but had little effect on goodness (see Fig. 7.1). This is also true for cluster patterns in Hamada (2020) (see Fig. 9.8). Furthermore, in this experiment, the complexity of the pmm repetitive pattern consisting of 8-dot D_2 linear motifs was the lowest and the goodness was medium (see Fig. 10.3). As discussed in Experiment 3 in the previous chapter, the symmetry axis is detected by an anisotropic spatial filter at the primary stage of the cognitive system. In other words, by anisotropic spatial filtering of the pmm repetitive pattern consisting of 8-dot D_2 linear motifs, we obtain a clear vertical rod (0°, 180°), horizontal rod (90°, 270°), and diagonal rod (45°, 135°) output that cannot be obtained with any repetitive pattern other than the pmm. This anisotropic spatial filter contributes to a special reduction in the complexity of the pmm repetitive pattern ($M = 1.5$ on a 7-point scale). On the other hand, as shown in Fig. 10.5b, the goodness of the diffused repetitive pattern of $p4m$ with the circular motif is exceedingly higher for upright ($M = 5.2$) and oblique ($M = 5.6$). Similarly, the complexity is exceedingly lower for the repetitive pattern with the circular motif ($M = 1.8$ and 1.9). Thus, the circular motif also specifically increases goodness and simplicity.

10.4 Similarity (Experiment 2)

Two repetitive patterns generated by translation or glide-reflection on a motif are lined up side by side to investigate how the possibility of mutual transformation of the pattern pairs defines the similarity. We also set up a relationship in which the repetitive patterns match each other when 45° inclination is applied and a relationship in which the repetitive patterns match each other when translation or glide-reflection is combined with $45°$ inclination. In this section, Hamada (1996, Experiment 2) will be reviewed.

10.4.1 Stimulus patterns and procedures

The repetitive patterns were drawn by shrinking the 16×16 imaginary grid used in Experiment 1 in the previous section and lined up on the left and right. Pattern pairs were printed in black on thick white cards (50 mm long $\times$ 110 mm wide). To reduce the number of stimulus-pattern pairs, $p4$, $p4g$, and $p2$ consisting of C_4 and C_2 motifs were not used. Examples of repetitive pattern pairs are shown in Fig. 10.6.

The participants were 88 undergraduate students at Tokushima University, who were randomly assigned to repetitive pattern pairs with D_n ($n = 1$, 2, 4) motifs (44 students) and C_1 motifs (44 ones). For D_n, both repetitive pattern pairs consisting of the D_{1vh} and D_{1d} motifs separated by the dotted lines in Fig. 10.2 were used by another two sets of 22 participants. However, because the motifs for D_4, D_{2vh}, and D_{2d} were limited to those shown in Fig. 10.2, they were duplicated in two pairs of 22 participants each. The two repetitive patterns consisting of C_1 motifs separated by the dotted lines in Fig. 10.2 were used in another two sets of 22 participants.

All participants used 60 cards of repetitive pattern pairs. In a set of 60 cards, half of the cards were concentrated repetitive pattern pairs and the other half were diffused ones. In addition, the number of upright and oblique patterns was made equal. To further offset the effects of the left and right positions of the cards and the direction of placement of the repetitive patterns within the participants, the paired repetitive patterns were rotated $90°$ clockwise and their left and right positions were swapped simultaneously. In addition, the entire pair of repetitive patterns was rotated $180°$ to offset the effect of the direction of observation of the cards.

In Fig. 10.6, Nos. 112 and 113 (or 342 and 328) are examples of concentrated and diffused patterns in a complementary relationship. No. 134 (or 310) is a pair of upright patterns, and No. 127 (or 354) is a pair of oblique patterns. No. 152 is an example of (upright: oblique), and No. 145 is an example of (oblique: upright). No. 145 (or 351) is a pattern in which the repetitive pattern of No. 152 (or 316) is rotated $90°$ clockwise and the left and right positions are swapped.

The participants' task was to rate the similarity of the repetitive pattern pairs on a 7-point integer scale. Three sessions were repeated, and the means of the second and third sessions were analyzed.

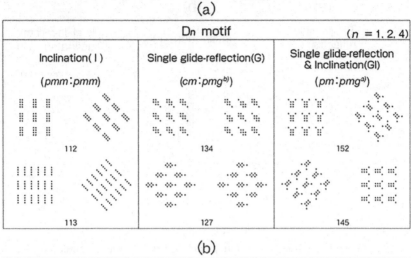

Fig. 10.6 Examples of repetitive pattern pairs. (a) is created from the D_n motif ($n=1$, 2, 4) and (b) is created from the C_1 motif. *(From Hamada, J. (1996). Symmetry and pattern cognition: The general effect of glide-reflection and selective effect of inclination upon pattern cognition. Japanese Psychological Review, 39, 338–360. (Japanese text with English abstract and figures).)*

10.4.2 Results and discussion

The mean ratings of similarity by 44 participants, including two pairs of participants because they were not significant, are shown separately for the concentration pattern (white bars) and diffusion pattern (gray bars) in Figs. 10.7 and 10.8. Also, the similarity for the repetitive pattern pair consisting of D_n ($n=1$, 2, 4) (Fig. 10.7) and the C_1 motif (Fig. 10.8) is shown.

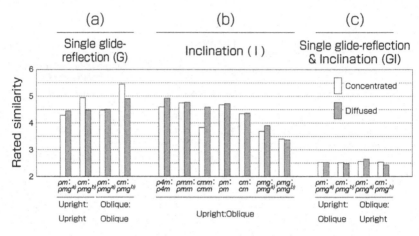

Fig. 10.7 Similarity for repetitive pattern pairs (a–c) created from D_n motifs ($n = 1, 2, 4$). *(From Hamada, J. (1996). Symmetry and pattern cognition: The general effect of glide-reflection and selective effect of inclination upon pattern cognition. Japanese Psychological Review, 39, 338–360. (Japanese text with English abstract and figures).)*

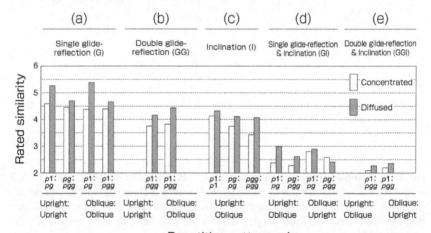

Fig. 10.8 Similarity for repetitive pattern pairs (a–e) generated from the C_1 motif. *(From Hamada, J. (1996). Symmetry and pattern cognition: The general effect of glide-reflection and selective effect of inclination upon pattern cognition. Japanese Psychological Review, 39, 338–360. (Japanese text with English abstract and figures).)*

10.4.2.1 Effect of glide-reflection

Figs. 10.7a and 10.8a show the similarity ratings for upright and oblique patterns when the translation of a repetitive pattern is replaced with glide-reflection (G: glide-reflection). It is also clear from the comparison of Fig. 10.8a and b that the similarity rating of double glide-reflection (GG) is lower than that of single glide-reflection (G).

10.4.2.2 Effect of 45° inclination

Comparing upright and oblique patterns, we can examine the effect of 45° inclination (I: Inclination) on similarity. In Fig. 10.7b, for the pair of repetitive patterns with D_n motifs ($n = 1, 2, 4$), the similarity of the 45° inclination pattern pair (I) decreases as the number of reflection axes of the patterns decreases, and as the glide-reflectional axis is present. For the repetitive pattern pair consisting of C_1 motifs in Fig. 10.8c, the similarity decreases in the order of no glide-reflectional axis ($p1:p1$), one glide-reflectional axis ($pg:pg$), and two glide-reflectional axes ($pgg:pgg$). Thus, the effect of 45° inclination (I) on decreasing similarity is strengthened as the number of glide-reflectional axes of the patterns increases.

10.4.2.3 Comparison of glide-reflection and 45° inclination

As can be seen from the comparison of Fig. 10.7a and b as well as Fig. 10.8a and c, the effect of 45° inclination (I) on decreasing similarity tends to be stronger than that of glide-reflection (G). The degree of similarity reduction tends to be greater for 45° inclination than for glide-reflection not only in Fig. 10.7a and b but also in Fig. 10.8a and c. In Experiment 1 of the previous section, the effect of glide-reflection on goodness and complexity was stronger than of 45° inclination. However, there was a contrasting inverse relationship for similarity, that is, 45° inclination tending to reduce similarity more strongly than glide-reflection.

10.4.2.4 Effect of combining glide-reflection and 45° inclination

Similarity ratings for (GI), which combines a single glide-reflection (G) with a 45° inclination (I), are shown for D_n motifs (Fig. 10.7c) by (upright: oblique) and (oblique: upright). Also, the similarity of the repetitive pattern pair consisting of C_1 motifs (Fig. 10.8d) is shown by (upright: oblique) and (oblique: upright). Regardless of the repetitive pattern pairs, these ratings are in good agreement with each other. Also, the degree of similarity reduction is clearly stronger for the combined transformation of glide-reflection and 45° inclination (GI) than for the single transformation of glide-reflection (G) and 45° inclination (I). The similarity between double glide-reflection (GG) and 45° inclination (GGI) is shown in Fig. 10.8e. It is clear that the degree of similarity reduction by GGI (in Fig. 10.8e) is stronger than that by GG (in Fig. 10.8b) and GI (in Fig. 10.8d). Similarly, comparing Fig. 10.8c with

(d) and (e), the degree of similarity decrease is stronger for the single transformation of 45° inclination (I in c), the combined transformation with single glide-reflection (GI in d), and the combined transformation with double glide-reflection (GGI in e), in that order. Thus, as the number of glide-reflection axes in each individual pattern increases, the similarity decreases. Also, compared to the single transformations of glide-reflection and 45° inclination, the similarity significantly decreases when they are combined.

As described above, the more the transformations required to match two repetitive patterns and the less the possibilities for mutual transformation, the lower the similarity becomes. The similarity decreases as the number of reflectional axes decreases and as the number of glide-reflectional axes increases.

10.4.2.5 Effect of linear and circular motifs on similarity

To compare with the goodness and complexity of the previous section (Experiment 1), we examined the similarity of repetitive pattern pairs with linear or circular motifs. Then, the similarity ratings are ($M = 4.9$) for the diffused pattern of $p4m$, which consists of circular motifs, and ($M = 4.8$ and 4.8) for the concentrated and diffused patterns of pmm, which consists of linear motifs. On the other hand, for example, the concentrated and diffused patterns of pmm without linear and circular motifs are ($M = 4.7$ and 4.7), and these rating values are similar. This result indicates that unlike goodness and complexity, linear and circular motifs have no effect on similarity.

10.4.2.6 Correlation of similarity with goodness and complexity

Goodness and complexity are judgments for individual patterns (Experiment 1), and similarity is a judgment for repetitive pattern pairs (Experiment 2). To examine the relationship between these cognitive judgments, the correlation coefficients between the similarity ratings and the difference in the goodness (or complexity) ratings for the two corresponding repetitive patterns were calculated. Here, we used the average of the repetitive pattern pairs used to cancel out the left and right positions and the direction of the repetitive pattern as the similarity value. For example, in Fig. 10.6, we calculated the average of the similarity ratings for the repetitive pattern pairs numbered 152 and 145. The difference in goodness (or complexity) between the right and left sides of the numbered 152 and 145 repetitive pattern pairs was then calculated. We calculated 30 pairwise correlation coefficients for this comparable similarity and difference in goodness (or complexity). In Experiment 2, the repetitive pattern pairs consisting of D_n ($n = 1, 2, 4$) and C_1 motifs were rated in different participant populations, so their correlation coefficients were calculated separately. The correlation coefficients between the similarity ratings and the difference in goodness ratings were $r = -.27$ for the pair of repetitive patterns consisting of D_n motifs and $r = -.25$ for them consisting of C_1 motifs. Similarly, the correlation coefficients between the similarity ratings and the difference in complexity ratings were $r = -.28$ for the repetitive pattern consisting of D_n motifs and $r = -.25$ for them consisting of C_1 motifs. All these correlations were not significant. Therefore, the similarity is not based on the goodness or complexity of the left and right repetitive patterns.

CHAPTER ELEVEN

Cognitive judgments for black-white filled patterns based on transformational group structure theory

11.1 Goodness and complexity of one-dimensional patterns (Experiment 1)

Imai (1972, 1977b) devised a one-dimensional (1D) filled pattern consisting of black-white ellipses arranged horizontally, and proposed a transformational structure theory of the similarity for these pattern pairs. He postulated that the cognitive system applies three kinds of cognitive transformations (i.e., the mirror-image transformation M, the phase transformation P, and the black-white reversal transformation R) to the presented pattern pairs, cognizes the possibility of mutual transformations (mutual matching), and makes similarity judgments based on them. To simplify, the greater the possibility of mutual transformation, the more similar they are. Ito (1975) reconfirmed the role of transformational structures in the similarity for visual and auditory pattern pairs, and at the same time clarified the differences in similarity between visual and auditory pattern pairs. On the other hand, Imai's transformational structure theory can be applied to the goodness of individual patterns by reading the possibility of mutual transformations as invariance. To simplify, the higher the invariance to transformational structure in an individual pattern, the better it is. For details of the transformational structure theory, please refer to Imai (1977a, 1986, 1992).

Amano and Imai (1989, 1992) defined the transformational group structure by adopting the transformation group as the unit of cognitive transformation, and showed that the order of similarity and goodness can be predicted in a form similar to the transformational structure theory. In their transformational group structure theory, the basic assertion that the more possibility of mutual transformations is, the more similar a pattern pair is, and the more invariant an individual pattern is, the better it is, is the same as the transformational structure theory. Note that, with respect to goodness, invariance to transformational groups is used in the sense of invariance to transformations other than the identity transformation.

Imai, Ito, and Ito (1976b) devised a 1D black–white filled pattern consisting of elliptic elements, as illustrated in Fig. 11.1, to examine the goodness and complexity of patterns, and clarified the role of cognitive transformational groups. They also focused on invariance within the pattern (the possibility of a perfect match to itself) and employed the mirror-image transformational group structure M, the phase transformational group structure P, and the black–white reversal transformational group structure R as unitary transformational group structures. The

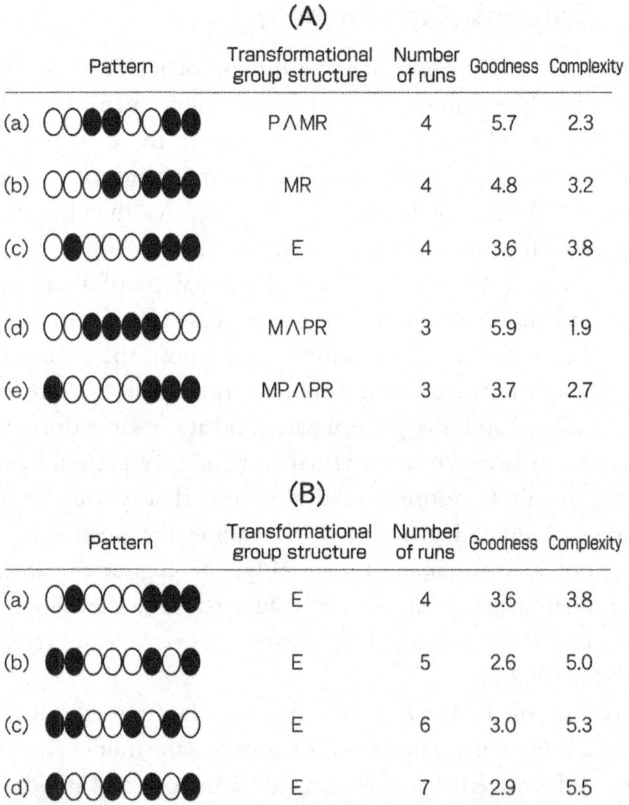

(A)

Pattern	Transformational group structure	Number of runs	Goodness	Complexity
(a) ⬭⬭⬛⬛⬭⬭⬛⬛	P∧MR	4	5.7	2.3
(b) ⬭⬭⬭⬛⬛⬭⬛⬛⬛	MR	4	4.8	3.2
(c) ⬭⬛⬭⬭⬭⬛⬛⬛	E	4	3.6	3.8
(d) ⬭⬭⬛⬛⬛⬛⬭⬭	M∧PR	3	5.9	1.9
(e) ⬛⬭⬭⬭⬭⬭⬛⬛⬛	MP∧PR	3	3.7	2.7

(B)

Pattern	Transformational group structure	Number of runs	Goodness	Complexity
(a) ⬭⬛⬭⬭⬭⬛⬛⬛	E	4	3.6	3.8
(b) ⬛⬛⬭⬭⬭⬛⬛⬛	E	5	2.6	5.0
(c) ⬛⬛⬭⬭⬛⬭⬛⬭⬭	E	6	3.0	5.3
(d) ⬛⬭⬭⬭⬛⬭⬛⬭⬛	E	7	2.9	5.5

Fig. 11.1 Examples and average rating values of black–white filled patterns. Goodness and complexity are shown for runs of 4 and 3 (A), and for runs of 4, 5, 6, and 7 (B). *(Adapted from Imai, S., Ito, S., & Ito, T. (1976b). Effects of intra-pattern transformation structures and the number of runs upon goodness and complexity judgments of patterns. Japanese Psychological Review, 19, 77–94. (Japanese text with English abstract).)*

mirror-image transformational group structure M shows invariance when the sequence order of the entire ellipses of the pattern is inverted. The phase transformational group structure P shows invariance when the phase of the entire ellipses is moved to the right (or left) direction and the ellipses that are out of the imaginary framework are sequentially added to the other end. And the black-white reversal transformational group structure R shows invariance when the black-white color of the entire ellipses is reversed. On the other hand, a multiple transformational group structure is one that shows invariance to multiple different transformational group structures. For example, that of both the mirror-image transformational group M and the phase transformational group P is denoted by M ∧ P. Furthermore, it is the product transformational group structure that shows invariance only when multiple different transformation groups are stacked. For example, that of the mirror-image transformational group M and the black-white reversal transformational group R is denoted by MR. The above transformational group structures have the invariance that when a certain transformation is applied to a pattern stimulus the resulting pattern is consistent with the original ellipse pattern, but the one that does not show invariance to any of these transformations is the empty transformational group structure E. In this section, Imai et al.'s (1976b) transformational structure theory will be replace into the style of the transformational group structure theory, and the goodness and complexity will be reviewed.

11.1.1 Stimulus patterns and procedures

Stimulus patterns were printed on thick white cards (7×9.5 cm) with four black and white ellipses (1 cm long, 0.7 cm short) in a single horizontal row without gaps on a gray background. A total of 46 8-ellipse patterns were used, eight of which are shown in Fig. 11.1. Fifty undergraduate students at Hokkaido University each participated in the rating of goodness or complexity. Twenty-six patterns selected from 46 cards, taking into account the transformation group structure, were distributed to two different groups of 25 participants each, and they rated on a 7-point integer scale for goodness or complexity. No restrictions or suggestions were given as to what goodness or complexity meant as a pattern, and they were instructed to rate the patterns based on their own judgment. They shuffled the cards thoroughly at the beginning of each session. The experiment was conducted in two sessions at their own pace, and only the data from the second session were analyzed.

11.1.2 Results and discussion

11.1.2.1 Dependence on transformational group structure

The number of runs (i.e., the number of white and black ellipse clumps) ranged from 2 to 7. Only patterns with run numbers of 4 and 3 are shown in Fig. 11.1A. For run number 4 (a to c), the multiple transformational group structure P ∧ MR, the product transformational group structure MR, and the empty transformational group structure E, are well-ordered, with goodness falling and complexity rising. Also, when the number of runs is 3 (d and e), the multiple transformational group structure M ∧ PR is better and simpler than MP ∧ PR. In summary, the more invariant a pattern is to transformations, the better and simpler it is. Thus, both goodness and complexity strongly depend on the transformational group structure. It is also worth noting that pattern with a single transformational group structure M (d) is the best $(M = 5.9)$ and simplest $(M = 1.9)$. This corresponds to Wagemans' (1995) finding that mirror symmetry is special for two-dimensional dot patterns.

11.1.2.2 Effect of run numbers

Fig. 11.1B shows the rating values for patterns with empty transformational group structure E and run numbers from 4 to 7. According to the results, complexity increases monotonically as the number of runs increases, but there is no such regular change in goodness. To summarize the above, goodness and complexity strongly depend on the transformational group structure, and complexity increases as the number of runs increases, but there is no consistent effect on goodness. This corresponds to the fact that, as shown in Figs. 9.4, 9.5, and 9.8 of Chapter 9, the goodness and complexity of the dot patterns in the square grid strongly depend on the group order, and that increasing the numerosity from 8 to 13 and then to 21 has no consistent effect on the goodness while the complexity increases.

11.2 Transformational group structure theory for similarity and goodness

Imai and Amano (1998) expressed the order relationship of 1D black-white filled patterns on similarity and goodness in the form of a hierarchical graph (Hasse's diagram) using a transformation group. Subsequently, Amano et al. (2001) and Konishi et al. (2003) attempted rating experiments on the similarity of pattern pairs and the goodness of individual patterns, respectively. On the other hand, Amano et al. (2008) conducted a rating experiment on the similarity of 1D black-white filled 12-ellipse pattern pairs lined up side by side based on the transformational group structure theory. The results show that the similarity decreases in the following order as will be experimentally discussed later: (i) the identity transformational group structure (the left and right patterns are the same), (ii) the multiple transformational group structure (the multiple different transformational groups can be mutually transformed), (iii) the unitary transformational group structure (the pairs of different patterns can be mutually transformed by an unitary transformational group), (iv) the product transformational group structure (the multiple different transformational groups can be mutually transformed only when they are stacked), and (v) the empty transformational group structure (the mutual transformation is impossible). In addition, Konishi et al. (2003) measured the goodness of individual 1D black-white filled 8-ellipse patterns based on the transformational group structure theory, where the unitary transformational group structure, the multiple transformational group structure, the product transformational group structure, and the empty transformational group structure as described above were employed.

They examined whether the experimental results were predicted by the hierarchical graph (Hasse's diagram) of similarity and goodness shown in Figs. 11.2 and 11.3. They predict that between two transformational group structures connected by a solid line, the similarity and goodness of the patterns with the higher structure is greater than that of the patterns with the lower structure. However, they cannot predict the order between transformational group structures that are not connected by a solid line. As will be discussed later, their rating experiments showed that the higher the possibility of mutual transformation in pattern pairs, the higher the similarity, and the higher the invariance in individual patterns, the higher the goodness. And both the similarity and goodness ratings followed the order predicted by the Hasse's diagram.

In the transformational group structure theory, there is a difficulty associated with the increase in the number of ellipses (m) that make up the pattern. In other words, in the case of similarity judgments, there are a total of $2^m \times 2^m$ pattern pairs, of which the percentage of pattern pairs with the empty transformational group structure increases rapidly from 66, 93, and 99% as m increases from 4 through 8 to 12. As a result, the differences in similarity cannot be explained for almost all pattern pairs. However, in practice, there are often large differences in the similarity of such pattern pairs (Amano et al., 2008). This problem is also true for pattern goodness (Konishi et al., 2003). Therefore, Amano et al. (2008, 2013) tried to solve

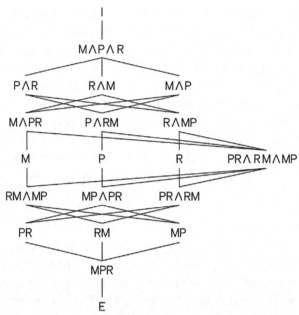

Fig. 11.2 Hasse's diagram predicting the order of similarity in 1D black-white filled pattern pairs. *(From Amano, K., Okano, D., Ogata, H., Shibata, Y., Konishi, T., Fukushi, K., et al. (2001). Transformational group structure theory on similarity judgment of patterns. IPSJ Journal, 42, 2733–2742. (Japanese text with English abstract and captions).)*

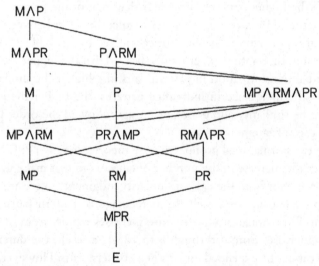

Fig. 11.3 Hasse's diagram predicting the order of goodness in 1D black- white filled patterns. *(From Konishi, T., Okano, D., Ogata, H., Shibata, Y., Amano, K., Fukushi, K., et al. (2003). IPSJ Journal, 44, 2274–2283. 42, 2733–2742 (Japanese text with English abstract and captions).)*

this problem by introducing Hamming's distance in the transformational group structure. In other words, when the 1D black-white filled pattern pair or the individual pattern has an empty transformational group structure, they defined the transformational group structure with distance as the Hamming's distance, which is the minimum number of black-white ellipses that need to invert the color to create the other transformational group structure. Distance 0 is the normal transformational group structure. The results of the rating experiment are represented by a Hasse's diagram with a double hierarchy: transformation group structure and Hamming's distance. As explained in the following experiments, the results support the prediction that similarity and goodness decrease with increasing Hamming's distance when the transformation group structure is the same.

11.3 Similarity of one-dimensional pattern pairs (Experiment 2)

Amano, Okano, Araki, and Konishi (2006) examined the similarity of a pair of 1D black-white filled patterns with 8-ellipse that have the same intra-pattern transformational group structure. As a result, the similarities were ordered in due course of the intra-pattern transformational group structure with higher invariance, if the inter-pattern transformational group structure was the same and not the empty transformational group structure E. Here, generally, in the opposite order for pattern pairs where the inter-pattern transformational group structure was the empty transformational group structure E. When we focus on the pattern pairs whose intra-pattern transformation group structure is the empty transformation group structure E, the similarity decreases in the order of (i) the identity transformational group structure I, (ii) the mirror-image transformational group structure M, (iii) the black-white reversal transformational group structure R, (iv) the phase transformational group structure P, (v) the product transformational group structure MPR, and (vi) the empty transformational group structure E. In this section, the similarity of Amano et al. (2008, Experiment 1) will be reviewed.

11.3.1.1 Stimulus patterns and procedures

For the stimulus patterns, they took a gray background area (6 × 16.5 cm) on a horizontal A5 sheet of card and placed a 12-ellipse pattern pair of ellipses (8 mm long, 5 mm short) in the center of the area. Forty-two pairs of elliptical patterns were used in the experiment, of which 26 are shown in Fig. 11.4.

No.	Pattern pair		Transformational group structure		Similarity	
1	OOOOOOOOOOOO	OOOOOOOOOOOO	I		9.1	9.1
2	O●O●O●O●O●O●	●O●O●O●O●O●O	MΛPΛR		8.7	8.7
3	O●●OO●●OO●●O	●OO●●OO●●OO●	PΛR		6.4	
4	O●●OOO●●●OOO	●OO●●●OOO●●O	RΛM		7.7	7.2
5	OOO●OOO●OOO●	●OOO●OOO●OOO	MΛP		7.5	
6	●●OO●●OO●●O●	●O●OOO●●OO●●	MΛPR		7.4	
7	●O●OOO●●OO●●	OO●●OO●●●O●O	PΛRM		5.6	6.4
8	OO●●OO●●●OO●	●●OOO●●OOO●●	RΛMP		6.2	
9	O●●●OO●●OO●O	O●OOO●●OO●●●	M		7.2	
10	OOO●OOO●OOO●	OO●OOO●OOO●O	P		5.6	6.4
11	OOOOOOOOOOOO	●●●●●●●●●●●●	R		6.5	
12	●●OO●OOO●●O●	O●OO●●●O●O●O	RMΛMP		5.5	
13	●OOO●O●●●OO●	●●OO●●●O●OOO	MPΛPR		3.6	4.9
14	OOO●OOO●OOO●	O●●●O●●●O●●●	PRΛRM		5.5	
15	OOO●OOO●OOO●	●●O●●●O●●●O●	PR		3.9	
16	●●●O●OOO●●O●	●●●O●●●O●OOO	RM		5.7	4.4
17	●●●OOO●●OO●O	OO●O●OO●●●O●	MP		3.5	
18	O●O●O●OOO●●●	O●●O●O●OOO●●	MPR		2.7	2.7
19	OOOOOOOOOOOO	OOOOOOOOOOO●		I_1	5.9	
20	OOOOOOOOOOOO	OOOOOOOOOO●●		I_2	4.4	
21	OOOOOOOOOOOO	OOOOOOO●●●●●		I_5	3.0	
22	OOOOOOOOOOOO	O●●●●●●●●●●●	E	R_1	3.3	3.0
23	OOOOOOOOOOOO	OOO●OOO●OOO●		I_3	3.0	
24	OO●●OO●●OO●●	OOOOOOOOOOOO		I_6	1.7	
25	OO●OOO●●●O●●	O●O●●O●OO●●●		M_4	1.8	
26	●●●●●●●●●●●●	O●OO●●O●O●O●		R_6	1.2	

Fig. 11.4 1D black-white filled pattern pairs, transformational group structure, and similarity ratings. (From Amano, K., Araki, M., Okano, D., Konishi, T., Fukushi, K., Hamada, J. (2008). Effects of quasi-transformational group structures on similarity judgments of pattern pairs, IPSJ Journal, 49, 2667–2678. (Japanese text with English abstract and captions).)

The participants were 41 undergraduate students at Ehime University. They judged the similarity of the 42 pattern pairs by an 11-point scale with a minimum of 0 point and a maximum of 10. They were instructed that the similarity was a completely personal judgment, and that they were free to change the criterion if they wanted to, without worrying about consistency. After looking through the cards in random order, they conducted two sessions of rating, and only the data from the second session were analyzed. The cards were thoroughly shuffled at the beginning of each session.

11.3.2 Results and discussion

Twenty-six examples of 12-ellipse 1D black-white filled pattern pairs, the transformational group structure, and the experimental results are shown in Fig. 11.4. The mean value of similarity decreases monotonically from $M = 9.1$ for the identity transformational group structure I to $M = 3.0$ for the empty transformational group structure E. The similarity of the MPR is lower than that of E because the pattern pairs of the specific empty transformational group structure E were selected to study the Hamming's distance, as explained next. Their ordinal relations are predicted by the nine-level Hasse's diagram for similarity in Fig. 11.2, so Fig. 11.5 shows the experimental results,

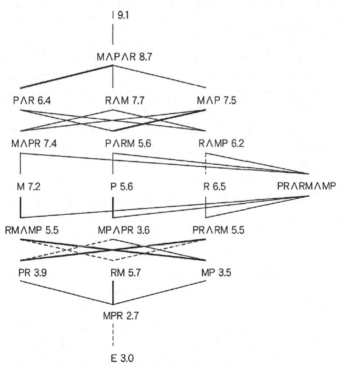

Fig. 11.5 Rated values of similarity in Hasse's diagrams for 1D black-white filled pattern pairs. *(From Amano, K., Araki, M., Okano, D., Konishi, T., Fukushi, K., Hamada, J. (2008). Effects of quasi-transformational group structures on similarity judgments of pattern pairs, IPSJ Journal, 49, 2667–2678. (Japanese text with English abstract and captions).)*

and averaged values for each transformational group structure. Here, there are no pattern pairs for PR ∧ RM ∧ MP. In this Hasse's diagram, thick solid lines indicate significant agreement with the prediction, thin solid lines indicate agreement with the prediction but not significant, and thin dotted lines indicate that the prediction is not consistent but not significant, respectively.

11.3.2.1 Hamming's distance

Note the six pattern pairs numbered 1, 11, 19, 20, 21, and 22 in Fig. 11.4. Then, the mean decreases monotonically from number 1 ($M = 9.1$), where the left and right patterns are all white, to number 19 ($M = 5.9$), where there is one black ellipse, to number 20 ($M = 4.4$), where there are two black ellipses, to number 21 ($M = 3.0$), where there are five black ellipses, and then increases at number 22 ($M = 3.3$), where there is one white ellipse. The number 11 ($M = 6.5$), where the pattern on the right side is all black ellipses, shows a large increase in similarity. Here, the number 1 is the pattern pair of the identity transformational group structure I with the same pattern on the left and right, and the number 11 is the pattern pair of the reversal transformational group structure R with all white on the left and all black on the right, and their similarity is high. The pattern pairs numbered 19, 20, 21, and 22 all have the empty transformational group structure E, and by reversing some black or white of ellipses, they become the identity transformational group structure I or the reversal transformational group structure R. The number 19 has a Hamming's distance of 1, the number 20 has the distance of 2, and the number 21 has the distance of 5, all of which result in identity transformational group structure I, and the similarity decreases monotonically in this order. On the other hand, the number 22 has a Hamming's distance of 1 and a black–white reversal transformational group structure R, and the similarity approaches the number 11. In Fig. 11.4, the numbers of underlined and subscripted number in the empty transformational group structure E indicates the Hamming's distance, which means that inverting the white or black color of the ellipse by that number will result in a transformational group structure other than E.

Next, we would like to consider the effect of Hamming's distance on the numbers 19 to 26. The similarity of Hamming's distances of 3 and 5 (i.e., numbers 23 and 21) in the pattern pairs, which result in the identity transformational group structure I is the same (i.e., 3.0), but the similarity of the five pattern pairs having I are all decreasing in the order of alignment, including this one. Similarly, for the reversal transformational group structure R, the number 26 has a longer Hamming's distance than 22 and has less similarity. Thus, the similarity of the pattern pairs of the empty transformational group structure E depends on the approaching transformational group structure and the Hamming's distance. Incidentally, the pattern pair of number 25 becomes the mirror-image transformational group structure M when the white or black colors of the four ellipses are reversed.

In Amano et al. (2008, Experiment 2), a rating experiment was also conducted using 22 8-elliptic 1D black-white filled pattern pairs, including 2 identity transformational group structures I and 20 empty transformational group structures E. The similarity of the pattern pairs, including those with Hamming's distances between 1 and 4, was analyzed in detail using Hasse's diagrams, and the similarity followed the predictions of the Hasse's diagram.

11.3.2.2 Hypothesis of order conservation

Imai (1986) proposed the following hypothesis of order conservation for similarity (or goodness). The order relation of similarity (or goodness) between transformational group structures T_1 and T_2 is also valid between multiple transformational structures $T_1 \wedge T_3$ and product transformational group structures $T_1 T_3$. Applying this hypothesis to Fig. 11.4, we first find that the mirror-image transformational group structure M ($M = 7.2$) is more similar to the phase transformational group structure P ($M = 5.6$). The order relation is also conserved between the multiple transformational group structures $R \wedge M$ ($M = 7.7$) and $P \wedge R$ ($M = 6.4$). It is also conserved between the product transformational group structures RM ($M = 5.7$) and PR ($M = 3.9$). Therefore, the experimental results support Imai's hypothesis of order conservation. In addition, according to Amano et al. (2001), the hypothesis of order conservation in similarity is generally supported. Furthermore, this hypothesis has been experimentally confirmed by Konishi et al. (2003) for goodness judgment.

11.4 Similarity of two-dimensional filled pattern pairs (Experiment 3)

11.4.1 Similarity to two-dimensional patterns

Oyama, Miyano, and Yamada (2002) and Endo, Saiki, Nakao, and Saito (2003) examined similarity and complexity using contour patterns. There, stimulus patterns were created with the aim of representing a wide variety of patterns in a unified manner with as few variables as possible, and it was shown that the degree of similarity could be expressed in terms of complexity, regularity, and curvilinearity (linearity). On the other hand, using dot patterns in 3×3 grid, Otsuka (1984) measured the similarity of 5-dot pattern pairs and showed that the similarity changes depending on the transformational structure between the patterns. Hamada (1996) created a repetitive pattern consisting of 8-dot motifs by employing the following transformations as the generators: translation, glide-reflection, reflection, 90° rotation, 180° rotation, and 360° rotation. And he found that the similarity of these patterns are defined by the group theory (see the previous chapter for details).

Tversky's (1977) feature matching theory (contrast model) is widely known for pattern similarity. In this theory, an object (pattern) is represented as a set of mutually independent features, and similarity is higher the more features are shared by the paired patterns and lower the more features are not shared. This theory has a wide range of application, and in his paper, it has been applied to various objects such as letters, figures, signals, and nations, and interesting findings have been described. However, this model assumes that the object of comparison is described as a set of features, and it may be difficult to apply it to dots pattern pairs.

Imai (1986) extended Imai's (1972, 1977b) one-dimensional filled pattern to two dimensions and showed that the similarity of 4-dot black–white filled pattern pairs in 2×2 grid followed the transformational structure theory. Here, in addition to the mirror-image, phase, and black–white reversal transformations described above, a rotational transformation was added, resulting in the pattern pairs with more possible mutual transformations became higher similarity.

In accordance with the transformational structure theory, Amano and Imai (1989) showed that the order of similarity can be predicted by adopting a transformational group as the unit of cognitive transformation. The possibility of mutual transformation by transformational groups other than the identity transformation group I (i.e., identity transformation e) was defined as the possibility of mutual agreement by transformations other than e. Shibata et al. (2002) adopted a total of five cognitive transformational groups for the similarity of black–white filled pattern pairs of $n \times n$ grid arranged on the left and right sides: in addition to the identity transformational group I, and as the unitary transformational groups there are the dihedral transformational group D, the translational transformational group P, the black–white reversal transformational group R structure. Moreover, there is the empty transformational group E. Here, (i) the identity transformation group structure I has the same pattern on both sides. In addition, (ii) the dihedral transformational group structure D is either a mirror-image transformation along the four axes or a rotational transformation of 90°, 180°, or 270°, (iii) the translation transformational group structure P translates the dots in each row or column and sequentially incorporates the dots that are out of the imaginary grid at the other end, and (iv) the black–white reversal transformational group structure R can match the left and right patterns by reversing the black and white of all dots, respectively. In addition, they also adopted the multiple transformational group structure, which indicates the possibility of mutual transformations for multiple transformational groups. For example, the case where there is both a mirror-image transformational group M and a translation transformational group P is denoted by M ∧ P. They also adopted the product transformational group structure, which indicates the possibility of transformation only when multiple different transformation groups are stacked. For example, if the possibility of a transformation is shown only when the mirror-image transformational group M and the black–white reversal transformational group R are stacked, we write MR. In the above transformational group structure, if some transformation is applied to the right or left of a pattern pair, it will match the other. However, (v) the empty transformational group structure E is the one that does not show the possibility of mutual transformation for any of these transformations.

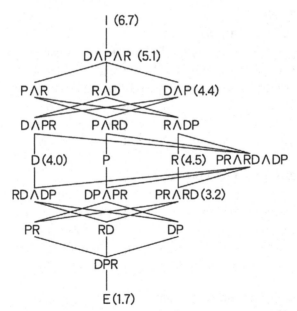

Fig. 11.6 Hasse's diagram predicting the order of similarity in an $n \times n$ black-white filled pattern (numbers are experimental results for $n = 2$). *(From Shibata, Y., Takasaki, M., Konishi, T., Okano, D., Ogata, H., Amano, K. (2002). Extension of the transformational group structure theory on similarity judgments to two-dimensional dot patterns. IPSJ Journal, 43, 4067–4070. (Japanese text with English abstract and captions).)*

They showed that similarity can be predicted by the hierarchical graph (Hasse's diagram) in Fig. 11.6. In two transformational group structures connected by a solid line in this figure, the higher structure is more likely to be mutually transformed than the lower structure, and the pattern pairs with the higher structure are predicted to be more similar than those with the lower structure. However, the order between transformational group structures that are not connected by solid lines cannot be predicted. They showed that the similarity decreases in the following order: (i) the identity transformational group structure (the left and right patterns are the same), (ii) the multiple transformational group structure (the multiple different transformation groups can be mutually transformed), (iii) the unitary transformation group structure (the different pattern pairs can be mutually transformed by an unitary transformational group), (iv) the product transformational group structure (the multiple different transformational groups can be mutually transformed by stacking them), and (v) the empty transformational group structure (the mutual transformation is impossible). In this section, Shibata et al. (2002), who used 4-dot black-white filled pattern pairs in 2 × 2 grid, will be reviewed.

11.4.2 Method

11.4.2.1 Stimulus patterns

The number of 4-dot black-white filled pattern pairs in the 2 × 2 grid used was 46. These were selected from among the existing 24 × 24 = 256 patterns so that the transformational group structure and the black-white ratio of the dots would not be biased. Seven of them are shown in Fig. 11.7. The pattern pairs are printed on a horizontal A7 card with a gray background (4 × 9 cm) and black-and-white small circles (8 mm diameter, 4 mm spacing) of equal contrast.

11.4.2.2 Participants and procedures

The participants were 43 undergraduate students at Ehime University. Before starting the experiment, they shuffled the 46 cards and looked through them. Then, they shuffled them again and rated the similarity of the pattern pairs on a 7-point integer scale. The cards were then reshuffled again for the next session, and only the data from the second session were analyzed.

11.4.3 Results and discussion

Fig. 11.7 shows examples of the transformational group structure and similarity ratings of the seven two-dimensional filled pattern pairs. The Hasse's diagram in Fig. 11.6 also shows the average ratings of all 46 pattern pairs by transformational group structure. Here, the similarity decreases as expected

No.	Pattern pair	Transformational group structure	Similarity
1	●O ●O / ●O ●O	I	6.8
2	O● ●O / ●O O●	D∧P∧R	5.1
3	●● ●O / O● ●●	D∧P	4.6
4	●● ●O / OO ●O	D	4.0
5	OO ●● / ●O O●	R	4.3
6	OO ●O / ●O ●●	PR∧RD	3.3
7	●● ●● / ●● OO	E	1.8

Fig. 11.7 Black-white filled pattern pairs and similarities in 2 × 2 grid. *(Adapted from Shibata, Y., Takasaki, M., Konishi, T., Okano, D., Ogata, H., Amano, K. (2002). Extension of the transformational group structure theory on similarity judgments to two-dimensional dot patterns. IPSJ Journal, 43, 4067–4070. (Japanese text with English abstract and captions).)*

in the order of (i) the identity transformational group structure, (ii) the multiple transformation group structure, (iii) the unitary transformational group structure, (iv) the product transformational group structure, and (v) the empty transformational group structure. Note that the order of similarity ($M = 4.0$ and 4.5) of the pattern pairs with the unitary transformational group structure of dihedral transformational group structure D and the black-white reversal transformational group structure R is not predicted by the Hasse's diagram. There were all significant differences between the means for the comparable transformation group structures in this Hasse's diagram. That is, there were significant differences between D ∧ P ∧ R and D ∧ P ($M = 5.1$ and 4.4), between D ∧ P and D ($M = 4.4$ and 4.0), and even between R and PR ∧ RD ($M = 4.5$ and 3.2).

The use of 4-dot black-white pattern pairs of 2×2 grid in this experiment has the advantage of enabling systematic selection of pattern pairs, but at the same time, it has the disadvantage of limiting the number of transformational group structures that appear. For example, the translational group structures P of the unitary transformational group structure does not appear. On the other hand, 11 transformational group structures including P appear when 9-dot black-white pattern pairs with 3×3 grid are used, and all 20 transformational group structures appear when 16-dot black-white pattern pairs with 4×4 grid are used. Konishi, Okano, and Amano (2008) studied in detail the similarity of 37 pattern pairs with 20 transformational group structures using a 4×4 grid 16-dot black-white filled pattern pairs.

11.5 Goodness of one-dimensional patterns (Experiment 4)

In this section, the goodness of 1D black-white filled patterns consisting of ellipses by Amano et al. (2013, Experiment 1) will be reviewed.

11.5.1 Stimulus patterns and procedures

Fig. 11.8 shows all 28 stimulus patterns used, the transformational group structure, and the results of the rating. The stimulus pattern was eight black-white ellipse (8 mm long and 6 mm short) with a gray background area (7.5×3.5 cm) printed on a horizontal A7 sheet of card.

The participants were 36 undergraduate students at Ehime University. They rated the goodness of the 28 patterns on a 7-point integer scale. They were instructed that goodness was a completely personal judgment and that they were free to change the criteria if they wanted to, without worrying about consistency. After looking through the cards in random order, they performed two sessions of rating, and only the data from the second session were analyzed. The cards were thoroughly shuffled at the beginning of each session.

11.5.2 Results and discussion

According to Fig. 11.8, the goodness ratings generally decrease monotonically from the multiple transformation group structure M ∧ P ($M = 5.9$) to the product transformational group structure MPR ($M = 2.8$), although there are deviations in the phase transformational group structure P ($M = 4.3$) and the multiple transformational group structure PR ∧ MP

No.	Pattern	Transformational group structure		Goodness	
1		M∧P		5.7	5.9
2				6.1	
3		M∧PR		6.0	5.8
4				5.6	
5		P∧RM		5.3	5.7
6				6.0	
7		M		5.8	5.9
8				6.0	
9		P		3.6	4.3
10				5.0	
11		MP∧RM∧PR		6.3	5.0
12				3.8	
13		PR∧MP		2.7	2.6
14				2.6	
15		RM		4.2	4.0
16				3.8	
17		MP		2.8	2.9
18				3.1	
19		MPR		3.1	2.8
20				2.6	
21		E	(M∧P)₁	2.6	2.9
22				3.2	
23			(M∧PR)₁	2.5	2.6
24				2.7	
25			(P∧RM)₁	2.4	2.5
26				2.5	
27			(MP∧RM∧PR)₁	2.4	2.3
28				2.1	

Fig. 11.8 1D black-white filled patterns, transformational group structure, and goodness ratings. *(From Amano, K., Ooya, T., Araki, S., Osanai, T., Endo, K., Okano, D., et al. (2013). Effects of quasi-transformational group structures on goodness judgments of patterns. IPSJ Journal, 54, 2254–2264. (Japanese text with English abstract and captions).)*

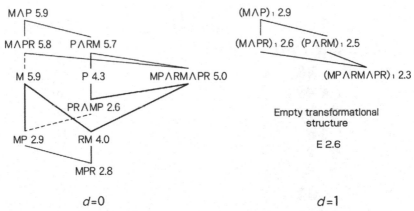

$d=0$ $d=1$

Fig. 11.9 Hasse's diagram and goodness rating values. *(From Amano, K., Ooya, T., Araki, S., Osanai, T., Endo, K., Okano, D., et al. (2013). Effects of quasi-transformational group structures on goodness judgments of patterns.* IPSJ Journal, *54, 2254–2264. (Japanese text with English abstract and captions).)*

($M = 2.6$), which consists of the product transformational group structures where P is involved. And the goodness of the empty transformational group structure E decreases monotonically from (M ∧ P)$_1$ to (MP ∧ RM ∧ PR)$_1$ without exception, consistent with the prediction of the transformational group structure and Hamming's distance above-mentioned. Here, the underline of the ellipse and the subscript 1 of the transformational group structure mean that reversing one of the black or white color of that ellipse will result in the transformation group structure in parentheses, which is not the empty transformational group structure E. Therefore, the Hamming's distance for these structures is 1. The rating results are predicted by a seven-level Hasse's diagram for goodness (Fig. 11.3), and the mean values are shown in Fig. 11.9. Again, thick solid lines indicate that the predictions are significant and consistent, thin solid lines indicate that the predictions are consistent but not significant, and thin dotted lines indicate that the predictions are not consistent but not significant. This result indicates that goodness follows the transformational group structure theory.

In Amano et al. (2013, Experiment 2), a rating experiment was also conducted using 35 12-elliptic 1D black-white filled patterns, including 24 empty transformational group structures E. There, the Hamming's distance was set to 1 and 2, and the relationship with goodness was analyzed in detail, and goodness followed the prediction of the Hasse's diagram.

PART FOUR

Size of a circle in geometrical illusions

CHAPTER TWELVE

The Ebbinghaus illusion as a circle size contrast

Geometric illusions have been published as psychological papers since the middle of the 19th century (Oppel, 1855). Goto and Tanaka (2005) describe the recent research on the illusion in detail. In Part 4, we would like to discuss the studies on the size illusion starting from Obonai (1933, 1955) and Morinaga (1935, 1969) and others (Morinaga, 1959; Oyama, 1960; Ehrenstein & Hamada, 1995; Noguchi, Kitaoka, & Takashima, 2008; Shiina & Oyama, 2008) in Japan. A typical example of the size illusion is the Ebbinghaus illusion shown in Fig. 12.1 (Wundt, 1898; Titchener, 1901; Ebbinghaus, 1908). Compared to the single circle (a) in the control condition, the central circle in (b) and (c) appears larger in the former and smaller in the latter, resulting in a size contrast. However, when the peripheral large circle in (c) is divided and only the neighboring area is left as in (d), the central circle clearly appears larger than in (c) due to size assimilation. The central circle in (e), which is complementary to (d), appears to be almost the same size as that in (c), and the contrast remains. Morinaga (1959, 1969) discovered Morinaga's paradox Type III by decomposing the peripheral large circles of the Ebbinghaus pattern (c) into the complementary (d) and (e) as shown in Fig. 12.1 (Noguchi, 1982; Noguchi et al., 2008).

Fig. 12.2B shows the complementary division of the peripheral circles of the Ebbinghaus pattern, extracted from Morinaga (1969). The central circle of the small arc (left) appears to be larger than that of the large arc (right), though they have the same diameter. This Morinaga's paradox Type III remains in (A), where the 60° arc in (B) is enlarged to 120°, and in (C), where the distance between the circumferences of (B) is increased by a factor of 5. Morinaga's paradox remains in these three figures. However, when these patterns are tilted by 45°, the appearance changes. In other words, the paradox remains in (b), but it is not clear in (a) and (c). This visual phenomenological method has its limitations and needs to be examined by psychophysical experiments. In the next section, we will examine the effects of the distance between the circumferences and the tilt angle on the illusion in the Ebbinghaus pattern, putting aside Morinaga's paradox Type III.

Psychophysics and Experimental Phenomenology of Pattern Cognition
https://doi.org/10.1016/B978-0-323-95286-6.00012-0

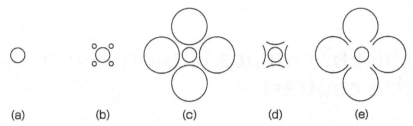

(a)   (b)   (c)   (d)   (e)

Fig. 12.1 The Ebbinghaus illusion (b and c) and Morinaga's paradox Type III (c–e). (a) is a control condition. *(Adapted from Hamada, J. (2020). Psychophysics of pattern cognition. Tokyo: Kazama Press (Japanese text) and Morinaga, S. (1969). Perceptional psychology. Tokyo: Meigen Press (Japanese, German, and English texts).)*

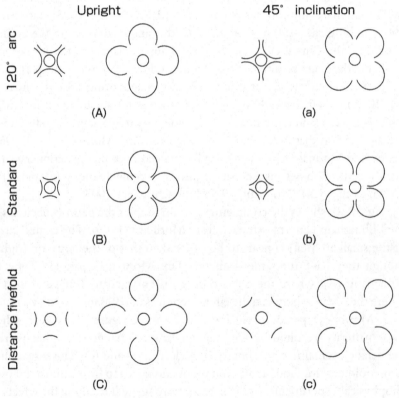

Fig. 12.2 Modification of Morinaga's paradox Type III in the Ebbinghaus illusion (A–C, and a–c).

12.1 Rotation angle and distance between the circumference of large, small, and mixed circles (Experiment 1)

Fig. 12.3 shows Ebbinghaus patterns consisting of surrounding large circles, surrounding small circles, and mixed circles. Kuroda and Noguchi (1984) and Ehrenstein and Hamada (1995) devised the mixed circles independently (Shulman, 1992). These central circles appear to be different in size even though they are all the same in diameter. In this illusion, the surrounding circles induce underestimation or overestimation of the central circle (Obonai, 1954; Morinaga & Noguchi, 1966; Massaro & Anderson, 1971). In this section, Ehrenstein and Hamada (1995, Experiment 1) will be reviewed.

Mach (1918) and Rock (1974) reported that the apparent size of a square is different when it is tilted 45° to form a diamond. Therefore, we will compare the amount of illusion when the surrounding circles are placed vertically and horizontally, and when they are tilt-rotated by 45°. In other words, we will examine the anisotropy of the geometric illusion. The effect of the distance between the circumferences on the strength of the illusion will also be examined.

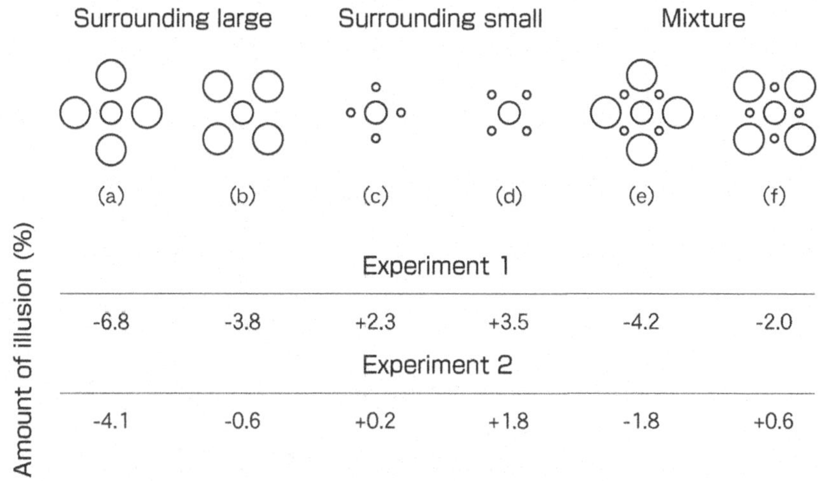

	Surrounding large		Surrounding small		Mixture	
	(a)	(b)	(c)	(d)	(e)	(f)
Experiment 1						
	-6.8	-3.8	+2.3	+3.5	-4.2	-2.0
Experiment 2						
	-4.1	-0.6	+0.2	+1.8	-1.8	+0.6

Amount of illusion (%)

Fig. 12.3 Examples of the Ebbinghaus patterns used in Experiments 1 and 2 (a–f). The *lower panel* shows the amount of illusion (%) when the distance between the circumferences of the central and surrounding circles is 1.6 mm. *(From Ehrenstein, W.H., & Hamada, J. (1995). Structural factors of size contrast in the Ebbinghaus illusion. Japanese Psychological Research, 37, 158–169.)*

12.1.1 Method

12.1.1.1 Stimulus pattern

As shown in Fig. 12.3, the Ebbinghaus patterns (hereafter abbreviated as standard patterns) used had vertical horizontal directions (a, c, and e), 45° inclined directions (b, d, and f), and three different distance between the circumferences of the central and surrounding circles (1.6, 4.8, and 8.0 mm). In addition, one single circle was used as a control condition with no surrounding circles. The stimuli used were six standard patterns, three distances, and one single circle, for a total of 19 types. To measure the subjective size of the central circle in the 19 patterns relative to the comparison circle by the constant method, we used the standard pattern and the comparison circle illustrated in Fig. 12.4.

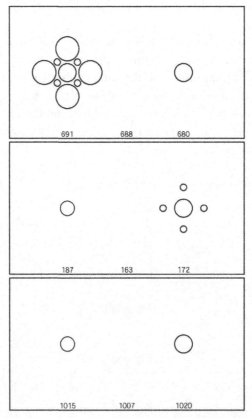

Fig. 12.4 Examples of the stimulus cards used in Experiment 1. The mixed circle is on the left and the comparison circle is on the *right (top panel)*, the surrounding small circle is on the right and the comparison circle is on the *left (middle panel)*, and the single circle is on the right and the comparison circle is on the *left (bottom panel)*. *(From Ehrenstein, W.H., & Hamada, J. (1995). Structural factors of size contrast in the Ebbinghaus illusion. Japanese Psychological Research, 37, 158–169.)*

The diameter of the single circle in the control condition and the central circle of the standard pattern was 9.5 mm, that of the surrounding small circle was 3.6 mm, and that of surrounding large circle was 13.1 mm. The number of comparison circles was nine (7.2, 7.7, 8.3, 8.9, 9.5, 10.2, 10.9, 11.7, and 12.5 mm), since the diameter was varied by 0.03 logarithmic units. The standard pattern was placed on the left or right side of the card, while the comparison circle was placed on the other side. The distance between the centers of the standard pattern and the comparison circle was 65 mm. The stimulus pattern was printed on a thick white card (7 × 13 cm) with black lines about 0.3 mm thick.

12.1.1.2 Participants and procedures

Ninety-six undergraduate students at Tokushima University participated in the experiment as groups. The participants were divided into six groups of 16 students each, that is, 3 (distance between the circumferences) × 2 (standard pattern on the left or right side). They looked through all $(3 \times 2 + 1) \times 9 = 63$ cards to get an overview of the patterns prior to the experiment. After a practice trial with 10 cards, they conducted two sessions. At the beginning of each session, they shuffled the cards. Their task was to determine, by pairwise comparison, whether the central circle of the standard and the single circles or the comparison circle was larger. In other words, on the response sheet they wrote the number directly below the circle that they felt was "larger". However, if the size of the two circles was felt to be "the same", the number in the middle was entered on it (see Fig. 12.4). The observation distance was the reading distance. The experiment was conducted at the participant's own pace, and no time constraints were imposed.

12.1.2 Results

The average of the upper and lower thresholds by the constant method was used as the point of subjective equality. Since the points of subjective equality not only in the standard pattern on the left and right sides but also in the first and second sessions showed a similar trend, these values were combined for analysis. In the control condition, the point of subjective equality for a single circle with a diameter of 9.5 mm was 9.77 mm, indicating overestimation. Then, the amount of illusion is defined as follows, based on the size of the single circle. In other words, the amount of illusion $(\%) = 100 \ (E - C)/C$. Here, E and C are the point of subjective equality of the center circle of the standard pattern and the single circle (i.e., 9.77 mm), respectively. The amount of illusion (%) as a function of the distance between the circumferences is shown in Fig. 12.5. Negative value indicates underestimation and positive values indicate

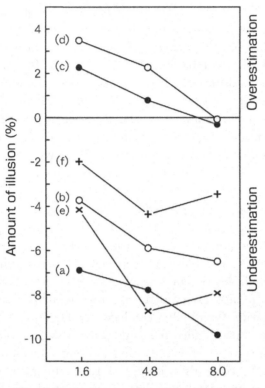

Fig. 12.5 The amount of illusion as a function of the distance between the circumferences. (a)–(f) correspond to Fig. 12.3. *(From Hamada, J. (2020). Psychophysics of pattern
cognition. Tokyo: Kazama Press (Japanese text); adapted from Ehrenstein, W.H., &
Hamada, J. (1995). Structural factors of size contrast in the Ebbinghaus illusion.* Japanese
Psychological Research, 37, 158–169.)

overestimation, meaning that the circle appears to be smaller and larger than that
of a single circle, respectively. When the distance between the circumferences is
short (i.e., 1.6 mm), the overestimation appears in the surrounding small circles
and the underestimation in the surrounding large circles. However, when the
distance is moderate (i.e., 4.8 mm), the underestimation in the large surrounding circles (a and b) is stronger than the overestimation in the small surrounding circles (c and d). As the distance increases (i.e., 8.0 mm), the
overestimation of the surrounding small circles disappears, and conversely,
the underestimation of the surrounding large circles increases. The mixed circle has a V-shape with respect to the distance expansion. Thus, the
Ebbinghaus size illusion depends on the distance between the circumferences.

When the three distances between the circumferences were averaged, the illusion was stronger in the vertical-horizontal direction (Fig. 12.3a: $M = -8.1\%$) than in the inclined direction (Fig. 12.3b: $M = -5.4\%$) in the large circle, while in the small circle, the illusion was stronger in the inclined direction (Fig. 12.3d: $M = +1.9\%$) than in the vertical-horizontal direction (Fig. 12.3c: $M = +0.9\%$). Averaged over the three distances between the circumferences and two orientations, the surrounding large circle and the mixed circle are underestimated, with average values of $M = -6.8$ and $M = -5.1\%$, respectively. On the other hand, the surrounding small circle is overestimated with $M = +1.4\%$.

12.1.3 Discussion

12.1.3.1 Control condition
The point of subjective equality for a single circle with a diameter of 9.5 mm was 9.77 mm, resulting in overestimation. The overestimation occurred even when the single circle was placed on the left or the right side, so it was not caused by the spatial error caused by the difference in placement. This overestimation may indicate an adaptation effect of fixing the diameter of not only the single circle, but also the center circle of the standard pattern to 9.5 mm and using it for all 63 cards.

12.1.3.2 The Ebbinghaus illusion
In the direction of the surrounding circles, the underestimation is larger in the vertical-horizontal direction (a) than in the 45° inclined direction (b). However, in the small circle, the overestimation is larger in the direction of 45° tilt (d) than in the vertical-horizontal direction (c). This feature appears in all distance conditions. This effect of the orientation, that is, the anisotropy of the geometric illusion, will be experimentally investigated in detail in the next Experiment 2.

As shown in Fig. 12.5, in the small circles the effect of the distance between the circumferences on the overestimation decreases as a function of distance and disappears at a distance of 8.0 mm. On the other hand, in the large circles, the underestimation increases as the distance increases. Thus, as the distance between the circumferences increases, the overestimation becomes stronger at short distances and weaker at long distances in the case of surrounding small circles. However, underestimation relatively is weaker at short distances for large circles and stronger at long distances. These trends are consistent with the results of Girgus, Coren, and Agdern (1972), Goto (1987), and Goto and Ohya (1989). In the large surrounding circles, the illusion may disappear when the distance is further increased. In the mixed circles, the underestimation is maximum at the distance of 4.8 mm between the circumferences and it exhibits a V-shape. If the distance is increased, the underestimation may become zero, as in the case of the large circle. These effects of the distance between the circumferences should be investigated in the future.

Finally, we would like to consider the counteracting effect of over- and under-estimation in mixed circles. When we averaged over the three distances between the circumferences in Fig. 12.5, the underestimation by the large surrounding circles ($M = -6.8\%$ for a and b) is stronger than the overestimation by the small surrounding circles ($M = +1.4\%$ for c and d). The average illusion in the mixed circles (e and f) is $M = -5.1\%$, which is almost the same as the sum of the illusions in the large and small circles ($M = -5.4\%$). Thus, in the mixed circles, the underestimation of the large circles and the overestimation of the small circles cancel each other out. This result is consistent with the report by Kuroda and Noguchi (1984) and Noguchi (2001, 2003, 2005) that the strength of the mixed circle illusion is due to the offset between under-estimation of the surrounding large circle and overestimation of the surrounding small circle, using the Ebbinghaus pattern corresponding to Fig. 12.3b, c, f. However, in this experiment, as shown in Fig. 12.5, the amount of the illusion as a function of the distance between the circumferences was monotonous for the surrounding large circles and the surrounding small ones, but V-shaped for the mixed ones. This suggests that there is not only an effect from the surrounding circles to the central circle but also an interaction between the surrounding large and small circles in the mixed circles.

12.2 Anisotropy of the Ebbinghaus illusion (Experiment 2)

In the previous experiment, the stimulus pattern was drawn in black on a white card, and the presentation time was not controlled, so the participants judged the size of the patterns at their own pace. In Experiment 2, we used a computer screen and fixed the presentation time of the pattern to one second. In this section, Ehrenstein and Hamada (1995, Experiment 2) will be reviewed.

12.2.1 Method
12.2.1.1 Stimulus patterns
The shape and size of the stimulus pattern on the computer screen (NEC-5924) were the same as in Experiment 1. However, in Experiment 2, the

polarity of black and white was reversed, and white circles were drawn on a light-free background. The luminance of the white circle was 47.5 cd/m^2 and that of the light-free background was 1.2 cd/m^2. The Ebbinghaus patterns (hereafter abbreviated as standard patterns) are Fig. 12.3a, c and e, and they are set in six directions of right rotation (0°, 15°, 30°, 45°, 60°, and 75°). The patterns for angle 45° are Fig. 12.3b, d and f. The patterns for angles 15° and 75° and for angles 30° and 60° are the same. The distance between the circumferences was 1.6 mm, the same as the minimum distance in Experiment 1. The stimuli used were three standard patterns, six directions, and one single circle, for a total of 19 types. There were 9 comparison circles as in Experiment 1, and the positions of the standard patterns and comparison circles were on the right and left sides. Thus, a total of 342 stimulus pairs were used.

12.2.1.2 Participants and procedures

Participants were eight undergraduate students at Tokushima University who participated in the experiment individually. They judged the size of the circles by pairwise comparisons based on the constant method as in Experiment 1. One second after the participant pressed a key on the computer, the standard pattern and the comparison circle were presented simultaneously for one second. They verbally reported whether the right or left side appeared to be larger for the central circle of the standard pattern and the single circle as a control condition comparing to the comparison circle. However, if they appeared to be the same size as the comparison circles, the participants reported that they were the same. The experimenter then marked it on a response sheet. The participant's head was fixed on a chin rest, and the viewing distance was 40 cm. The duration of one session was about 15 min. Each participant repeated four sessions on different days.

12.2.2 Results and discussion

Regardless of whether the single circle was on the right or left side, its point of subjective equality was higher than its actual size (9.5 mm in diameter) as in Experiment 1, so the amount of illusion (%) was calculated and analyzed. Fig. 12.6 shows it as a function of the rotation angle of the standard pattern. According to the results, surrounding small circles show overestimation, surrounding large ones show underestimation, and mixed ones are located in the middle of them. In all patterns, the amount of the illusion tends to increase as the rotation angle increases. In other words, the anisotropy of the geometrical illusion appears.

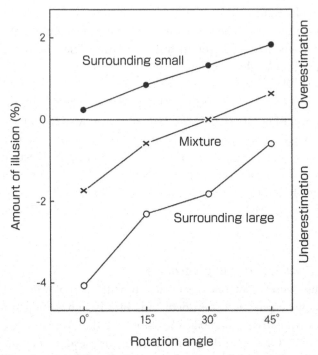

Fig. 12.6 The amount of the illusion as a function of the rotation angle of the Ebbinghaus pattern (Fig. 12.3a, c and e). *(From Hamada, J. (2020). Psychophysics of pattern cognition. Tokyo: Kazama Press (Japanese text); adapted from Ehrenstein, W.H., & Hamada, J. (1995). Structural factors of size contrast in the Ebbinghaus illusion. Japanese Psychological Research, 37, 158–169.)*

In the bottom panel of Fig. 12.3, there was a significant correlation between the amounts of illusion (%) obtained in Experiment 1, in which the cards were used, and Experiment 2, in which the face was fixed and the pattern was presented on the computer screen. Therefore, the method using cards in Experiment 1 is highly reliable. Here, the former shows a stronger illusion than the latter. Next, we discuss the presentation time of the Ebbinghaus pattern in both experiments. The difference between the above two experiments may be due to the fact the presentation time of both standard and comparison patterns were simultaneously limited to 1 s in Experiment 2, but in Experiment 1 they were judged with no time limit. Therefore, it is necessary to experimentally and theoretically investigate the nature of the Ebbinghaus illusion by changing the presentation time of the stimuli in the future.

CHAPTER THIRTEEN

The Delboeuf illusion by comparative judgments

13.1 Examination by method of limits

The outer circle in the left (a) and the inner one in the right (b) of Fig. 13.1 appear to be different, although they are the same in diameter. The inner circle in the left (a) towed the outer one and causes underestimation, whereas the outer circle in the right (b) towed the inner one and causes overestimation, resulting in size assimilation. This size illusion is called the Delboeuf illusion (Delboeuf, 1865; Oyama, 1970; Robinson, 1972).

Morinaga (1935) and Ogasawara (1952) examined the Delboeuf illusion by the method of limits with the comparison circles and concentric ones shown in Fig. 13.2. For example, Ogasawara measured the amount of the illusion by comparing the apparent size of the inner and outer circles of the concentric circles with that of the comparison ones. In the stimulus series for measuring the inner circle, the diameter of the inner circle was fixed at three large, medium, and small diameters (60, 40, and 20 mm, respectively), and the diameter of the outer circle was sequentially varied to measure the diameter of the comparison circle that matched the apparent size of the inner circle. In the same way, in the stimulus series for measuring the outer circle, the diameter of the outer circle was fixed at three different sizes (80, 60, and 40 mm, respectively), and the diameter of the inner circle was sequentially changed to measure the amount of the outer circle illusion. The observation distance was about 90 cm. As shown by the dashed line in Fig. 13.3, the inner circle was overestimated and the outer circle was underestimated. Moreover, the overestimation and underestimation were both maximized when the diameter ratio of the inner circle to the outer one was about 2:3. This diameter ratio is consistent with the findings of Morinaga (1935). According to the method of limits using concentric and comparison circles, the Delboeuf illusion depends on the diameter ratio

Psychophysics and Experimental Phenomenology of Pattern Cognition Copyright © 2023 Elsevier Inc.
https://doi.org/10.1016/B978-0-323-95286-6.00013-2

of the inner and outer circles, causing overestimation of the inner circle and underestimation of the outer one, resulting in size assimilation.

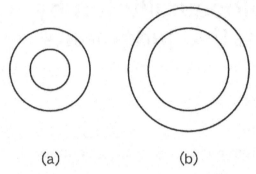

(a)   (b)

Fig. 13.1 The Delboeuf illusion (a and b). *(From Hamada, J. (2005). Size-illusion of Delboef (Concentric circle illusion). In T. Goto, & H. Tanaka. (Eds.),* Handbook of the science of illusion *(pp. 126–135). Tokyo: Tokyo University Press (Japanese text).)*

Comparison   Concentric
circle   circle

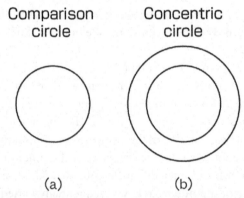

(a)   (b)

Fig. 13.2 Comparison and concentric circles for measuring the Delboeuf illusion (a and b). *(From Hamada, J. (2005). Size-illusion of Delboef (Concentric circle illusion). In T. Goto, & H. Tanaka. (Eds.),* Handbook of the science of illusion *(pp. 126–135). Tokyo: Tokyo University Press (Japanese text).)*

13.2 Examination by constant method

In this section, the Delboeuf illusion measured by Hamada (2002) using card-based free-viewing tasks and the constant method will be reviewed, referring to a part of the results of Ogasawara (1952) by the method of limits.

13.2.1 Method
13.2.1.1 Stimulus patterns and procedures
A stimulus pattern was printed on a thick white card (83 mm long × 150 mm wide) with black lines of approximately 0.3 mm. Concentric circles with a

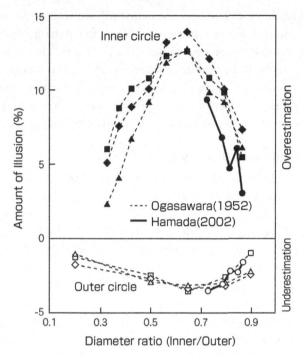

Fig. 13.3 Overestimation and underestimation in the Delboeuf illusion by the method of limits *(dotted lines)* and the constant method *(solid lines). (From Hamada, J. (2002). Examination of Delboef illusion by magnitude estimation and constant method. In: Proceedings of the 66th annual convention of Japanese Psychological Association, 442. (Japanese text).)*

small diameter difference ($\Delta d = 5.5\,\text{mm}$) were used, with five different combinations of inner and outer diameters (mm): (36.8:42.3), (31.3:36.8), (25.8:31.3), (20.3:25.8), and (14.8:20.3). In addition, eight single circles were used. The comparison circle was placed on the left side, and the concentric and single ones were placed on the right. The distance between their centers was 70 mm. A small random pattern number was marked directly below each circle.

The participants were 40 undergraduate students at Tokushima University, and the experiment was conducted in two groups. Half of the participants (20) were randomly assigned to the inner circle judgment condition, and the other half were assigned to the outer circle judgment condition. Eight comparison circles for five types of concentric ones were used in each condition. In addition, seven comparison circles were used to five single circles for the inner or outer circles. The number of cards distributed was

75 for each participant. They observed the cards at a reading distance by bin-ocular free vision. Two sessions were repeated after 10 trials of practice. The cards were shuffled at the beginning of each session. They compared the apparent size of the inner or outer concentric circle and the single circle with that of the comparison circle. They then wrote the pattern number of the circle that appeared larger on the response paper at their own pace. They were not allowed to answer that they look the same size.

13.2.2 Results and discussion

The point of subjective equality was defined as the diameter of the compar-ison circle where the inner or outer circle was judged to be 50% larger than the comparison one. The amount of illusion was calculated by the following formula: The amount of illusion (%) $= 100(E_i - C_i)/C_i$. E_i is the measured value for an inner or outer circle with diameter i ($i = 1, 2, ..., 5$), and C_i is the measured value for a single circle with the same diameter. The amount of the illusion by the constant method is shown by the solid lines in Fig. 13.3. According to the results, overestimation occurs in the inner circle, and it becomes stronger as the diameter ratio decreases. In the outer circle, under-estimation occurs, and it becomes stronger as the diameter ratio decreases. Although not measured in this experiment, it is likely that if the diameter ratio is further reduced, the amount of illusion would be maximized at 2:3.

As shown in Fig. 13.3, the results obtained by the method of limits (dashed lines) of Ogasawara (1952) and the constant method (solid line) of Hamada (2002) are in good agreement. In particular, the outer circle shows almost perfect agreement. Thus, in the comparative judgment by the method of limits and the constant method, the Delboeuf illusion results in overestimation, where the outer circle tows the inner one, and underes-timation, where the inner circle tows the outer one, resulting in size assim-ilation. The agreement between the results of the two methods indicates that the method of card-based free-viewing tasks is highly reliable.

CHAPTER FOURTEEN

Concentric circle illusion and judgment-order effect by absolute judgments

As reported in the previous chapter, according to comparative judgment, the outer circle surrounding the small circle is smaller than the inner circle placed by the large one (see Fig. 13.1). Here, the diameter of the former is the same as that of the latter, and size assimilation appears. On the other hand, Hamada, Paramei, and Ehrenstein (2000), Hamada, Nisimura, Paramei, and Ehrenstein (2002), Hamada (2005), and Kawahara, Nabeta, and Hamada (2007) made absolute judgments of the sizes of the inner and outer circles of concentric circles by numerals without using comparison circles. As a result, the appearance of the size differed greatly between comparative and absolute judgments. Furthermore, in absolute judgment, the size illusion differed depending on whether the inner circle or the outer one was judged first or second, and a judgment-order effect appeared. We distinguish between the illusion of comparative judgment and that of the absolute one and call the former the Delboeuf illusion and the latter the concentric circles illusion.

In comparative judgments, when the concentric and the comparison circles are presented simultaneously, participants will compare the apparent sizes of these circles with each other. Therefore, some interaction between the two circles may occur. Therefore, Hamada et al. (2000), Hamada et al. (2002), Paramei, Hamada, and Ehrenstein (2003), and Ehrenstein, Hamada, and Paramei (2004) avoided this interaction by using Helson's (1964) category rating method and Stevens' (1961) magnitude estimation method (Aiba, 1970; Guirao, 1991), which do not use comparative circles but instead use numerals, to examine the concentric circles illusion. In this chapter, Hamada et al. (2000) and Hamada (2005) will be reviewed.

14.1 Examination by absolute judgment methods
14.1.1 Method

14.1.1.1 Stimulus pattern

The concentric circles consisted of seven circles ranging from 12.0 to 45.0 mm in diameter, with intervals from 5.5 to 33.0 mm. A total of 21 concentric circles and seven single circles were used for a total of 28 stimulus patterns as shown in Fig. 14.1. The diameter ratios of the inner and outer circles of these concentric ones ranged from 0.27 to 0.88. The diameters of the outer circle in each row and the inner one in each column are all the same. The diameters of the concentric circles along the diagonal axis from the lower left to the upper right are the same. The smallest diameter difference ($\Delta d = 5.5$ mm) is the same as that used in the constant method in the previous chapter. Each stimulus

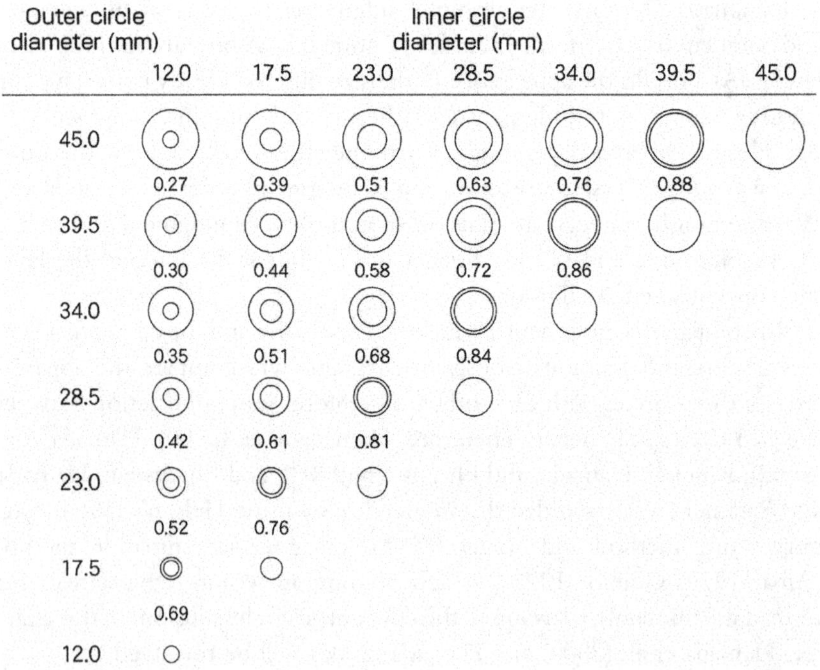

Outer circle diameter (mm)	Inner circle diameter (mm)						
	12.0	17.5	23.0	28.5	34.0	39.5	45.0
45.0	0.27	0.39	0.51	0.63	0.76	0.88	
39.5	0.30	0.44	0.58	0.72	0.86		
34.0	0.35	0.51	0.68	0.84			
28.5	0.42	0.61	0.81				
23.0	0.52	0.76					
17.5	0.69						
12.0							

Fig. 14.1 Concentric and single circles used. Seven types of circles with isometrically different diameters are combined. (*From Hamada, J., Paramei, G.V., & Ehrenstein, W.H. (2000) Judgment-order effect on apparent size in the Delboeuf illusion.* Journal of Human Science, Faculty of Integrated Arts and Sciences, Tokushima University, 8, *1–13. (Japanese text with English abstract and captions).)*

pattern was printed on the center of a thick white card (83 mm long × 80 mm wide) with a black line about 0.3 mm thick, and the pattern number was written at the bottom center. A total of 56 cards, two of each stimulus pattern, were used to obtain two ratings in one experiment.

Participants and procedures. Undergraduate students at Tokushima University participated in the experiments as groups for three conditions. They observed the cards at a reading distance under binocular-free vision and the free-viewing tasks. Assuming an observation distance of 30 cm, the diameters of the smallest and largest circles, 12 mm and 45 mm, corresponded to visual angles of 2.3° and 8.5°. Their task was to make absolute judgments about the apparent size of inner or outer circle and single circle and to assign small integers to circles that appeared small and large ones to circles that appeared large. In the category rating method, integers from 1 to 7 or from 1 to 11 were applied. Participants were not instructed to use all integers from 1 to 7 for the former or from 1 to 11 for the latter. In the magnitude estimation method, positive integers except for 0 were applied. In these experiments, participants were not taught the criteria for judgment; they were free to set them.

There were 66 participants for the 7-category rating and 76 for the 11-category, and 78 for the magnitude estimation. They participated in the experiments as three different groups without overlap. They were randomly assigned to the inner circle prior and the outer circle prior conditions. The number of participants in each condition was an even number. In the inner-circle condition, the participants filled out the response sheet in the order of inner circle to outer one. In the outer-circle condition, the order was reversed, from the outer circle to the inner one. To get a general outline of the cards prior to the experiment, they went through all the cards. They wrote the pattern number on the response sheet and then wrote two ratings for the inner or outer circle for concentric circles and one rating for a single circle. These tasks were carried out one card at a time at a self-paced pace. The cards were well shuffled at the beginning of the experimental session; three sessions were repeated, and the average of the data from the second and third sessions was analyzed.

14.1.2 Results and discussion

In order to examine the apparent size of single circles and inner/outer circles, the amount of illusion was calculated for each participant by the following

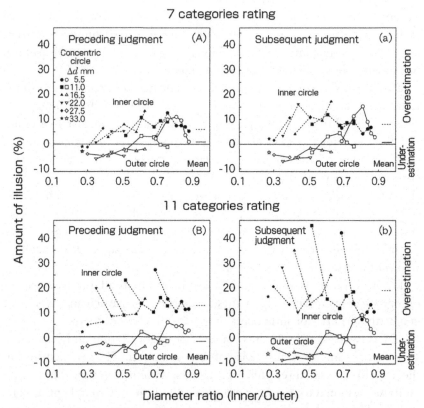

Fig. 14.2 The amount of the concentric circle illusion as a function of the diameter ratio by the category raring method. *(From Hamada, J., Paramei, G.V., & Ehrenstein, W.H. (2000) Judgment-order effect on apparent size in the Delboeuf illusion.* Journal of Human Science, Faculty of Integrated Arts and Sciences, Tokushima University, 8, 1–13. *(Japanese text with English abstract and captions) for (A and a); Hamada, J. (2005). Size-illusion of Delboef (concentric circle illusion). In: T. Goto & H. Tanaka (Eds.),* Handbook of the science of illusion *(pp. 126–135). Tokyo: Tokyo University Press. (Japanese text) for (B and b).)*

formula: The amount of illusion (%) $= 100\,(E_i - C_i)/C_i$. E_i is the rated value for an inner or outer circle with diameter i ($i = 1, 2, …, 6$), and C_i is the rated value for a single circle with the same diameter ($i = 1, 2, …, 7$). Figs. 14.2 and 14.3 show the mean amount of illusions (%) of all participants for 21 inner and outer circles as a function of the diameter ratio of the inner and outer circles. The former is the result of the category grading method (7 and 11 categories), and the latter is the result of the magnitude estimation method. In both figures, the left panel shows the amount of the illusion for the preceding judgment and the right for the subsequent one. The inner circles are indicated by dotted lines with solid symbols, and the outer ones are indicated by solid lines

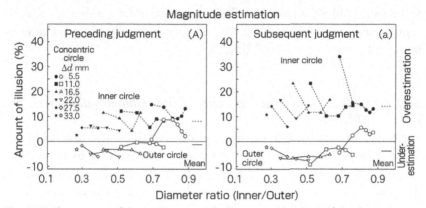

Fig. 14.3 The amount of the concentric circle illusion as a function of the diameter ratio by the magnitude estimation method (A and a). *(From Hamada, J., Paramei, G.V., & Ehrenstein, W.H. (2000) Judgment-order effect on apparent size in the Delboeuf illusion. Journal of Human Science, Faculty of Integrated Arts and Sciences, Tokushima University, 8, 1–13. (Japanese text with English abstract and captions).)*

with open symbols. The diameter difference between the inner and outer circles is indicated by Δd. The short horizontal lines at the rightmost of each panel are the mean values of the 21 inner and outer circles.

14.1.2.1 The concentric circle illusion in preceding judgment

As shown in the left panels of Figs. 14.2 and 14.3, according to the category grading method and the magnitude estimation one, the amount of the preceding illusion depends on the diameter difference. In other words, the preceding judgment of the inner circle shows overestimation, resulting in size assimilation to the outer one. On the other hand, for the outer circle, when the diameter difference is relatively large, underestimation relative to the inner one occurs, and assimilation occurs. However, at the six prepared minimum diameter differences of $\Delta d = 5.5$ mm, overestimation, not underestimation, occurs. When the overestimation of the outer circle was tested by including the six values, significant differences were found in both the category grading method (7 and 11 categories) and the magnitude estimation one. Thus, at the minimum diameter difference of $\Delta d = 5.5$ mm, the overestimation appears in both the outer and inner circles, resulting in the expansion of the entire concentric circle. This expansion tends to occur even when the diameter difference $\Delta d = 11.0$ mm in the 7-category rating. This phenomenon does not appear in the Delboeuf illusion by the method of limits and the constant method in the previous chapter.

Moreover, unlike the Delboeuf illusion, the maximum illusion of the concentric circles illusion does not always occur when the diameter ratio of inner and outer circles is 0.67 (i.e., 2:3).

14.1.2.2 Expansion of concentric circles with minimum diameter difference

For concentric circles with the smallest diameter difference ($\Delta d = 5.5$ mm) in this experiment, both the inner and outer circles were overestimated, resulting in an expansion of the concentric circle. This overestimation depends on the size of the concentric circles. Six of these concentric circles were used as shown in Fig. 14.1. However, as shown in Figs. 14.2 and 14.3, the overestimation of the outer circle is the largest for concentric circles of a medium size, whereas the illusion does not occur for the smallest and largest concentric circles. This phenomenon appears in both the category rating method and the magnitude estimation one, and it is extremely robust, appearing not only in the preceding judgment but also in the subsequent one. Incidentally, Noguchi and Rentschler (1999) and Noguchi (2001, 2003, 2005) reported that in the Oppel-Kundt circle segmentation illusion, when the outer circle is filled with multiple concentric circles, the whole circle expands (Gyoba, 2004). Considering the expansion of concentric circles obtained in this experiment, the Oppel-Kundt circle segmentation illusion does not require a large number of circles, but the expansion of the whole concentric circle may occur even if only two circles with a small diameter difference are used. This expansion may also occur in a narrow double square (Obonai, 1954).

14.1.2.3 Judgment order effects in subsequent judgment

For each of the inner circle (solid symbols) and the outer circle (open symbols) in Figs. 14.2 and 14.3, the judgment-order effect is defined as the amount of the subsequent illusion (right panel) minus that of the preceding illusion (left panel). In common with the category rating (7 or 11) method and the magnitude estimation one, the subsequent judgments of the inner circle showed larger illusions than the preceding judgments, indicating the significant judgment-order effect. On the other hand, the category rating method for the outer circle shows no significant difference between the amounts of the preceding and the subsequent illusions. However, in the magnitude estimation method, the amount of the subsequent illusion for outer circle was stronger than that of the preceding illusion, and the judgment-order effect was significant.

Judgment-order effect. The Delboeuf illusion measured by comparative judgment is qualitatively different from the concentric circles illusion measured by absolute judgment. On the other hand, as reported by Hamada and Ehrenstein (2008), the judgment-order effect did not occur with the brightness contrast induction (see Fig. 4.1). Similarly, this effect also did not occur when judging in succession the goodness of the solid-dot patterns juxtaposed to the right and left (Kawano, N., 2002, unpublished paper). Therefore, the judgment-order effect may be unique to the size illusion.

14.1.2.4 Excessive overestimation in the smallest inner circle

According to the results of the 11-category rating method shown in Fig. 14.2 (below), both the preceding (B) and subsequent (b) judgments overestimated the inner circle, with the largest value at the smallest inner circle of a diameter of 12.0 mm (see also Fig. 4.1). Similarly, this over-estimation is also clearly observed in the results of the subsequent judgment of the magnitude estimation method in Fig. 14.3a, however, it is weaker for the preceding judgment (A). This overestimation is only noticeable in the smallest inner circle and is rarely seen elsewhere. This phenomenon does not appear in the results of the 7-category rating condition shown in Fig. 14.2 (above), which is common to both the preceding and subsequent judgments. In addition, for the outer circle, this phenomenon is not seen in all judgments, and the outer circle may play a role as a framework. It is unclear at this point what this overestimation in the minimum inner circle means.

14.1.3 Future work

In this experiment, the inner and outer circles were presented simultaneously, and the participants were asked to judge the apparent size at their own pace. Therefore, it is necessary to examine the concentric circles illusion and the judgment-order effect when the presentation time of the inner and outer circles is shortened. In addition, the fact that the excessive overestimation appeared only in the smallest inner circle, but not in the other inner circles and all outer circles, seems to be an issue to be examined in the future. In addition, the effect of these factors on the size contrast of the Ebbinghaus illusion should be examined. In the concentric circles, the inner circle is smaller than the outer circle, so the experimenters can avoid the mistake in the order of judgment between these two circles. However, in the Ebbinghaus pattern, it is necessary to design the experiment in such a way that the participants do not make a mistake in the order of judgment between the surrounding circles and the central circle.

14.2 Trends in research on the induction field of vision and DOG in Japan

In Japan, the induction field of vision has been studied experimentally and theoretically for a long time and has influenced many studies on geometric illusions (Koyadu, 1969; Mori, 1970). First, Motokawa (1948) and Motokawa and Akita (1957) measured the retinal sensitivity to flashes in a dark room for squares, triangles, and circles and drew retinal induction fields. Yokose (1956, 1957) proposed a basic formula for the visual potential field. He relied on Köhler's (1940) proposal of the perceptual electric current theory that the theory of perception should be a field theory. Yokose conducted experiments to verify his basic formula and measured the field created by the contour figures using the light threshold. He drew equipartition lines and found that they were quite consistent with Motokawa's equipartition lines. On the other hand, Obonai (1955, 1957) proposed qualitatively a Mexican hat-like neural activity consisting of excitation and inhibition, influenced by Hering's (1920) opponent-colors theory and Pavlov's (1927) conditioned reflex. He hoped that it would be expressed in a mathematical model in the future.

Obonai's expectation came to fruition as a two-dimensional lateral inhibition model of Fujii, Matsuoka, and Morita (1967). They expressed Obonai's induction as DOG (a difference of two Gaussians) and showed that the Müller-Lyer and Poggendorff illusions were explained by the shift of peaks in the convolutional integration of the illusory figures and DOG. Their DOG did not have luminance dependence. Therefore, Hamada (1976a, 1976b, 1984b) added luminance dependence to DOG by using Stevens' power law. He then constructed a four-level serial processing mathematical model in which the inflection points resulting from the convolutional integration of luminance and DOG are detected as edges and undergo information reduction. He simulated a border contrast in brightness perception (see Fig. 2.2). Furthermore, Hamada, Fukuda, Uchiumi, Fukushi, and Amano (2019) showed that Hamada's mathematical model can be used to judge the complexity of the dot patterns via an anisotropic spatial filter (see Fig. 9.7). Fukouzu, Itoh, Yoshida, and Shiraishi (1998) and Yoshida, Fukouzu, and Itoh (2005) arrived at a DOG-based visual space transfer model from an engineering point of view, starting from the basic formula of Yokose's visual potential field and referring to the lateral inhibition model of Fujii et al. (1967). This model has been used by Shiraishi, Fukouzu, Yoshoda, and Itoh (2000) and others to analyze geometric illusions. As described above, DOG-based research has developed independently with influences from abroad in Japan.

PART FIVE

Visual and auditory memory in successive recalls

CHAPTER FIFTEEN

Modality effect for random digit sequences

Atkinson and Shiffrin (1968, 1971), using a free recall method, proposed a memory model in which the human memory mechanism consists of three stages: sensory registers, short-term memory, and long-term memory. They postulated that stimuli from the outside world pass through sensory registers such as visual, auditory, and tactile, and are registered in short-term memory, where they are rehearsed and transferred to long-term memory (Loftus & Loftus, 1976; Lindsay & Norman, 1977). Sperling (1960, 1967) and Darwin, Turvey, and Crowdwe (1974) clarified the existence of sensory registers and their decay process for visual and auditory stimuli, respectively, using the partial report method.

Differences in memory performance between visual and auditory stimuli have been studied as modality effects. The study using random alphanumeric characters revealed the following differences in memory between visual presentation by letters and auditory one by sounds. With visual presentation, the serial position curve is almost a monotonically decreasing function, and the performance at the end of the series increases only slightly. However, with auditory presentation, the serial position curve shows a U-shape and the performance at the beginning and end of the series is high (Murray, 1966; Corballis, 1966; Watkins & Watkins, 1980; Greene & Crowder, 1986; Greene, 1987).

In the present study, we adopt a method developed by Imai (1979), in which random digits are presented one by one in succession, and the recall time is controlled in succession by auditory signals at a fixed period. In this study, we will examine the modality effect by this method and clarify the relationship between visual and auditory memory for random 10 digits.

15.1 Independence of visual and auditory memory in paired digits (Experiment 1)

We will examine the serial position curves and correct recall (%) for digits presented visually as letters (called visual digits), audibly as sounds

Psychophysics and Experimental Phenomenology of Pattern Cognition
https://doi.org/10.1016/B978-0-323-95286-6.00015-6

(called auditory digits), and paired digits with different visual and auditory digits. In this section, Hamada (1990b) will be reviewed.

15.1.1 General method

A 10-digit random sequence of digits from 0 to 9 was created based on a random number table, taking care not to have consecutive numbers next to each other (e.g., 56 or 65). These were input into a personal computer (Oki Electric IF800 model 20), and then presented in the center of the screen as a single-digit number (6.0 cm in length × 4.5 cm in width), which was continuously recorded on a VTR (SONY VO2900) to form a visual digit sequence. Similarly, the digit presented in the corner of the screen was recited in normal pronunciation by the stimulus creator and recorded on the VTR to become an auditory digit sequence.

In the following four experiments, 24 undergraduate students at Tokushima University participated in each experiment. They participated in the experiment in groups of three or less. The participants in the four experiments were different and did not overlap except for Experiments 2 and 4. Different digit series A and B were used in the experiments on the different two days. 12 participants used A on the first day and B on the second day, while the other 12 participants used B on the first day and A on the second day. The order of implementation of A and B was counterbalanced between the groups of the same participants in the different two days. Since A and B showed similar trends in the experimental results, they were combined and analyzed. In this way, a total of 48 participants each participated in each experiment.

Participants were taught to intentionally and actively rehearse the digit sequences in the order specified, which was done internally, and not aloud. The interval between trials of the sequence was 5 s. After the completion of one condition, there was a break of several minutes. A few practice trials were conducted before each condition to familiarize with the memorization, rehearsal, and recall methods. When writing the digits, a carbon paper was inserted between two response sheets, and the first sheet was written with a steel pen. Therefore, they were not able to see the handwriting. When calculating the correct recall (%), only numbers that were correctly entered in the specified reproduction position were considered correct, and all cases in which it was shifted, or adjacent digits were switched were considered wrong. The general method described above was the same for Experiments 1 to 4.

15.1.2 Control and paired conditions in Experiment 1

In the control condition, 10-digit visual and auditory digit sequences were randomly arranged in 8 series each (16 series in total). In the paired condition, two different digits were simultaneously presented, one visual and the other auditory. Thus, in the paired condition, two different digit sequences of five were presented audio-visually in succession. After its presentation, it was specified whether the visual or auditory digit sequence should be recalled first by the letters on the screen. The first digit sequence to be recalled is called the preceding recall digit sequence, and the next one is called the following one. The participants are not told in advance whether the visual or auditory digit sequence should be recall first. The preceding visual and following auditory order, and the preceding auditory and following visual digit sequences were randomly arranged in 8 series each (16 series in total).

15.1.3 Presentation and recall of the sequence of digits

The time course of the experiment is shown in Fig. 15.1. In the control condition, visual or auditory digit sequences was presented in succession at a rate of one digit every 1.6 s, and the end of presentation and the start of recall were signaled audio-visually. A recall started after a 2.4 s blank period, and

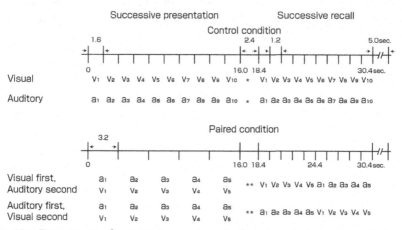

Fig. 15.1 Time course of presentation and recall of random digits in the control and paired conditions. v_i and a_i indicate visual and auditory digits; * indicates cue for end of presentation and start of recall; ** indicates end of presentation and specification of recall order. *(From Hamada, J. (1990b). Some differences between the visual and auditory memories in the short-term memory.* Japanese Journal of Psychology, 61, 8– *14. (Japanese text with English abstract).)*

the digits were entered one by one on the response sheet in the order of presentation in accordance with the sound signal issued in 1.2 s cycles. In the paired condition, different visual and auditory digits were simultaneously presented in pairs every 3.2 s. Immediately after the presentation of the digit sequence, the letters on the screen specified whether the visual or auditory task should be recalled first, and the recall proceeded along the same time course as in the control condition. For the time course of visual digits, the presentation and pause times were both 0.8 s each (1.6 s in total) in the control condition, and both times were doubled (3.2 s in total) in the paired one. The time course of auditory digits was one digit per 1.6 s for presentation in the control condition but double the time in the paired condition (3.2 s in total).

15.1.4 Results

15.1.4.1 Serial position curves

Fig. 15.2a and b show the correct recall (%) as a function of serial position. In the control condition (a), both visual and auditory responses are similarly good at the beginning of the serial position. For visuals, the performances fall almost monotonically and the improvement in performance at the end of the serial position is negligible. However, the correct recall (%) in the center of the auditory sequence was lower than that of the visual sequence, and the improvement in performance at the beginning and end of the serial position

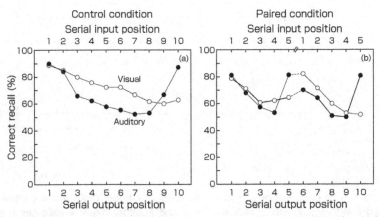

Fig. 15.2 Serial position curves in control and paired conditions (a and b). The *thick line* in the paired condition (b) indicates the visual first and auditory second, and the *thin line* is the opposite. *(From Hamada, J. (1990b). Some differences between the visual and auditory memories in the short-term memory. Japanese Journal of Psychology, 61, 8–14. (Japanese text with English abstract).)*

was clearly evident, and the serial position curve showed a U-shape. The average visual and auditory recalls were 73 and 68% with significant difference as shown in Table 1. Under the paired condition of Fig. 15.2b, the shapes of the visual and auditory serial position curves are similar to that in the control condition, regardless of whether the digits for visual or auditory is recalled first.

15.1.4.2 Comparison of control and paired conditions
In order to match the presentation time of 3.2 s in the paired condition, the relative serial positions were used for control condition. That is, the average recall rates of two neighboring positions (e.g., 1 and 2, 3 and 4, etc.) were calculated starting from serial positions 1 and 2 in the control condition and are shown in Table 15.1. This table also shows the preceding and following recall rates in the paired conditions for visual and auditory. The mean of preceding recall rate of 68% in the visual condition is significantly lower than the 73% in the control one. However, in the auditory condition, the mean of preceding recall rate of 68% is the same as in the control one.

15.1.4.3 Correct recall (%) of the preceding and following in paired conditions
Comparing the correct recall (%) of the preceding and following recall-digit sequences, the latter is 3% lower than the former, in common with visual and auditory but not significantly so.

Table 15.1 Correct recall (%) on the relative serial position curve in the control condition and on the preceding and following digit sequences in the paired condition.

	Visual					
Relative serial position	1	2	3	4	5	Mean
Control condition	87	78	73	64	62	73
Proceding recall	81	71	62	63	65	68*
Following recall	83	74	63	53	51	65

	Auditory					
Relative serial position	1	2	3	4	5	Mean
Control condition	87	64	57	54	77	68
Proceding recall	79	68	58	54	82	68
Following recall	74	66	52	51	81	65

*$P < .05$ (%)

From Hamada, J. (1990b). Some differences between the visual and auditory memories in the short-term memory. *Japanese Journal of Psychology, 61*, 8–14. (Japanese text with English abstract).

15.1.5 Discussion

Imai and Hosoda (1988) reported that the serial position curve decreased monotonically when 9-digit random visual digits were presented one by one in succession and made to recall in succession. The 10-digit visual digit sequence obtained in the control condition of the present experiment also showed a monotonous decrease in the serial position curve for visual digits, consistent with their results. On the other hand, the present experiment by successive recalls revealed that the serial position curve for auditory becomes U-shaped. Thus, the modality effect in the successive recalls was clarified. Crowder and Morton (1969), based on experiments by the immediate recall method, found that there was no difference in correct recall (%) between visual and auditory stimuli at the beginning and center of the serial position. In contrast, the modality effect occurred in terms of the performance for audition was higher than that of vision at the end of the serial position. However, in the control condition of the present experiment, the mean correct recall (%) of vision was higher than that of audition, and the performance in the center of the serial position was higher for vision. This discrepancy can be attributed to the difference between the immediate and successive recall methods.

15.1.5.1 Independence of visual and auditory memory

The visual and auditory serial position curves were different in the control and paired conditions; however, the shapes of them were the same in both conditions. Moreover, there was no significant difference in the mean performance between the preceding and following recalls for both the visual and auditory sequences in the paired condition, and the inversion of the recall order (i.e., preceding or following) did not affect the performances. This indicates that there are independent mechanisms for visual and auditory sequences in the human memory system.

15.1.5.2 Inhibitory effect of auditory digits on visual memory

As shown in Fig. 15.1, the time elapsed between the presentation and recall of the digit in the serial position ranged from 18.4 s to 30.4 s in the control condition. However, in the paired condition, the time from the start of the presentation of the digit to the end of the preceding recall is 18.4 to 24.4 s, which is 6.0 s earlier than the control one. Despite this difference in the method of memorization and retention period, the mean performance in the preceding recall in the paired condition with a shorter retention period for visual digits (68%) was significantly lower than that in the control one with a longer retention period (73%), resulting in poor performance (* mark in top panel of Table 15.1). Thus, these differences in mean performance are not due to a longer or shorter retention period, but rather to the inhibitory effect of auditory digits on visual memory. On the other hand, the mean performance in the auditory control condition (68%) was consistent with that (68%) of the auditory preceding digits (bottom panel of Table 15.1). This result means that the difference in retention period between the control and the paired conditions do not affect the performance of the auditory digit sequence, and that the visual digit sequence in the paired condition does not have any effect on auditory memory. From the above, we concluded that visual digits do not inhibit auditory memory in the paired condition, but auditory digits unidirectionally inhibit visual memory.

The mean performance of the preceding and following recall digits in the paired condition was 3% lower in the latter than in the former, regardless of visual or auditory, but this was not significant (Table 15.1). As shown in Fig. 15.1, 18.4 to 24.4 s elapse from the start of the presentation of the preceding digit sequence to the recall, and the recall of the following digit sequence starts 6.0 s later. This result indicates that the difference of 6.0 s in retention period does not affect the performance. In addition, the visual performance of the preceding and following digits were both similarly low compared to the control condition. Thus, the inhibitory effect of auditory digits on visual memory is approximately equal for preceding and following recall digits. The fact that the difference in retention period for visual digits does not make a difference in memory indicates that this inhibitory effect of auditory digits on visual performance occurs during the memorization phase, not during the retention and rehearsal phase.

15.1.5.3 Comparison of performances in the center of the serial position with immediate and successive recalls

In Crowder and Morton's (1969) theoretical curve of modality effects in immediate recalls, there was no difference between the visual and the auditory performance at not only the beginning but also the center of serial position, in contrast, auditory performance was high at the end of it. On the other hand, in the controlled condition of the successive recalls in the present study, visual performance was higher than auditory one at the center of the series. The difference in the recall methods cause a difference in the performance of the center parts of serial position curve. The immediate recall does not have enough time to process the visual information, but the successive recalls have enough time to rehearse the visual digits, which increases the performance. However, there may be no increase in performance of auditory digits in the successive recall method due to rehearsal. These processing characteristics are robust to the paired condition as well.

15.2 Inhibitory effects on overlap digits in forward and backward recalls (Experiment 2)

In Experiment 2, in addition to visual and auditory digits, overlap digits, which are the same digits presented audio-visually at the same time, were added. The digits were presented one by one in random order in a cyclic fashion. After that, the participants were forced to perform a successive recall in which they were asked to perform a forward or backward rehearsal. Forward rehearsal is done in the order of presentation during the presentation of digits, and backward rehearsal is done in the reverse order. In this way, the modality effect is examined by controlling the rehearsal during the retention period of the digits sequence. In this section, Hamada (1986, Experiment 1) will be reviewed.

15.2.1 Experimental conditions

The method used in Experiment 2 was the same as the general method described in the previous experiment. The time course of the presentation and recall of the digit sequence is shown in Fig. 15.3. The presentation time and pause time for visual digits were both 0.8 s (total 1.6 s), and auditory digits were uttered at a rate of 1 every 1.6 s. A total of 15 sequences of 5 visual, 5 auditory, and 5 overlap digit sequences were presented in random order.

The forward and backward conditions were established based on the difference in the direction of the recalls. In the forward condition, the last digit in the digit sequence was recalled after the rehearsal period of the digits, however, in the backward one, that is recalled immediately after its presentation, so there is little possibility of rehearsal. Thus, the last digit in the input sequence ends the recall after 16.0 s in the forward direction, but 5.2 s in the backward one. The recall of the first digit in the input sequence ends after 19.6 s in the forward direction, but 30.4 s in the backward one. By setting these conditions, we examine how the modality effect behaves in visual, auditory, and overlap presentations.

15.2.2 Results and discussion

Fig. 15.4a and b shows the serial position curves and the average correct recall (%) in the forward and backward conditions. The tracing period of short-term

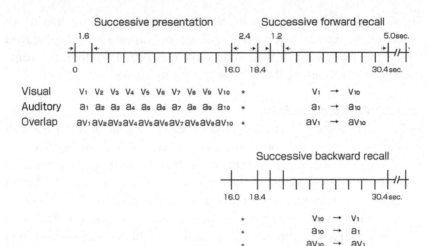

Fig. 15.3 Time course of successive presentations and recalls in the forward and backward conditions. v_i, a_i, and av_i indicate visual, auditory, and overlapping digits, respectively. * indicates cues for end of presentation and start of recall. *(From Hamada, J. (1986). Interaction between visual and auditory memory for random digits series under forward and backward rehearsal/recall conditions. Japanese Journal of Psychonomic Science, 5, 55–61. (Japanese text with English abstract and captions).)*

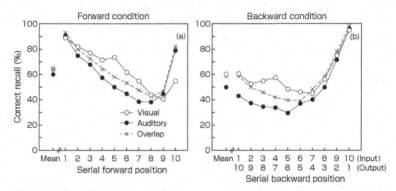

Fig. 15.4 Serial position curves and mean correct recall (%) in forward and backward conditions. *(Adapted from Hamada, J. (1986). Interaction between visual and auditory memory for random digits series under forward and backward rehearsal/recall conditions. Japanese Journal of Psychonomic Science, 5, 55–61. (Japanese text with English abstract and captions), Experiment 1.)*

memory is about 5 to 20 s according to Craik and Lockhart (1972). In the present experiment, both presentation and recall for digits proceeded in succession, taking 30.4 s in the forward condition. If this time is the only issue, the results in this experiment reflect the processing in short-term memory.

However, since memory processing progresses with the passage of time in successive recalls, it seems that the results of this experiment cannot be discussed within the framework of their short-term memory. Therefore, the name "short-term memory" will not be used in the following.

15.2.2.1 Forward condition

In Fig. 15.4a, the visual, auditory, and overlap digit sequences all have high correct recall (%) at the end of the serial position. For example, there is a significant difference in the performance of the visual digit sequence at serial positions 9 and 10. This is likely because the forward and backward conditions were implemented as one. The visual correct recall (%) decreases almost monotonically until serial position 9. The performance at the end of this serial position is almost equally high for auditory and overlap digit sequences. The results for overlap are intermediate between visual and auditory in serial positions 3 to 7, and almost identical to auditory at serial positions 9 and 10. In the center of the serial position, overlap performance is lower than that of vision. Taking into account the inhibitory effect of auditory digits on visual memory in paired digits in the previous experiment, this result suggests that visual memory also receives inhibitory effect from auditory digits in overlap digits. Looking at the whole series position, the mean performances of visual and overlap digits both agreed at 65%, which are significantly higher than auditory 60%.

15.2.2.2 Backward condition

In Fig. 15.4b, the average performance in the backward condition is 60% for vision, 58% for overlap, and 49% for audition. Among the three types of serial position curves, auditory performance is the lowest. There was no difference between visual and overlap in input serial positions 1 and 2, and auditory performance was low. The retention period was 30.4 s in input serial position 1 and 27.6 s in input serial position 2, during which the inhibition effect from auditory digits to visual memory disappeared and the performance of overlap condition was consistent with that of vision. In addition, the performance of overlap was lower than that of vision in the input series from position 3 to 6. Here, the retention periods were 24.8 s in position 3 and 16.4 s in position 6, indicating an inhibitory effect from auditory digits to visual memory, as in the forward condition. There is no difference between the overlap and visual memory in the input series from position 7 to 10. The retention time was 13.6 s in position 7 and 5.2 s in position 10, and the performance increased rapidly as the time to recall became shorter. On the other hand, auditory performance is lower than visual and overlap in the input series positions 1 to 5. And the specific improvement in auditory digits at output series position 10, which occurred in the forward condition, disappears at output series position 10 in the backward condition. Thus, as shown in Fig. 15.4b, the performance of all modalities on the output series in the backward condition first rapidly decreases and then slightly improves as the recall time increases. The reason for this phenomenon is unknown.

15.3 Inhibitory effects on overlap digits in short- and long-cycle presentations (Experiment 3)

In the previous experiment, in common with forward and backward recalls, overlaps were lower than visuals for performance in the center of the serial position. This result implies that visual memory receives inhibition from auditory digits in the overlap condition, where the same digits are presented audio-visually. Therefore, in Experiment 3, the presentation cycles of visual, auditory, and overlap digit sequences were set to short and long. Then, we impose forward recall and compare the serial position curves of these digit sequences to study the modality effect. The reason why the results of overlap in the center of the serial position did not match the visual in the previous experiment will also be clarified. In this section, Hamada (1988b) will be reviewed.

15.3.1 Experimental conditions
The method used in the present experiment was the same as the general method described in Experiment 1. The time course of the presentation and recall of the digit sequences is shown in Fig. 15.5. The experimental conditions consisted of short- and long-cycle. The presentation time of visual digits was 0.8 s, and the pauses were 0 and 1.6 s in the short- and the long-cycle conditions, respectively, however, auditory digits were uttered at a rate of one digit every 0.8 and 2.4 s in the conditions, respectively.

15.3.2 Results and discussion
Fig. 15.6a and b shows the serial position curves and average correct recall (%) for visual, auditory, and overlap digit sequences in the short- and long-cycle conditions. These series are divided into two components at position 8 or 9.

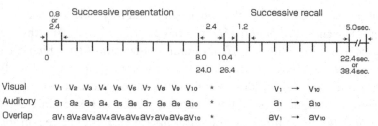

Fig. 15.5 Time course of presentation and recall of random digits in short- and long-cycle conditions. v_i, a_i, and av_i indicate visual, auditory, and audio-visual digits, respectively. ∗ indicates cues for end of presentation and start of recall. *(From Hamada, J. (1988b). Superiority between auditory and visual primacy effects depended on memorization rate. Japanese Journal of Psychonomic Science, 7, 85–89. (Japanese text with English abstract).)*

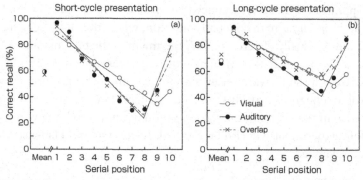

Fig. 15.6 Serial position curves and mean correct recall (%) in short- and long-cycle conditions. Two straight lines are fitted to the serial position curve. *(From Hamada, J. (1988b). Superiority between auditory and visual primacy effects depended on memorization rate. Japanese Journal of Psychonomic Science, 7, 85–89. (Japanese text with English abstract).)*

15.3.2.1 Short-cycle condition

As shown in Fig. 15.6a, the serial position curve at serial positions 1 to 8 in the overlap does not match with the curve of the high performance in the visual, but that of the low performance in the auditory. In other words, visual memory for overlap digits is completely inhibited from auditory digits. A straight line with a slope of −6.3% is fitted to visual serial positions 1 to 9 with a high correlation coefficient ($r = -.99$), and there is a slight increase in performance at the final serial position. A line with a slope of

−10% is fitted to the auditory serial positions 1 to 8 ($r=-.98$), and its downward slope is larger than that of the visual. A straight line with a slope of 26% was fitted to the auditory serial positions 8 to 10 ($r=.97$), showing a significant increase in performance. In the overlap condition, a straight line with a slope of −9.3% applies to serial positions 1 to 8 ($r=-.98$) and a straight line with a slope of 20% applies to serial positions 8 to 10 ($r=.96$).

15.3.2.2 Long-cycle condition

As shown in Fig. 15.6b, the serial position curve of overlap condition coincides with the visual and auditory envelopes. This means that the inhibitory effect of auditory digits on visual memory, which appeared in the short-cycle condition, has disappeared. A straight line with a slope of −4.8% is fitted to the visual serial positions 1 to 9 with a high correlation coefficient ($r=-1.00$), and there is a slight increase in performance at the final serial position. A straight line with slopes of −6.8 and −5.2% is fitted to serial positions 1 to 8 for auditory and overlap ($r=-.97$ and $=-.95$). And for auditory and overlap serial positions 8 through 10, straight lines with slopes of 20 and 14% are fitted ($r=.96$ and $=.94$).

15.3.2.3 Comparison of short- and long-cycle conditions

When the presentation cycle was extended from 0.8 to 2.4 s, the mean performance changed as follows: the visual performance increased from 59 to 68%, the auditory from 59 to 66%, and the overlap from 57 to 72%, all significantly.

15.3.2.4 Up until serial position 8 inhibitory effects of auditory digits on visual memory and their disappearance

The auditory digit was uttered as a normal recitation at a rate of one per 0.8 and 2.4 s. And the presentation time of the visual digit was fixed at 0.8 s, and their pause intervals were 0 and 1.6 s in the present experiment but 0.8 s in Experiment 2. In this way, the presentation cycle of visual and auditory digits was extended from 0.8 to 2.4 s in the present experiment. At the beginning and center of the serial position in the short-cycle condition, overlap performance is almost completely consistent with auditory, rather than visual which has higher performance. Then, visual memory receives inhibition from auditory digits. In contrast, at these locations in the long-cycle condition, the performance of the overlap is consistent with vision, unlike in the short-cycle one. This result indicates that the inhibitory effect from auditory digits to visual memory in the overlap disappears when the presentation cycle is prolonged. That is, a longer presentation cycle is

necessary for visual information to contribute effectively to the memorization of overlap digit sequences.

In the previous experiment, when the presentation period was set to
1.6 s, which is the middle of the present experiment, the performance in
the center of the overlap sequence was between visual and auditory, but
when it was set to 2.4 s, it matched with visual. This indicates that when
the presentation cycle was increased, the auditory inhibition weakened
and the visual information started to be used, and the middle of serial position in the overlap condition was improved. In addition, 1.6 s in Experiment
2 was the transition period when the inhibitory effect disappeared.

In Fig. 15.7, we examine the mechanism of memory based on the change
in performance at the center of the serial positions. In the control condition
(A), the performance of visual and auditory memory improved as the presentation cycle increased. Similarly, in the overlap condition (B), the visual
and auditory memory performance improved. However, in this condition,

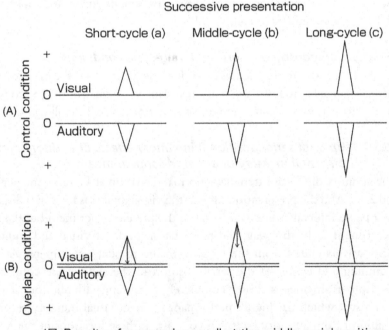

Fig. 15.7 Schematic summary of results and inhibitory effects of successive recall in the
center of the serial position.

auditory digits completely inhibit visual memory in the short-cycle (a), and the inhibition is weakened in the medium-cycle (b). In the long-cycle (c), auditory digits do not inhibit visual memory. In this way, inhibition is gradually weakened by prolonging the presentation cycle. Thus, in the short-cycle condition, visual memory receives the full inhibitory effect from the auditory digit sequence. However, latent visual memory that is not manifested restores performance as the inhibition disappears when the presentation cycle is lengthened.

15.3.2.5 Auditory dominance at the end of the series in the forward conditions

In the short-, middle-, and long-cycle conditions, the visual serial position curve showed only a slight increase in performance at the end of the serial position, while the auditory and overlap curves were more pronounced. Thus, auditory performance at the end of the serial position in overlap was superior to visual performance regardless of the length of the presentation cycle.

15.4 Modality effects appearing in forward and backward recalls in interchanging conditions (Experiment 4)

In the present experiment, in order to examine the modality effect by interchange of visual and auditory digits, we imposed forward and backward recalls. The results of Experiment 1, in which different digits were presented in audio-visual pairs, showed that visual and auditory memory exist independently. In the present experiment, we will examine the effect of presenting visual and auditory digits interchangeably on memory. In this section, Hamada (1986, Experiment 2) will be reviewed.

15.4.1 Procedures and participants

The method used in the present experiment was the same as the general method described in Experiment 1. The time course of the presentation and recall of the digit sequence is shown in Fig. 15.8. The presentation and pause times for the visual digits were both 0.8 s (total of 1.6 s), and the auditory digits were uttered at a rate of one per 1.6 s, the same as in the control condition of Experiment 1. In this experiment, there will be a halving presentation in which five visual and five auditory digits are presented in a lump, and an alternate presentation in which one visual and one auditory digits are presented alternately. In other words, as shown in Fig. 15.8, there is a visual-audio

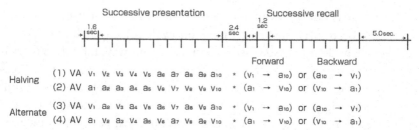

Fig. 15.8 Time course of successive presentation and recall in forward and backward recall conditions. v_i and a_i denote visual and auditory digits. *(From Hamada, J. (1986). Interaction between visual and auditory memory for random digits series under forward and backward rehearsal/recall conditions. Japanese Journal of Psychonomic Science, 5, 55–61. (Japanese text with English abstract and captions.)*

halving sequence (1, VA) in which five visual digits are presented first, followed by five auditory digits, and an audio-visual halving sequence (2, AV) in the reverse order. Then, there is a visual-audio alternating digit sequence (3, VA), in which visual and auditory digits are presented alternately, one after the other, and an audio-visual alternating digit sequence (4, AV), in the reverse order. A total of 16 types of these digit sequences were prepared, four for each. Based on the difference in the direction of the recall of the 10-digit sequence, forward and backward recall was provided. In other words, participants were required to recall the digit sequence in the order of successive forward or backward.

The participants were the same in Experiments 2 and 4, which were conducted on the same two days.

15.4.2 Results and discussion

Fig. 15.9A and a and Fig. 15.9B and b show the input series position curves and the average correct recall (%) for forward and backward recalls, respectively; Fig. 15.9A and B and Fig. 15.9a and b show halving and alternating presentations, respectively.

In the forward recall condition (A), the series position curves for VA and AV drop almost monotonically, but the performance of auditory digits specifically improves at series position 10 in VA, while that of visual digits is low in AV. On the other hand, the specific improvement in auditory performance at series position 10 in VA had an inhibitory effect on visual performance between series positions 1 and 5. In other words, there is a significant difference between the average correct recall of 85% for auditory and 79% for visual in these series positions. Here, the correct recall of the entire serial

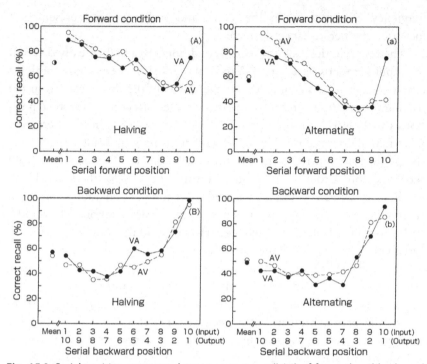

Fig. 15.9 Serial position curves and mean correct recall (%) of forward and backward recall as a function of input series position for halving and alternating presentations. *(Adapted from Hamada, J. (1986). Interaction between visual and auditory memory for random digits series under forward and backward rehearsal/recall conditions. Japanese Journal of Psychonomic Science, 5, 55–61. (Japanese text with English abstract and captions).)*

positions for VA and AV is 71% for both, and there is no difference in whether visual (or auditory) is presented first or visual (or auditory) is presented later.

In the alternating presentation condition (a), the average recall rate from series positions 1 to 10 is 60% for AV and 57% for VA, which is not significant. As in the halving-presentation condition (A), auditory performance in VA specifically increased at series position 10 in the alternating-presentation condition (a), and there was a significant difference in the average correct recall between series positions 1 and 5: 67% for VA and 78% for AV. This indicates that the auditory inhibition from serial position 10 affects not only vision but also audition in the first half of the series position.

Comparing the performance of serial positions 1 to 10 with the halving and alternating presentation conditions, the halving (71%) is significantly higher than the alternating (59%) presentation condition. Thus, as the frequency of switching in the visual and auditory digits presentation increases, the performance decreases.

The results in the backward recall conditions (B) and (b) are divided into the input serial positions 1 to 4, 5 to 7, and 8 to 10. There is no significant difference between VA and AV for the results of the three sections in the halving presentation condition, and the average correct recall for serial positions 1 to 10 is 57% for the former and 54% for the latter. In the alternating presentation condition of VA and AV, there is no significant difference in the performance in these three sections, and the average recall rate from serial positions 1 to 10 is 48% for the former and 51% for the latter. Here, on the performance in the halving and alternating presentation conditions, there was no significant difference in the input series positions 1 to 4 and 8 to 10, so no modality effect appeared. However, in the middle of the input series positions 5 to 7, halving (50%) was significantly higher than the alternating (37%) presentation condition, indicating that the frequent switching between visual and auditory presentation reduced performance.

As shown above, the performance of halving was higher than that of alternating presentation in both forward and backward recall conditions. This result indicates that the performance of 5 digits presented in a lump is higher than that of 5 digits presented one by one in alternation, and that frequent switching of the modality decreases the performance in alternation. This result may indicate that visual and auditory digits interfere with each other at the time of memorization.

In this chapter, the modality effect was examined by imposing successive presentations and recalls, so the difference between successive and immediate recalls needs to be examined.

Afterword

In Part 1, in order to elucidate contour perception and the brightness illusion, I proposed a four-level serial processing mathematical model consisting of an excito-inhibitory transduction level assuming luminance-dependent DOG (a difference of two Gaussians), a response gradient extraction level in which the gradient of the output is extracted, an edge detection level in which the inflection points are detected as edges, and finally an information reduction level in which the response gradients of the output in excito-inhibitory transduction level are averaged across edges. Then, the border contrast of brightness was simulated by this model. Using this as a reference, I experimentally and theoretically investigated the contour enhancement effect and the Craik-O'Brien-Cornsweet brightness illusion. As a result, adding a luminance step (i.e., edge) to the uniform luminance field caused a decrease in the brightness levels, and different degrees of this darkening effect resulted in the contour enhancement effect and the brightness illusions. Therefore, I proposed a five-level qualitative model in which a decrease in the brightness levels is induced in the upper level of the four-level serial processing mathematical model. In addition, the simultaneous contrast and assimilation of brightness were examined by a qualitative model. In those experiments, the asymmetry between light and dark was revealed, and a decrease in the brightness levels occurred without exception when luminance steps were added to the uniform field. In order to explain the Ehrenstein illusion for radial patterns of eight black or white lines on a gray background, I proposed a three-level qualitative model in which the edge detection level for straight lines and circles are set above the antagonistic process of excitation and inhibition, and in which lateral spread is blocked by the edges. The Ehrenstein illusion caused by the difference in brightness levels between the background and circular field after edge detection is explained by this model. Furthermore, when the Ehrenstein illusion was examined by rotating the four black and white lines in 45° each, an anisotropy of brightness illusion appeared.

In Part 2, when participants were asked to make relative and absolute judgments for two weight stimuli raised in succession, a negative time-order effect emerged that it was stronger for the 3 s than for the 1 s interval in both judgments. Furthermore, in absolute judgments, compared to a single stimulus, the preceding stimulus was judged lightly and the following stimulus was judged heavily. When the presentation interval was shortened from 3 s to 1 s, the weight sensations for the lightly judged preceding stimulus and those for the heavily judged following ones converged closer to those for the single ones in the control condition. The mechanism of the negative time-order effect in weight sensation was explained by the disinhibition based on the antagonistic process of excitation and inhibition.

In Part 3, we drew two-dimensional dot patterns in a hexagonal grid, while I drew them in square grids. Based on them, we investigated goodness, simplicity, unifiedness, and similarity based on psychological experiments, using group theory and an anisotropic spatial filter as cues. The results revealed the effects of group order (i.e., the number of transformations), grids, contrast polarity, numerosity (8, 13, and 21 dots), configuration, linearity or collinearity, and an anisotropic spatial filter on cognitive judgments. These cognitive judgments for 8-, 13-, and 21-dot patterns arranged in square grids increased as a function of group order regardless of the presence or absence of reflection axes. However, the simplicity and unifideness of the D_2 linear pattern with parallel edges did not follow group order and was significantly higher than that of the D_4 pattern with four reflection axes. The specific increase in simplicity and unifideness of the D_2 linear pattern is determined in the primary stage of the cognitive system where an anisotropic spatial filter functions. Then, the goodness, simplicity, and unifiedness bypassed the primary stage and were subjected to group-theoretic processing. We assumed that unifiedness is determined at the secondary stage where the reflection axes cannot be cognized, while goodness and simplicity of patterns other than the D_2 linear pattern are determined at the tertiary stage where the reflection axes can be cognized. Thus, we proposed a three-stage serial processing model of symmetry cognition. Goodness, simplicity, and unifiedness were affected by the difference in configuration as well as group order. The behavior of goodness and simplicity for dot patterns in hexagonal and square grids was different, and the effects of reflection axes, contrast polarity, and linearity varied regularly and variably.

On the other hand, similarity decreased when the difference in dot numbers between the 21-dot standard and the comparison pattern (8- and 13-dot) pairs was large. Similarity was also specified in the group order, but the similarity between the 21-dot standard and 13-dot comparison pattern pairs was determined by the configuration of dot patterns. In other words, the similarity between them was not affected by group order and by contrast polarity.

Both goodness and simplicity of repetitive patterns differed between upright and 45° oblique patterns, indicating an anisotropy of symmetry cognition. And the simplicity of the repetitive pattern consisting of linear motifs increased specifically due to the effect of the anisotropic spatial filter, but no consistent effect for goodness. In addition, the goodness and simplicity of the repetitive pattern consisting of circular motifs also increased specifically. Moreover, the similarity of the repetitive pattern pairs decreased as the coupling of the transformations increased, that is, as the possibility of mutual transformations weakened. The similarity also decreased not only as the number of reflection axes of the repetitive pattern decreased but also as the number of glide-reflection axes increased.

On the other hand, the similarity, goodness and complexity of one-dimensional black-white elliptic filled patterns (1D) arranged horizontally are also specified by group theory, and the transformational group structure theory was proposed. In other words, as the possibility of mutual transformations of pattern pairs increases, similarity increases. And as the invariance of individual patterns increases, goodness and simplicity also increase. However, while simplicity decreased as the number of runs (the number of white and black oval blobs) increased, goodness was unaffected. Both the similarity of the pattern pairs and the goodness of the individual patterns followed the predictions of the Hasse's diagram. The similarity of the pattern pairs without the possibility of mutual transformation and the goodness of the individual patterns without invariance decreased with the Hamming's distance. The similarity of two dimensional black-white filled dot patterns (2D) were also specified the transformational group structure theory.

Based on the discussion in Parts 1 and 3, serial processing models for not only the contour perception and brightness illusions, but also for the goodness, simplicity, and unifiedness of the 8-, 13-, and 21-dot patterns in the original condition in a 9×9 square grid are shown in Fig. A.1. Here, it is assumed that stimuli from the outside world are sent to the antagonistic process of excitation and inhibition, from which the final cognitive decision is made while undergoing serial processing (see also Figs. 2.10 and 9.12). The negative time-order effect in Part 2 is also thought to occur in the antagonistic process.

In Part 4, we examined circle size as a geometric illusion, that is, the Ebbinghaus, the Delboeuf, and the concentric circles illusions. When the direction of the Ebbinghaus pattern was rotated clockwise in $15°$ increments, the overestimation of the Surrounding small increased, the underestimation of the Surrounding large decreased, and the illusion of the Mixture circle was intermediate between them. Thus, the Ebbinghaus illusion showed an anisotropy of the geometric illusion. In addition, in this illusion, when the distance between the circumferences was increased in the Surrounding large and Surrounding small conditions, the underestimation was enhanced in the

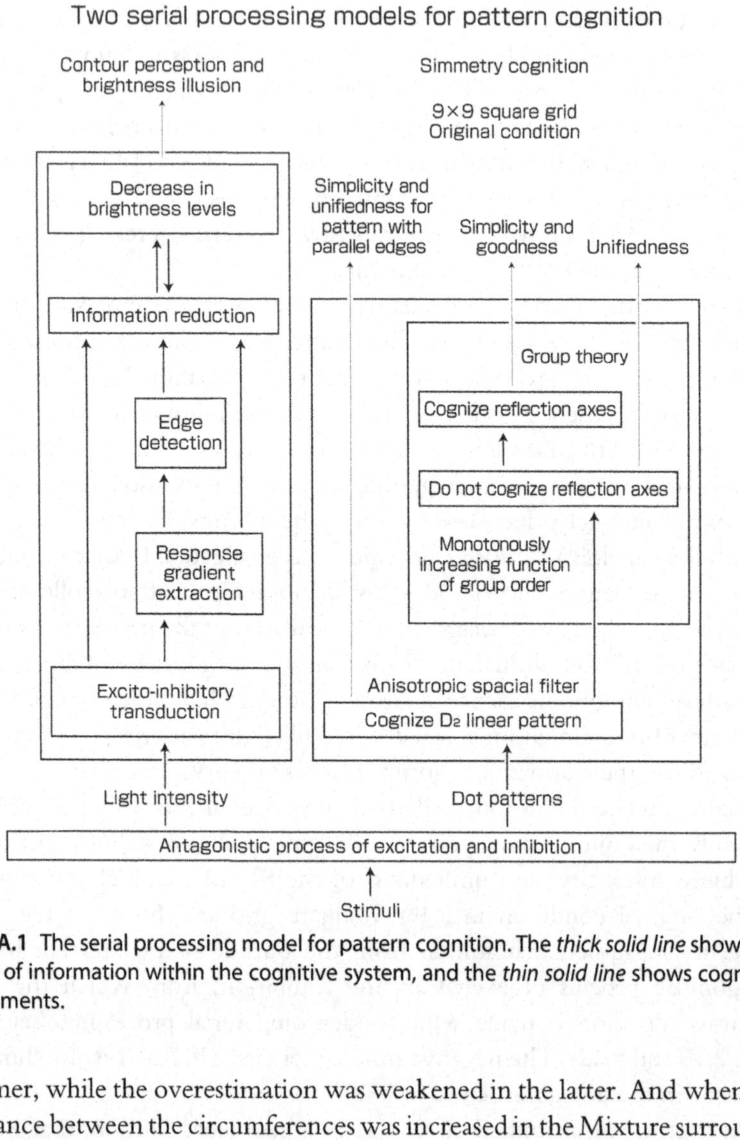

Two serial processing models for pattern cognition

Contour perception and
brightness illusion

Simmetry cognition

9×9 square grid
Original condition

| Decrease in brightness levels |
| Simplicity and unifiedness for pattern with parallel edges |

Simplicity and goodness　Unifiedness

Information reduction

Group theory

Cognize reflection axes

Do not cognize reflection axes

Edge detection

Monotonously increasing function of group order

Response gradient extraction

Excito-inhibitory transduction

Anisotropic spacial filter
Cognize D₂ linear pattern

Light intensity

Dot patterns

Antagonistic process of excitation and inhibition

Stimuli

Fig. A.1 The serial processing model for pattern cognition. The *thick solid line* shows the flow of information within the cognitive system, and the *thin solid line* shows cognitive judgments.

former, while the overestimation was weakened in the latter. And when the distance between the circumferences was increased in the Mixture surrounding condition, which is a superposition of large and small circles, the underestimation first strengthened and then weakened, resulting in a V-shape. On the other hand, the results of the Delboeuf illusion measured by the constant method using a comparison circle showed the same size assimilation as found in the past by the method of limits. However, when concentric circles were presented alone and the apparent size of the inner and outer circles was judged absolutely by the number, the amount of illusion differed greatly from that of the Delboeuf illusion due to comparative judgment. In other words, the property that the illusion is maximized at the ratio of inner and outer circle diameters of 2:3, which was obtained by the comparative judgment, was not valid by the absolute judgment. We named this illusion the concentric circle illusion to distinguish it from the Delboeuf illusion. When the diameter difference between the inner and outer circles was 5.5 mm, which was the smallest, the inner circle was overestimated and the outer circle was also overestimated, causing the whole concentric circle to be expanded. The difference in the order of judgments between the inner and outer concentric circles caused a change in the amount of the concentric circle illusion, resulting in the judgment-order effect.

In the future, it is expected to clarify the anisotropy that appears in two-dimensional patterns, such as the anisotropy of the brightness illusion in Part 1, that of symmetry cognition in Part 3, and that of geometric illusion in Part 4.

In Part 5, the modality effect on random sequences of digits was investigated by the successive recall method. The different digits were presented audio-visually in the paired condition. As a result, it was found that visual and auditory memory mechanisms exist independently, and that auditory digits have an inhibitory effect on visual memory. In the overlap condition, in which the same digit was presented audio-visually, this inhibitory effect disappeared over time, and the visual and auditory information functioned effectively to improve memory performance. In addition, memory performance was better when the five visual and auditory digits were presented in clumps than when they were presented alternately one by one.

I believe that the theoretical origin of the five themes discussed in this book lies in the antagonistic process of excitation and inhibition. As described above, this book discusses symmetry cognition in dot patterns and the organizations of perception and memory from the standpoint of psychophysics and experimental phenomenology, based on psychological experimental results and theoretical models.

References

Adelson, E. H. (2000). Lightness perception and lightness illusion. In M. S. Gazzaniga (Ed.), *The new cognitive neurosciences* (2nd ed., pp. 333–359). Cambrige, MA: MIT Press.

Aiba, T. S. (1970). New psychohysics of Stevens. In T. Oyama (Ed.), *Psychological lectures, 4 perception* (pp. 261–287). Tokyo: Tokyo University Press (Japanese text).

Akita, M. (1969). Color vision and color theory. In R. Osaka (Ed.), *Psychological lectures, 3 sensation* (pp. 19–82). Tokyo: Tokyo University Press (Japanese text).

Akita, M., & Hamada, J. (1973). Increment threshold obtained under center-surround and center-backgrround conditions. In *JCIE Symposium on Color Science, Tokyo, 1973* (pp. 152–162).

Amano, K., Araki, M., Okano, D., Konishi, T., Fukushi, K., & Hamada, J. (2008). Effects of quasi-transformational group structures on similarity judgments of pattern pairs. *IPSJ Journal, 49,* 2667–2678 (Japanese text with English abstract and captions).

Amano, K., & Imai, S. (1989). Group theoretical approach to the cognition of transformational structures and similarity of patterns. *Japanese Journal of Psychology, 60,* 297–303 (Japanese text with English abstract).

Amano, K., & Imai, S. (1992). Group theoretical approach to the cognition of transformational structures and goodness of patterns. *Japanese Journal of Psychology, 63,* 181–187 (Japanese text with English abstract).

Amano, K., Okano, D., Araki, M., & Konishi, T. (2006). On the effectof transformational group structures in similarity judgments. *IPSJ Journal, 47,* 2807–2810 (Japanese text with English abstract and captions).

Amano, K., Okano, D., Ogata, H., Shibata, Y., Konishi, T., Fukushi, K., Hamada, J., & Imai, S. (2001). Transformational group structure theory on similarity judgment of patterns. *IPSJ Journal, 42,* 2733–2742 (Japanese text with English abstract and captions).

Amano, K., Ooya, T., Araki, S., Osanai, T., Endo, K., Okano, D., Konishi, T., Fukushi, K., & Hamada, J. (2013). Effects of quasi-transformational group structures on goodness judgments of patterns. *IPSJ Journal, 54,* 2254–2264 (Japanese text with English abstract and captions).

Arai, H. (2007). *Illusional illustration collection for mathematical studies of vision* (pp. 14–15). Sakigake: Graduate School of Mathematical Sciences, Tokyo University, Japan Science and Technology Agency (Japanese text).

Atkinson, R. C., & Shiffrin, R. M. (1968). Human memory: A proposed system and its control processes. In K. W. Spence, & J. T. Spence (Eds.), *Vol. 2. The psychology of learning and motivation: Advance in research and theory.* New York: Academic Press.

Atkinson, R. C., & Shiffrin, R. M. (1971). The control processes of short-term memory. *Scientific American, 224,* 82–90 (Tokyo: Nikkei Science, Japanese translation 1971).

Beck, J. (1972). *Surface color perception.* Cornell University Press.

Beitel, R. (1934). Spatial summation of subliminal stimuli in the retina of the human eye. *Journal of General Psychology, 10,* 311–325.

Beitel, R. (1936). Inhibition of threshold excitation in the retina of the human eye. *Journal of General Psychology, 14,* 31–61.

Békésy, G. v. (1959). Neural funneling along the skin and between the inner and outer hair cells of the cochlear. *Journal of Acoustical Society of America, 31,* 1236–1249.

Békésy, G. v. (1960). Neural inhibitory units of the eye and skin. Quantitative description of contrast phenomena. *Journal of the Optical Society of America, 50,* 1060–1070.

Békésy, G. v. (1967a). Mach band type lateral inhibition in different sense organs. *Journal of General Physiology, 50,* 519–532.

Békésy, G. v. (1967b). *Sensory inhibition.* Princeton University Press (Tokyo: Igaku Press, Japanese translation 1969).

Békésy, G. v. (1968). Mach- and Hering- type lateral inhibition in vision. *Vision Research, 8,* 1483–1499.

Békésy, G. v. (1972a). Mach bands measured by a compensation method. *Vision Research, 12,* 1485–1497.

Békésy, G. v. (1972b). Compensation method to measure the contrast produced by contours. *Journal of the Optical Society of America, 62,* 1247–1251.

Bergström, S. S. (1966). A paradox in thr perception of luminance gradients. I. *Scandinavian Journal of Psychology, 7,* 209–224.

Berman, P. W., & Liebowitz, H. W. (1965). Some effects of contour on simultaneous brightness contrast. *Journal of Experimental Psychology, 69,* 251–256.

Bernard, C. (1865). *Introduction à l'étude de la médecine expérimentale.* Tokyo: Iwanami Press (Paris, Japanese translation 1970).

Bertamini, M. (2010). Sensitivity to reflection and translation is modulated by objectness. *Perception, 39,* 27–40.

Bertamini, M., & Makin, A. D. J. (2014). Brain activity in response to visual symmetry. *Symmetry, 6,* 975–996.

Bertamini, M., Silvanto, J., Norcia, A. M., Makin, A. D. J., & Wagemans, J. (2018). The neural basis of visual symmetry and its role in middle and high-level visual processing. *Annals of the New York Academy of Sciences, 1426,* 111–126.

Bruce, V. G., & Morgan, M. J. (1975). Violations of symmetry and repetition in visual patterns. *Perception, 4,* 239–249.

Campbel, F. W., & Robson, J. G. (1965). Application of Fourier analysis to the visibility of gratings. *Journal of Physiology (London), 197,* 551–566.

Cohen, M. A., & Grossberg, S. (1984). Neural dynamics of brightness perception: Features, boundaries, diffusion, and resonance. *Perception & Psychophysics, 36,* 428–456.

Cooper, L. A., & Shepard, R. N. (1984). Turning something over in the mind. *Scientific American, 251,* 106–114 (Tokyo: Nikkei Science, Japanese translation 1985).

Corballis, M. C. (1966). Rehearsal and decay in immediate recall of visually and audrally presented items. *Canadian Journal of Psychology, 20,* 43–51.

Cornsweet, T. N. (1970). *Visual perception.* New York: Academic Press.

Coxeter, H. S. (1965). *Introduction to geometry.* New York: Wily (Tokyo: Meiji Press, Japanese translation 1965).

Craik, K. J. W. (1966). Brightness, discrimination, border, and subjective brightness. In S. L. Sherwood (Ed.), *The nature of psychology. A selection of papers, essays and other wrightings* (pp. 94–97). Cambridge University Press.

Craik, F. I. M., & Lockhart, R. S. (1972). Levels of processing: A framework for memory research. *Journal of Verbal Learning and Verbal Behavior, 11,* 671–684.

Crowder, R. G., & Morton, J. (1969). Precategorical acoustic storage (PAS). *Perception & Psychophysics, 5,* 365–373.

Dakin, S. C., & Herbert, A. M. (1998). The spatial region of integration for visual symmetry detection. *Proceedings of the Biological Sciences, 265,* 659–664.

Dakin, S. C., & Watt, R. J. (1994). Detection of bilateral symmetry using spatial filters. *Spatial Vision, 8,* 393–413.

Darwin, C. J., Turvey, M. T., & Crowdwe, R. G. (1974). An auditory analogue of Sperling paetial report procedure: Evidence for brief auditory storage. *Cognitive Psychology, 3,* 255–267.

Day, R. H., & Jory, M. K. (1978). Subjective contour, visual acuity, and line contrast. In J. C. Armington, J. Krauskopf, & B. R. Wooten (Eds.), *Visual psychophysics and physiology* (pp. 331–340). New York: Academic Press.

Day, R. H., & Jory, M. K. (1980). A note on a second stage in the formation of illusory contour. *Perception & Psychophysics, 27,* 89–91.

Davidson, M. (1968). Perturbation approach to spatial brightness interaction in human vision. *Journal of the Optical Society of America, 58,* 1300–1308.

Delboeuf, M. J. (1865). Note sur certaines illusions d'optique; essay d'une théorie psychphysique de la manière don't l'oeuil apprécie les distances et les angles. *Bulletin de l'Académie Royale des Sciences, des Lettres et des Beaux-Arts de Belgique, II Série, 19,* 195–216.

Diamond, A. L. (1953). Forveal simultaneous brightness contrast as a function of inducing- and test-field luminances. *Journal of Experimental Psychology, 45,* 304–314.

Dooley, R. P., & Greenfield, M. I. (1977). Measurement of edge-induced visual contrast and a spatial-frequency interaction of the Cornsweet illusion. *Journal of the Optical Society of America, 67,* 761–765.

Ebbinghaus, H. (1908). *Grundzüge der Psychologie. Vol. II.* Leipzig: Veit (Part 1).

Endo, N., Saiki, J., Nakao, Y., & Saito, H. (2003). Perceptual judgments of novel contoure shapes and hierarchical descriptions of geometrical properties. *Japanese Journal of Psychology, 74,* 346–353 (Japanese text with English abstract and captions).

Ehrenstein, W. (1941). Über Abwandlungen der L. Hermannschen Helliskeitserscheinung. *Zeitschrift für Psycholgie, 150,* 83–91 (English translated by Anne Hogg, 1987) Modifications of the brightness phenomenon of L. Hermann. In: S. Petry, & G. E. Meyer (Eds.), *The perception of illusory contours* (pp. 35-39). New York: Springer-Verlag).

Ehrenstein, W. (1954). *Orobleme der ganzheitspsychologischen Wahrnehmungshehre.* Leipzig: Johann Ambrosius Barth.

Ehrenstein, W. H., & Hamada, J. (1995). Structural factors of size contrast in the Ebbinghaus illusion. *Japanese Psychological Research, 37,* 158–169.

Ehrenstein, W. H., Hamada, J., & Paramei, G. V. (2004). Size induction: Stimulus and brain correlates. In A. M. Oliveira, M. Teixeira, G. F. Borges, & M. J. Ferro (Eds.), *Fechner Day 2004 Proceedings of the Twentieth Annual Meeting of the International Society for Psychophysics* (pp. 70–75). Coimbra, Portugal: International Socierty for Psycophysics.

Evans, R. M. (1959). *Eye, film, and camera in color photography.* New York: Wiley.

Fiorentini, A., & Radici, T. (1957). *Binocular measurements of brightness on a field presentining a luminance gradient* (pp. 453–461). XII: Atti Fond. Giorgio Ronchi.

Fiorentini, A., Baumgartner, G., Magnussen, S., Schiller, P. H., & Thomas, J. P. (1990). The perception of brightness and darkness: Relations to neuronal receptive fields. In L. Spillmann, & J. W. Werner (Eds.), *Visual perception: The neurophysiological foundations* (pp. 129–161). San Diego: Academic Press.

Fry, G. A., & Alpern, M. (1953). The effect of a peripheral glare source upon the apparent brightness of an object. *Journal of the Optical Society of America, 43,* 189–195.

Fuld, K., & O'Donnell, K. (1984). Brightness matching and scaling of the Ehrenstein illusion. In L. Spillmann, & B. R. Wooten (Eds.), *Sensory experience, adaptation, and perception* (pp. 461–469). Hillsdale, NJ: Erlbaum.

Fujii, K., Matsuoka, A., & Morita, T. (1967). Analysis of the optical illusion by lateral inhibition. *Japanese Journal of Medical Electronics and Biological Engineering, 5,* 117–126 (Japanese text with English abstract and captions).

Fukouzu, Y., Itoh, A., Yoshida, T., & Shiraishi, T. (1998). An analysisof the figure by the visual space transfer model $F_{(1)}$: A study on elucidation and estimation of a scene on figure recognition (6). *Bulletin of Japanese Society for the Science of Design, 45,* 75–82 (Japanese text with English summary).

Furukawa, T., & Hagiwara, S. (1978). A nonlinear receptive field model of the visual system. *IEEE Transactions on Biomedical Engineering, BME-25*(1), 76–83.

Fushimi, K. (1967a). The science of patterns (1). *Mathematical Seminar, 5,* 50–55 (Japanese text).

Fushimi, K. (1967b). The science of patterns (6). *Mathematical Seminar, 11,* 20–26 (Japanese text).

Fushimi, K. (2013). *Kohji Fushimi collection. Vol. 1. The science of patterns.* Tokyo: Nippon Hyoron Press (Japanese text).

Garner, W. R. (1966). To perceive is to know. *American Psychologist, 21,* 11–19.

Garner, W. R. (1970). Good patterns have few alternatives. *American Scientist, 58,* 34–42.

Garner, W. R. (1974). *The processing of information and structure.* Hillsdale, NJ: Lawrence Erlbaum Associates.

Garner, W. R., & Clement, D. E. (1963). Goodness of pattern and pattern uncertainty. *Journal of Verbal Learning and Verbal Behavior, 2,* 446–452.

Gergeson, M. A. (1980). Spatial frequency analysis in early visual processing. *Philosophical Transactions of the Royal Society of London B, 290,* 11–22.

Gerrits, H. J. M., & Vendrik, A. J. H. (1970). Simultaneous contrast, filling-in process and information processing in man's visual system. *Experimental Brain Research, 11,* 411–430.

Girgus, J., Coren, S., & Agdern, M. (1972). The interrelationship between the Ebbinghaus and Delboeuf illusions. *Journal of Experimental Psychology, 95,* 453–455.

Glass, L. (1969). Moiré effect from random dots. *Nature, 223,* 578–580.

Glass, L., & Pérez, R. (1973). Perception of random dot intereference patterns. *Nature, 246,* 360–362.

Goto, T. (1987). Experimental study on size-illusion of contrastive circles (4): Effects of the combination of stimulus conditions and of the repeated observations on the magnitude of Ebbinghaus illusion. *Journal of the Faculty of Letters: Nagoya University (Philosophy), 33,* 53–76 (Japanese text with English abstract).

Goto, T., & Ohya, K. (1989). Experimental study on the contitions of stimulus presentation in the size illusion of contrastive circles. *Journal of the Faculty of Letters: Nagoya University (Philosophy), 35,* 37–59 (Japanese text with English abstract).

Goto, T., & Tanaka, H. (2005). *Handbook of the science of illusion.* Tokyo: Tokyo University Press (Japanese text).

Greene, R. L. (1987). Stimulus suffixes and visual presentation. *Memory & Cognition, 15,* 497–503.

Greene, R. L., & Crowder, R. G. (1986). Recency effects in delayed recall of mouthed stimuli. *Memory & Cognition, 14,* 355–360.

Grossberg, S. (1983). The quantized geometry of visual space: The coherent computation of depth, form, and lightness. *Behavioral and Brain Sciences, 6,* 625–692.

Grossberg, S. (1987). Cortical dynamics of three-dimensional form, color, and brightness perception, I: Monocular theory. *Perception & Psychophysics, 41,* 87–116.

Grossberg, S., & Mingolla, E. (1985). Neural dynamics of form perception: Boundary completion, illusory figure, and neon color spreading. *Psychological Review, 92,* 173–211.

Grossberg, S., & Mingolla, E. (1987). The role of illusory contours in visual segmentation. In S. Petry, & G. E. Meyer (Eds.), *The perception of illusory contours* (pp. 116–125). New York: Springer-Verlag.

Grossberg, S., & Kelly, F. (1999). Section 4. Neural dynamics of binocular brightness perceotion. *Vision Research, 39,* 3796–3816.

Grossberg, S., & Todorovic, D. (1988). Neural dynamic of 1-D and 2-D brightness perception: A unified model of classical and recent phenomena. In S. Grossberd (Ed.), *Neural networks and natural intelligence* (pp. 127–194). Cambridge: The MIT Press.

Guilford, J. P. (1954). *Psychometric method.* New York: McGraw (Tokyo: Baifu Press, Japanese translation 1959).

Guirao, M. (1991). A single scale based on ratio and partition estimates. In S. J. Bolanowski Jr.,, & G. A. Gescheider (Eds.), *Ratio scaling of psychological magnitude: In honor of the memory of S. S. Stevens* (pp. 59–78). Hillsdale, NJ: Lawrence Erlbaum Associates.

Gyoba, J. (1995). *Important research collection of cognitive psychology: Visual cognition.* Tokyo: Seishin Press (Japanese text).

Gyoba, J. (2004). Visual psychophysics (10): Figure perception and visual illusions. *Journal of the Institute of Image Information and Television Engineers, 58*, 1385–1390 (Japanese text).

Gyoba, J., Seto, I., & Ichikawa, S. (1985). Problems on the rating of pattern cognition: An analysis by the semantic differential method and its correspondence to Imai's transformation structure theory. *Japanese Journal of Psychology, 56*, 111–115 (Japanese text with English abstract).

Hamada, J. (1971). *Inhibitory and facilitational effects in visual field* (Bachelor thesis) (pp. 1–109). Tokushima, Japan: Tokushima University (Japanese text).

Hamada, J. (1976a). A mathematical model for brightness and contour perception. In *XXIst international congress of psychology, abstract guide* (p. 355).

Hamada, J. (1976b). A mathematical model for brightness and contour perception. *Hokkaido Report of Psychology, HRP-11-76-17*, 1–19.

Hamada, J. (1980a). *A model construction and psychophysical studies on light-dark contrast induction.* Ph.D. thesis Sapporo, Japan: Hokkaido University (1-202 (Japanese text).

Hamada, J. (1980b). An inducing mechanism of the Craik-O'Brien and the Cornsweet effects. *Japanese Journal of Psychology, 51*, 55–62 (Japanese text with English abstract and captions).

Hamada, J. (1980c). Lightness changes induced by incremental and decremental luminance patterns. *Institute of Electronics and Communication Engineers of Japan, IE79-80*, 19–27 (Japanese text).

Hamada, J. (1982). The contour enhancement effects produced by darkening effects. In H.-G. Geissler, & P. Petzold (Eds.), *Psychophysical judgment and the process of perception* (pp. 132–139). Amsterdam: North-Holland.

Hamada, J. (1983). Lightness decreas of the total area accompanying simultaneous lightness contrast. *Japanese Journal of Psychology, 54*, 115–122 (Japanese text with English abstract and captions).

Hamada, J. (1984a). Lightness decrease and increase in square-wave gratings. *Perception & Psychophysics, 35*, 16–21 (Springer Nature).

Hamada, J. (1984b). A multi-stage model for border contrast. *Biological Cybernetics, 51*, 65–70 (Springer Nature).

Hamada, J. (1984c). How humans perceive things. *Publicity from Tokushima University, 49*, 12–16 (Japanese text).

Hamada, J. (1985). Asymmetric lightness cancellation in Craik-O'Brien patterns of negative and positive contrast. *Biological Cybernetics, 52*, 117–122 (Springer Nature).

Hamada, J. (1986). Interaction between visual and auditory memory for random digits series under forward and backward rehearsal/recall conditions. *Japanese Journal of Psychonomic Science, 5*, 55–61 (Japanese text with English abstract and captions).

Hamada, J. (1987). Overall brightness decrease in the Ehrenstein illusion induced for both contrast polarities. *Perception & Psychophysics, 41*, 67–72 (Springer Nature).

Hamada, J. (1988a). Effects of symmetry groups on complexity and goodness in visual pattern. *Japanese Journal of Psychology, 59*, 137–143 (Japanese text with English abstract).

Hamada, J. (1988b). Superiority between auditory and vusual primacy effects depended on memorization rate. *Japanese Journal of Psychonomic Science, 7*, 85–89 (Japanese text with English abstract).

Hamada, J. (1990a). Examination of negative time order effect based on relative and absolute judgments. *Japanese Journal of Psycholomic Science, 9*, 1–10 (Japnese text with English abstract and captions).

Hamada, J. (1990b). Some differences between the visual and auditory memories in the short-term memory. *Japanese Journal of Psychology, 61*, 8–14 (Japanese text with English abstract).

Hamada, J. (1991). Asymmetries in the perception of lightness and darkness. *Trends in Biological Cybernetics, 2*, 93–105.

Hamada, J. (1993). Goodness and complexity ratings of repetitive patterns formed by wall-paper groups. *Journal of Human Science, Faculty of Integrated Arts and Sciences, Tokushima University*, *1*, 39–51 (Japanese text with English abstract and captions).

Hamada, J. (1994). Brightness perception. In T. Oyama, S. Imai, & T. Wake (Eds.), *Handbook of sensory and perceptual psychology* (pp. 344–348). Tokyo: Seishin Press (Japanese text).

Hamada, J. (1995). The Ehrenstein illusion: Effect of contrast polarity, gap size, and line orientation. *Japanese Psychological Research*, *37*, 117–124.

Hamada, J. (1996). Symmetry and pattern cognition: The general effect of glide-reflection and selective effect of inclination upon pattern cognition. *Japanese Psychological Review*, *39*, 338–360 (Japanese text with English abstract and figures).

Hamada, J. (2002). Examination of Delboef illusion by magnitude estimation and constant method. In *Proceedings of the 66th Annual Convention of Japanese Psychological Association* (p. 442). (Japanese text).

Hamada, J. (2005). Size-illusion of Delboef (concentric circle illusion). In T. Goto, & H. Tanaka (Eds.), *Handbook of the science of illusion* (pp. 126–135). Tokyo: Tokyo University Press (Japanese text).

Hamada, J. (2008). *The excitation and the compound inhibition in brightness illusion*. Tokyo: Kazama Press (Japanese text).

Hamada, J. (2010). The same thing looks different in brightness. In *Tokushima Newspaper, October 30* (Japanese text).

Hamada, J. (2020). *Psychophysics of pattern cognition*. Tokyo: Kazama Press (Japanese text).

Hamada, J., Amano, K., Fukuda, S. T., Uchiumi, C., Fukushi, K., & van der Helm, P. A. (2016). Group theoretical model of symmetry cognition. *Acta Psychologica*, *171*, 128–137. https://doi.org/10.1016/j.actpsy.2016.10.002

Hamada, J., & Ehrenstein, W. H. (2008). Long-range effects in brightness induction: An absolute judgment approach. *Gestalt Theory*, *30*, 61–69.

Hamada, J., Ehrenstein, W. H., Müller, M., & Cavonius, C. R. (1992). Global loss of brightness accompanying simultaneous brightness contrast. In *XXVth International Congress of Psychology*. Brussels.

Hamada, J., Fukuda, S. T., Uchiumi, C., Fukushi, K., & Amano, K. (2019). Effects of dot number and symmetry group order on goodness and complexity of dot patterns in a group theoretical approach. *Japanese Journal of Psychonomic Science*, *37*, 153–162 (Japanese text with English abstract and figure captions) https://doi.org/10.14947/psychono.37.22

Hamada, J., & Ishihara, T. (1987). A tortoise-shell pattern structure and human pattern cognition. In *Commemoration volume of the founding of the faculty of integrated arts and sciences* (pp. 305–316). The University of Tokushima (Japanese text with English captions).

Hamada, J., & Ishihara, T. (1988). Complexity and goodness of dot patterns varying in symmetry. *Psychological Research*, *50*, 155–161 (Springer Nature).

Hamada, J., Nabeta, T., Fukuda, S. T., Uchiumi, C., Fukushi, K., & Amano, K. (2017). Goodness and complexity of dot patterns in a matrix framework based on a group theoretical model. *Japanese Journal of Psychonomic Science*, *36*, 30–39 (Japanese text with English abstract and figure captions) https://doi.org/10.14947/pshchono.36.4

Hamada, J., & Nakahashi, T. (1995). Relationship between form and brightness in the Ehrenstein illusion. *Perception*, *24*(Supplement), 79.

Hamada, J., Nishimura, H., Patamei, G. V., & Eherenstein, W. H. (2002). Apparent size and judgment-order effect: A magnitude estimation study of the Delboeuf illusion. *Japanese Journal of Psychology*, *73*, 58–63 (Japanese text with English abstract).

Hamada, J., Paramei, G. V., & Ehrenstein, W. H. (2000). Judgment-order effect on apparent size in the Delboeuf illusion. *Journal of Human Science, Faculty of Integrated Arts and Sciences, Tokushima University*, *8*, 1–13 (Japanese text with English abstract and captions).

Hamada, J., Uchiumi, C., Fukushi, K., & Amano, K. (2011a). Goodness of compound patterns based on symmetry groups. *Japanese Journal of Psychology*, *82*, 1–8 (Japanese text with English abstract).

Hamada, J., Uchiumi, C., Fukushi, K., & Amano, K. (2011b). Complexity and goodness of dot patterns depending upon symmetry groups. *Japanese Psychological Review*, *54*, 138–152 (Japanese text with English abstract).

Hamada, J., Uchiumi, C., Fukushi, K., & Amano, K. (2013). Goodness and complexity of compound and filled patterns depending upon a hierarchy of perception. *Japanese Journal of Psychonomic Science*, *31*, 123–134 (Japanese text with English abstract and captions).

Hamada, J., Uchiumi, C., Sato, Y., Fukuda, T. S., Fukushi, K., & Amano, K. (2021). Examining disjointedness of dot patterns based on a three-stage serial processing model of symmetry cognition. *Journal of Human Science, Faculty of Integrated Arts and Sciences, Tokushima University*, *29*, 1–14 (Japanese text with English abstract and captions) https://repo.lib.tokushima-u.ac.jp/116654

Hartline, H. K., & Ratliff, F. (1957). Inhibitory interaction of receptor units in the eye of Limulus. *Journal of General Physiology*, *40*, 357–376.

Hayashi, K. (1937). Transitional comparison of equal weight (II). *Japanese Journal of Psychology*, *12*, 564–577 (Japanese text).

Heinemann, E. G. (1955). Simultaneous brightness induction as a function of inducing- and test-field luminances. *Journal of Experimental Psychology*, *50*, 80–96.

Helmholtz, H. V. (1867). *Handbuch der physiologischen Optik* (1st ed.). Hamburg and Leipzig: Voss.

Helson, H. (1947). Adaptation-level as frame of reference for prediction of psychophysical data. *American Journal of Psychology*, *60*, 1–29.

Helson, H. (1963). Studies of anomalous contrast and assimilation. *Journal of the Optical Society of America*, *53*, 179–184.

Helson, H. (1964). *Adaptation-level theory: An experimental and systematic approach to behavior*. New York: Harper & Row.

Helson, H., & Roles, F. H. (1959). A quantitative study of reversal of classical lightness-contrast. *American Journal of Psychology*, *72*, 530–538.

Hering, E. (1920). *Grundzüge der Lehre vom Lichtsinn*. Berlin: Julius Springer (*Outlines of a theory of the light sense*, translated by Hurvich, L. M., & Jameson, D. (1964). Cambridge, Massachusetts: Harvard University Press.).

Hochberg, J. E. (1971). Perception: 1. Color and shape. In J. W. Kling, & L. A. Riggs (Eds.), *Woodworth & Schlosberg's experimental psychology* (3rd ed., pp. 395–474). New York: Holt, Rinehart and Winston, Inc.

Hochberg, J. E. (1978). *Perception* (2nd ed.). Englewood Cliffs, New Jersey: Prentie-Hall, Inc. (Tokyo: Iwanami Press, Japanese translation 1981).

Horeman, H. W. (1963). Inducitive brightness depression as influenced by configurational conditions. *Vision Research*, *3*, 121–130.

Horeman, H. W. (1965). Relation between brightness and luminance under induction. *Vision Research*, *5*, 331–340.

Horst, S. (2005). Phenomenology and psychophysics. *Phenomenology and the Cognitive Sciences*, *4*, 1–21.

Hubel, D. G., & Wiesel, T. N. (1965). Receptive fields and functional aechitecture in two nonstriate visual areas (18 and 19) of the cat. *Journal of Neurophysiology*, *28*, 229–289.

Hubel, D. G., & Wiesel, T. N. (1979). Brain mechanisms of vision. *Scientific American*, *241*, 150–162 (Tokyo: Nikkei Science, Japanese translation 1979).

Ichikawa, S. (1985). Quantitative and structural factors in the judgment of pattern complexity. *Perception & Psychophysics*, *38*, 101–109.

Ichikawa, S., & Gyoba, J. (1984). Methodological problems on pattern psychophysics. *Japanese Psychological Review*, *27*, 132–157 (Japanese text with English abstract).

Imai, S. (1972). Effect of inter-pattern transformation structures upon similarity judgments of linear pattern pairs. In *Proceedings of the XXth International Congress of Psychology* (pp. 164–165).

Imai, S. (1977a). Various theories about the goodness of patterns. *Japanese Psychological Review, 20,* 258–272 (Japanese text with English abstract).

Imai, S. (1977b). Pattern similarity and cognitive transformations. *Acta Psychologica, 41,* 433–447.

Imai, S. (1979). Die antizipative Natur der Wiedergewinnung aus dem menschlichen Gedächtnis: Die Wirkung von Aufgabenwechsel und -unterbrechungs auf die Reproduktionsleistung. In F. Klix, K.-P. Timpe, & Hrsg (Eds.), *Arbeits- und Ingenieurpsychologie und Intensivierung* (pp. 32–36). Berlin: VEB, Deutscher Verlag der Wissenschaften.

Imai, S. (1986). The transformational structure theory of pattern cognition. In *17. Japanese Psychological Monographs*. Tokyo: Tokyo University Press (Japanese text with English summary).

Imai, S. (1992). Fundamentals of cognitive judgments of pattern. In H.-G. Geissler, S. W. Link, & J. T. Townsend (Eds.), *Cognition, information processing, and psychophysics: Basic issues* (pp. 225–265). New Jersey: Lawrence Erlbaum Associates.

Imai, S., & Amano, K. (1998). A theory of pattern cognition based on the concepts of transformation and mapping. *Bulletin of the Japan Society for Industrial and Applied Mathematics, 8,* 30–45 (Japanese text with English abstract).

Imai, S., & Hosoda, S. (1988). Paradoxical fall in repetitive learning of a random series of digits. *Japanese Journal of Psychology, 59,* 227–233 (Japanese text with English abstract).

Imai, S., Ito, T., & Ito, S. (1976a). Effect of intra-pattern transformation structures upon goodness judgments of two-dimensional patterns. *Japanese Journal of Psychology, 47,* 202–210 (Japanese text with English abstract and summary).

Imai, S., Ito, S., & Ito, T. (1976b). Effects of intra-pattern transformation structures and the number of runs upon goodness and complexity judgments of patterns. *Japanese Psychological Review, 19,* 77–94 (Japanese text with English abstract).

Ito, M., & Hamada, J. (1972). Experimental study on facilitation effects in visual field (continued from the last report). *Bulletin of Journal of Cultural and Social Sciences, University of Tokushima, Department of Liberal Arts, 7,* 163–172 (Japanese text with English abstract and captions).).

Ito, S. (1975). Similarity judgments of patterns depending upon perceived inter-pattern transformation structures. *Japanese Journal of Psychology, 46,* 10–18 (Japanese text with English abstract).

Jory, M. K., & Day, R. H. (1979). The relationship between brightness contrast and illusory contours. *Perception, 8,* 3–9.

Jung, R. (1973). Visual perception and neurophysiology. In R. Jung (Ed.), *Central processing of visual information, handbook of sensory physiology, VII/3A* (pp. 1–152). Berlin: Springer-Verlag.

Kaneko, T., & Obonai, T. (1952). Factors of intensity, quantity and distance in psychophysiological indaction. *Japanese Journal of Psychology, 23,* 73–79 (Japanese text with English abstract).

Kaneko, T., & Obonai, T. (1959). Spatio-temporal characteristics of excitation and inhibition in the retino-cerebral field. *Japanese Psychological Research, 1,* 1–5.

Kanizsa, G. (1955). Margini quasi-percettivi in campi con stimolazione omogenea. *Rivista di Psicologia, 49,* 7–30 (English translated by Gerbino, W., 1987) Quasi-perceptual margins in homogeneously stimulated fields. In: Petry, S., & Meyer, G. E. (Eds.), *The perception of illusory contours* (pp. 40–49). New York: Springer-Verlag.).

Kanizsa, G. (1976). Subjective contours. *Scientific American, 234,* 48–52 (Tokyo: Nikkei Science, Japanese translation 1976).

Kanizsa, G. (1979). *Organization in vision: Essays on gestalt perception.* New York: Praeger (Tokyo: Science Press, Japanese translation 1985).

Kawahara, J., Nabeta, T., & Hamada, J. (2007). Area-specific attentional effect in the Delboeuf illusion. *Perception, 36,* 670–685.

Kennedy, J. M. (1979). Subjective contoures, contrast, and assimilation. In C. F. Nodine, & D. F. Fisher (Eds.), *Perception and pictorial representaltion* (pp. 167–195). New York: Praeger.

Köhler, W. (1923). Zur Theorie des Sukzessivver-gleiches und der Zeitfehler. *Psychologische Forschung, 4,* 115–175.

Köhler, W. (1940). *Dynamics in psychology.* New York: Liveright (Tokyo: Iwanami Press, Japanese translation 1952).

Kingdom, F. A. (2003). Levels of brightness perception. In L. Harris, & M. Jenkin (Eds.), *Level of perception* (pp. 23–46). New York: Springer-Verlag.

Koffka, K. (1915). Zur Grundlegung der Wahrnehmungspsychogie: Eine Auseinandersetzung mit V. Benussi. *Zeitschrift für Psychologie, 73,* 11–90.

Koffka, K. (1923). Über Feldbegrenzung und Felderfüllug. *Psychelogie Forshung, 4.*

Koffka, K. (1931). *Pshchologie der optischen Wahrnehmung. Bethe's Handbuch der Physiologie. Vol. 12.* (2. Hälfte).

Koffka, K. (1935). *Principles of gestalt psychology.* New York: Harcourt Brace (Tokyo: Fukumura Press, Japanese translation 1988).

Konishi, T., Okano, D., & Amano, K. (2008). Statistical test of the order predicted by the transformational group structure theory. *Information, 11,* 239–248.

Konishi, T., Okano, D., Ogata, H., Shibata, Y., Amano, K., Fukushi, K., Hamada, J., & Imai, S. (2003). Transformational group structure theory on goodness judgments of patterns. *IPSJ Journal, 44,* 2274–2283 (42, 2733–2742 (Japanese text with English abstract and captions).).

Koyadu, T. (1969). Induction field of vision. In Y. Wada, T. Oyama, & S. Imai (Eds.), *Handbook of sensation and perception psychology* (pp. 504–536). Tokyo: Seishin Press (Japanese text).

Kuffler, S. W. (1953). Discharge patterns and functional organization of mammalian retina. *Journal of Neurophysiology, 16,* 37–68.

Kuroda, K., & Noguchi, K. (1984). Similarity grouping effects in the size-assimilation and size-contrast illusion. In *Proceedings of the 48th Annual Convention of Japanese Psychological Association* (p. 168). (Japanese text).

Lauenstein, O. (1933). Ansatz zur einer physiologishen Theorie des Vergleich und der Zeitfehler. *Psychologische Forschung, 17,* 130–177.

Ledermann, W., & Vajda, S. (1985). *Handbook of applicable mathematics: Vol. V. Combinatorics and geometry* (pp. 329–422). Chichester, UK: Wily.

Lindsay, P. H., & Norman, D. A. (1977). *Human information processing: An introduction to psychology.* New York: Academic Press (Tokyo: Science Press, Japanese translation 1983).

Liu, C. L. (1968). *Introduction to combinatorial mathematics.* New York: McGraw-Hill (Tokyo: Kyoritsu Press, Japanese translation 1972).

Loftus, G. R., & Loftus, E. F. (1976). *Human memory: The processing of information.* Hillsdale: Lawrence Erlbaum Associates (Tokyo: Tokyo University Press, Japanese translation 1980).

Mach, E. (1865). Über die Wirkung der räumlichen Vertheihung des Lichtreizes auf die Netzhaut. In *Sitzungsberichte der mathematisch-naturwissenschaftlichen Classe der kaiserlichen Akademic der Wissenschaften, 52* (pp. 303–322). (Ratliff, 1965).

Mach, E. (1918). *Die Analyse der Empfindungen und das Verhältnis des Physischen zum Psychischen.* Jena, Germany: Verlag von Gustav Fischer (Tokyo: Hosei University Press, Japanese translation 1971).

Magnussen, S., & Glad, A. (1975). Brightness and darkness enhancement during flicker: Perceptual correlates of neural B- and D-systems in human vision. *Experimental Brain Research, 22*, 399–413.

Makin, A. D. J., Wright, D., Rampone, G., Palumbo, L., Guest, M., Sheehan, R., Cleaver, H., & Bertamini, M. (2016). An electrophysiological index of perceptual goodness. *Cerebral Cortex.* https://doi.org/10.1093/cercor/bhw255

Marr, D. (1983). *Vision: A computational integration onto the human representation and processing of visual information.* San Francisco: W. H. Freeman and Company (Tokyo: Sangyo Press, Japanese translation 1987).

Marr, D., & Hildreth, E. (1980). Theory of edge detection. *Proceedings of the Royal Society of London, B207*, 187–217.

Massaro, D. W., & Anderson, N. H. (1971). Judgmental model of the Ebbinghaus circles illusion. *Journal of Experimental Psychology, 89*, 147–151.

Matsuda, T. (1978). Judgments of pattern goodness and intra-configurational transformation structures: An examination of Imai's theory. *Japanese Journal of Psychology, 49*, 207–214 (Japanese text with English abstract).

Metzger, W. (1953). *Gesetze des Sehens.* Frankfurt am Main: Verlag von Waldem Kramer (Tokyo: Iwanami Press, Japanese translation 1968).

Metzger, W. (2006). *Laws of seeing* (English translated by Spillmann, L., Lehar, S., Stromeyer, M. and Wertheimer, M.). Cambridge: MIT Press.

Minguzzi, G. F. (1987). Anomalous figures and the tendency to continuation. In S. Petry, & G. E. Meyer (Eds.), *The perception of illusory contours* (pp. 71–75). New York: Springer-Verlag.

Mori, T. (1970). Visual field. In T. Oyama (Ed.), *Psychological lectures, 4 perception* (pp. 139–166). Tokyo: Tokyo University Press (Japanese text).

Mori, T. (1977). Mach bands. In O. Fujita, T. Mori, & Y. Isogai (Eds.), *Vol. 2. Psychological laboratory* (pp. 93–123). Tokyo: Fukumura Press (Japanese text).

Morinaga, S. (1935). Conditions for size-assimilation and size-contrast. In *Memorial papers on modern psychology for Dr. Masuda* (pp. 28–48). Tokyo: Iwanami Press (Japanese text).

Morinaga, S. (1941). Beobachtungen über Grundlagen und Wirkungen anschaulich gleichmässiger Breite. *Archiv für die Gesamte Psychologie, 110*, 309–348.

Morinaga, S. (1959). Über die Raumwahrnehmung in Hinsicht auf die optischen Täuschungen. In *Proceedings of the 15th International Congress of Psychology* (pp. 273–274). Amsterdam: North-Holland.

Morinaga, S. (1969). *Perceptional psychology.* Tokyo: Meigen Press (Japanese, German, and English texts).

Morinaga, S., & Noguchi, K. (1966). An attempt to unify the size-assimilation and size-contrast illusions. *Psychologische Forschung, 29*, 161–168.

Motokawa, K. (1948). Physiological basis of sensation. *Science, 18*, 526–537. Tokyo: Iwamami Press (Japanese text).

Motokawa, K., & Akita, M. (1957). Electrophysiological studies of the field of retinal induction. *Psychologia, 1*, 10–16.

Moulden, B., & Kingdom, F. (1990). Light-dark asymmetries in the Craik-Cornsweet-O'Brien illusion and a new model of brightness coding. *Spatial Vision, 5*, 101–121.

Murray, D. J. (1966). Vocalization-at-presentaion and immediate recall, with varying recall methods. *Quarterly Journal of Experimental Psychology, 18*, 9–18.

Noguchi, K. (1964). Overview of reseach in adaptation-level. *Japanese Journal of Psychology, 35*, 96–108 (Japanese text).

Noguchi, K. (1982). Illusion theory - paradox of Morinaga's displacement. *Psychology, 8*, 40–47 (Japanese text).

Noguchi, K. (2001). The third approach to the study of perception: Experimental phenomenology and experimental aesthetics. *Pshchological Research, Nihon University, 22*, 20–25 (Japanesr text with English abstract and captions).

Noguchi, K. (2003). Aesthetic world approachrd through sensation and perception: The relationship between psychophysical and aesthetic judgments. *Japanese Journal of Sensory Evaluation, 7,* 92–97 (Japanese text).

Noguchi, K. (2005). Illusion and experimental aesthetics. In T. Goto, & H. Tanaka (Eds.), *Handbook of the science of illusion* (pp. 458–466). Tokyo: Tokyo University Press (Japanese text).

Noguchi, K., Kitaoka, A., & Takashima, M. (2008). Gestalt-oriented perceptual research in Japan: Past and present. *Gestalt Theory, 30,* 11–28.

Noguchi, K., & Rentschler, I. (1999). Comparison between geometrical illusion and aesthetic preference. *Journal of Faculty of Engineering, Chiba University, 50,* 29–33.

Obonai, T. (1933). Experiments on the illusion of contrast and confluence: Contributions to the study psycho-physiological induction (1). *Japanese Journal of Psychology, 8,* 1–20 (Japanese text with English abstract).

Obonai, T. (1954). Induction effect in estimates of extent. *Journal of Experimental Psychology, 47,* 57–60.

Obonai, T. (1955). *Visual perception: A study of psycho-physiological induction theory.* Tokyo: Nakayama Press (Japanese text).

Obonai, T. (1957). The concept of psycho-physiological induction. *Psychologia, 1,* 3–9.

Obonai, T. (1977). *Perception, learning, and thinking: Psycho-physiological induction theory.* Tokyo: The Hokuseido Press.

O'Brian, V. (1958). Contour perception, illusion and reality. *Journal of the Optical Society of America, 48,* 112–119.

Ogasawara, J. (1952). Displacement-effect of concentric circles. *Japanese Journal of Psychology, 22,* 224–233 (Japanese text with English abstract).

Oliva, A., Mack, M. L., Shrestha, M., & Peeper, A. (2004). Identifying the perceptual dimensions of visual complexity of scenes. In *Proceedings of the 26th Annual Meeting of the Cognitive Science Society.*

Otsuka, Y. (1984). The role of geometrical transformations in the cognitive judgments of patterns. *Japanese Journal of Psychology, 55,* 67–74 (Japanese text with English abstract).

Oppel, J. J. (1855). Über geometrisch-optishe Täuschung. *Jahresbericht des physikaliscen Vereins zu Frankfurt am Main,* 37–47.

Osgood, C. E., Suci, G. J., & Tannenbaum, P. H. (1957). *The measurement of meaning.* Urbana: University of Illinois Press.

Oyama, T. (1960). Japanese studies on the so-called geometrical-optical illusions. *Psychologia, 3,* 7–20.

Oyama, T. (1970). Geometric illusion. In T. Oyama (Ed.), *Psychological lectures, 4 perception* (pp. 91–109). Tokyo: Tokyo University Press (Japanese text).

Oyama, T. (2010). *Measuring perception: What experimental data tell us about visual psychology.* Tokyo: Seishin Press (Japanese text).

Oyama, T., Miyano, H., & Yamada, H. (2002). Application of multidimensional scaling to color and shape similarity perception. In H. Yanai, A. Okada, K. Shigemasu, H. Takagi, & M. Iwasaki (Eds.), *Handbook of multivariate analysis examples* (pp. 634–647). Tokyo: Asakura Press (Japanese text).

Palmer, S. E. (1982). Symmetry, transformation, and the structure of perceptual systems. In J. Beck (Ed.), *Organization and representation in perception* (pp. 95–144). Hillsdale: Lawrence Erlbaum Association.

Palmer, S. E. (1983). The psychology of perceptual organization: A transformational approach. In J. Beck, B. Hope, & A. Rosenfeld (Eds.), *Human and machine vision* (pp. 269–339). New York: Academic Press.

Palmer, S. E. (1991). Goodness, gestalt, groups, and garner: Local symmetry subgroups as a theory of figural goodness. In G. R. Lockhead, & J. R. Pomerantz (Eds.), *The perception of structure: Essays in honor of Wendell R. Garner* (pp. 23–39). Washington, DC: American Psychological Association.

Palumbo, L., Ogden, R., Makin, A. D. J., & Bertamini, M. (2014). Examining visual complexity and its influence on perceived duration. *Journal of Vision, 14*, 1–18.

Paramei, G. V., Hamada, J., & Ehrenstein, W. H. (2003). Size induction: A judgment-order effect. In B. Berglund, & E. Borg (Eds.), *Proceedings of the Nineteenthe Annual Meeting of the International Society of Psychophysics* (pp. 223–228). Stockholm: International Socierty for Psychophysics.

Patel, A. S. (1966). Spatial resolution by the human visual ststem. The effect of mean retinal illuminance. *Journal of the Optical Society of America, 56*, 689–694.

Pavlov, I. P. (1927). *Conditioned reflxes.* London and New York: Oxford University Press.

Petry, S., & Meyer, G. E. (1987). *The perception of illusory contours.* New York: Springer-Verlag.

Prazdny, K. (1983). Illusory contours are not caused by simultaneous brightness contrast. *Perception & Psychophysics, 34*, 403–404.

Pritchard, R. M. (1961). Stabilized images on the retina. *Scientific American, 204*. 72–78. (Aichi: Aichi Gakuin University, Japanese translation 1978).

Ratliff, F. (1965). *Mach bands: Quantitative studies on neural networks in the retina.* San Francisco: Holden-Day.

Ratliff, F. (1971). Contour and contrast. *Proceedings of the American Philosophical Society, 115*, 150–163.

Ratliff, F. (1972). Contour and contrast. *Scientific American, 226*(6), 90–101 (Tokyo: Nikkei Science, Japanese translation 1972).

Ratliff, F., & Hartline, H. K. (1959). The responses of limulus optic nerve fibers to patterns of illumination on the receptor mosaic. *Journal of General Physiology, 42*, 1241–1255.

Ratliff, F., & Riggs, L. A. (1950). In voluntary motions of the eye during monocular fixation. *Journal of Experimental Psychology, 40*, 687–701.

Rigss, L. A. (1971). Vision. In J. W. King, & L. A. Riggs (Eds.), *Woodworth & Schlosberg's experimental psychology* (3rd ed., pp. 273–314). New York: Holt, Rinehart and Winston, Inc.

Robinson, J. O. (1972). *The psychology of visual illusion.* London: Hutchinson University Library.

Robson, J. G. (1983). Frequency domain visual processing. In O. J. Braddick, & A. C. Sleigh (Eds.), *Physical and biological processing of images* (pp. 73–87). Berlin: Springer.

Rock, I. (1974). The perception of disoriented figures. *Scientific American, 230*, 78–85 (Tokyo: Nikkei Science, Japanese translation 1974).

Rock, I., & Anson, R. (1979). Illusory contours as the solution to a problem. *Perception, 8*, 665–681.

Rubin, E. (1921). *Visuell wahrgenommene Figuren: Studien in psychologischer Analyse.* Copenhagen: Gyldendalska Boghandel.

Sambin, M. (1987). A dynamic model of anomalous figures. In S. Petry, & G. E. Meyer (Eds.), *The perception of illusory contours* (pp. 131–142). New York: Springer-Verlag.

Schumann, F. (1900). Einige Beobachtungen über die Zusammenfassung von Gesichtseindrucken zu Einheiten. *Zeitschrift für Psychologie und Physiologie der Sinnesorgane, 23*, 1–32 (English translated by Hogg, A., 1987). Contributions to the analysis of visual perception—First Paper: Some observations on the combination of visual impressions into units. In: Petry, S., & Meyer, G. E. (Eds.), *The perception of illusory contours* (pp. 21-34). New York: Springer-Verlag).

Shapley, S., Caelli, T., Grossberg, S., Morgan, M., & Rentschler, I. (1990). Computational theories of visual perception. In L. Spillmann, & J. W. Werner (Eds.), *Visual perception: The neurophysiological foundations* (pp. 417–448). San Diego: Academic Press.

Shepard, R. N., & Metzler, J. (1971). Mental rotation of three-dimensional objects. *Science*, *171*, 701–703.

Shibata, Y., Takasaki, M., Konishi, T., Okano, D., Ogata, H., & Amano, K. (2002). Extension of the transformational group structure theory on similarity judgments to two-dimensional dot patterns. *IPSJ Journal*, *43*, 4067–4070 (Japanese text with English abstract and captions).

Shiina, K., & Oyama, T. (2008). Remembering Shiro Morinaga. *Gestalt Theory*, *30*, 6–10.

Shulman, G. L. (1992). Attentional modulation of size contrast. *The Quarterly Journal of Experimental Psychology*, *45A*, 529–546.

Shiraishi, T., Fukouzu, Y., Yoshoda, T., & Itoh, A. (2000). An analysis of the Müller-lyre illusion figure by the visual space transfer model $F_{(1)}$: A study on elucidation and estimation of a scene on figure recognition (7). *Bulletin of Japanese Society for the Science of Design*, *47*, 35–42 (Japanese text with English summary).

Sokolov, Y. N. (1963). *Perception and the conditioned reflex* (in English published). New York: Macmillan (Tokyo: Sekai Press, Japanese translation 1965).

Sokolov, E. N. (2005). Neurobiology of gestalts. In R. Miller, A. M. Ivanitsky, & P. M. Balaban (Eds.), *Complex brain functions. Conceptual advances in Russian neurocieace* (pp. 239–254). The Taylor & Francis e-Library.

Sokolov, E. N. (2013). *The psychophysiology of consciousness*. Oxford A.O: Oxford University Press.

Sperling, G. (1960). The infotmation available in brief visual presentations. *Psychological Monographs*, *74*, 1–29.

Sperling, G. (1967). Successive approximations to a model for short term memory. *Acta Psychologica*, *27*, 285–292.

Spillmann, L., Fuld, K., & Gerrits, H. J. M. (1976). Brightness contrast in the Ehrenste illusion. *Vision Research*, *16*, 713–719.

Spillmann, L., Fuld, K., & Neumeyer, C. (1984). Brightness matching, brightness cancellation, and increment threshold in the Ehrenstein illusion. *Perception*, *13*, 513–520.

Spillmann, L., & Werner, J. S. (1990). *Visual perception: The neurophysiological foundations*. San Diego: Academic Press.

Stevens, S. S. (1961). To honor Fecner and repeal his law. *Science*, *133*, 80–86.

Strother, L., & Kubovy, M. (2003). Perceived complexity and the grouping effect in band patterns. *Acta Psychologica*, *114*, 229–244.

Takahashi, M., & Uemura, Y. (1967). Test-threshold luminance under various luminance and area condition of a ring-shaped inducing field. *Japanese Psychological Research*, *9*, 199–204.

Tevlov, B. M. (1936). The dependence of the absolte visual threshold on the presence of an additional stumlus in the field vision. *Journal of General Psychology*, *15*, 3–11.

Titchener, E. B. (1901). *Experimental psychology. A manual of laboratory practice*. New York: Macmillan.

Torii, S., & Uemura, Y. (1965). Effect of inducing luminance and area upon the apparent brightness of test field. *Japanese Psychological Research*, *7*, 86–100.

Treder, M. S. (2010). Behind the looking-glass: A review on human symmetry perception. *Symmetry*, *2*, 1510–1543. https://doi.org/10.3390/sym2031510

Treisman, A., Cavanagh, P., Fischer, B., Ramachandran, V. S., & von der Heydt, R. (1990). Form perception and attention: Striate cortex and beyond. In L. Spillmann, & J. W. Werner (Eds.), *Visual perception: The neurophysiological foundations* (pp. 273–316). San Diego: Academic Press.

Tyler, C. W., & Hardage, L. (1996). Mirror symmetry detection: Predominance of second-order pattern processing throughout the visual field. In C. W. Tyler (Ed.), *Human symmetry perception and its computational analysis* (pp. 157–171). Zeist, The Netherlands: VSP.

Tversky, A. (1977). Features of similarity. *Psychological Review*, *87*, 327–352.

van der Helm, P. A. (2011). The influence of perception on the distribution of multiple symmetries in nature and art. *Symmetry, 3*, 54–71.

van der Helm, P. A. (2014). *Simplicity in vision: A multidisciplinary account of perceptual organization.* Cambridge, UK: Cambridge University Press.

van der Helm, P. A., & Leeuwenberg, E. L. J. (1996). Goodness of visual regularities: A nontransformation approach. *Psychological Review, 103*, 429–456.

Walker, J. T. (1978). Brightness enhancement and Talbot level in stationary grating. *Perception & Psychophysics, 23*, 356–359.

Wagemans, J. (1995). Detection of visual symmetries. *Spatial Vision, 9*, 9–32.

Wagemans, J. (1997). Characteristics and models of human symmetry detection. *Trends in Cognitive Sciences, 1*, 346–352. https://doi.org/10.1016/S1364-6613(97)01105-4

Watkins, O. C., & Watkins, M. J. (1980). The modality effect and echoic persistence. *Journal of Experimental Psychology: General, 109*, 251–278.

Watt, R. J., & Morgan, M. J. (1983). Mechanisms responsible for the assessment of visual location: Theory and evidence. *Vision Research, 23*, 97–109.

Wenderoth, P. (1996). The effects of the contrast polarity of dot-pair partners on the detection of bilateral symmetry. *Perception, 25*, 757–771.

Wenderoth, P., & Welsh, S. (1998). Effects of pattern orientation and number of symmetry axes on the detection of mirror symmetry in dot and solid patters. *Perception, 27*, 965–976.

Wertheimer, M. (1923). Untersuchungen zur Lehre von der Gestalt II. *Psychologische Forschung, 4*, 301–350.

Weyl, H. (1952). *Symmetry.* Princeton, NJ: Princeton University Press (Tokyo: Kinokuniya Press, Japanese translation 1970).

Wilson, H. R., & Bergen, J. R. (1979). A four mechanism model for threshold spatial vision. *Vision Research, 19*, 19–32.

Woodworth, R. S., & Schlosberg, H. (1954). *Experimental psychology* (2nd ed.). New York: Holt.

Wundt, W. (1898). *Die geometrisch-optischen Täuschungen.* Leipzig: Teubner.

Yodogawa, E. (1980). Quantitative descriptions of pattern goodness and complexity. *Institute of Electronics and Communication Engineers of Japan, PRL80-35*, 1–8 (Japanese text with English abstract).

Yodogawa, E. (1982). Symmetry, an entropy-like measure of visual symmetry. *Perception & Psychophysics, 32*, 230–240.

Yokose, J. (1956). *Psychology of vision (enlarged edition, 1968).* Kyoritsu Press (Japanese text).

Yokose, J. (1957). Theoretical formula of vector-field and its experimental proof. *Psychologia, 1*, 17–21.

Yoshida, T., Fukouzu, Y., & Itoh, A. (2005). Engineering (field) model of geometrical illusion. In T. Goto, & H. Tanaka (Eds.), *Handbook of the science of illusion* (pp. 365–377). Tokyo: Tokyo University Press (Japanese text).

Zeki, S. (1993). *A vision of the brain.* Oxford: Blackwell Science Ltd. (Tokyo: Igaku Press, Japanese translation 1995).

Index

Note: Page numbers followed by *f* indicate figures, and *t* indicate tables.

Printed in the United States
by Baker & Taylor Publisher Services